Technology Strategies for the Hospitality Industry

Technology Strategies for the Hospitality Industry

Third Edition

Peter D. Nyheim
Duy Tan University

with

Ashley Akright
Brian Cliette
Melissa Navarro
Bao Nguyen Le
Jessica Testa

 **Pearson**

330 Hudson Street, NY NY 10013

Vice President, Portfolio Management: Andrew Gilfillan
Portfolio Manager: Pamela Chirls
Editorial Assistant: Lara Dimmick
Field Marketing Manager: Bob Nisbet
Product Marketing Manager: Elizabeth Mackenzie-Lamb
Director, Digital Studio and Content Production:
    Brian Hyland
Managing Producer: Jennifer Sargunar
Content Producer: Rinki Kaur
Manager, Rights Management: Johanna Burke

Manufacturing Buyer: Deidra Smith
Creative Digital Lead: Mary Siener
Full-Service Management and Composition: Integra
    Software Services Pvt. Ltd.
Full-Service Project Manager: Ashwina Ragounath
Cover Design: Studio Montage
Cover Photos: Arina P Habich/Shutterstock
Printer/Binder: LSC Communications, Inc.
Cover Printer: LSC Communications, Inc.
Text Font: SabonLTPro

Library of Congress Cataloging-in-Publication Data

Names: Nyheim, Peter D., author.
Title: Technology strategies for the hospitality industry / Peter D. Nyheim,
    Duy Tan University.
Description: Third Edition. | Boston, Massachusetts : Pearson, [2018] |
    Includes bibliographical references.
Identifiers: LCCN 2018009727| ISBN 9780134484495 | ISBN 0134484495
Subjects: LCSH: Hospitality industry–Data processing. | Information
    technology.
Classification: LCC TX911.3.E4 N95 2018 | DDC 338.4/7910285—dc23 LC record available
    at https://lccn.loc.gov/2018009727

ISBN 10:   0-13-448449-5
ISBN 13: 978-0-13-448449-5

BRIEF CONTENTS

CONTENTS

PREFACE

New To This Edition

- New expanded digital marketing and social media content
- New expanded meeting planning technology content
- New content on augmented reality
- New content on virtual reality
- Database content includes big data and blockchain
- New discussion of cloud technology in hospitality

Welcome to the third edition! Hospitality organizations are embracing new technologies every day. Whether it is with a customer, supplier, or coworker, our industry is expected to embrace the digital world. In an industry where presentation is everything, this must be accomplished seamlessly, even though numerous boundaries and multiple parties are involved. Take heed that if along the way the technology breaks down, it will affect the property where the customer is located. If it works properly, well that was expected in the first place. The third edition of *Technology Strategies for the Hospitality Industry* not only takes away the confusion surrounding technology in our industry, but it also gives you the tools to succeed.

Obviously, the role of information technology (IT) or information systems (IS) is important and challenging for managers today. From daily operations to future planning, it is hard to find a process where some form of technology is not involved. Do you wish to understand it?

Ours is a fast-moving industry, where serving the customer right away often takes precedence over all other considerations. For this and other reasons, oftentimes the uses and advantages of technology are not employed to their fullest potential. With the entry of smartphones and cloud technology, today's customers are even more empowered and demanding. Given the competitive nature of our industry and the fact that technology will not go away, today's manager has no choice but to understand it. Simply put, technology is part of doing business in the new millennium.

Information technology (IT), information systems (IS), management information systems (MIS)...just what is the difference? The first two are often used interchangeably in this book and elsewhere; however, MIS is very different. The *M* in MIS stands for *management*. Managers are concerned with getting things done through other people. Managers are also evaluated on revenue and expenses. Although IS and IT are used, their purpose is to lead the reader in understanding technology within a management context, or MIS.

From a human resources perspective, those managers with this IT understanding find themselves with a leg up on their competition and often a brighter career path. Whether your role or career aspirations focus on food and beverage (F&B) management, asset and space management, marketing and sales, consulting, or perhaps even MIS, your specialty will only be enhanced with the right MIS knowledge base resulting in your becoming a coveted "knowledge worker."

Changing Roles In Hospitality Management

In the past, day-to-day operations in our industry involved pens, paper, and files. Although they are obviously still used, the focus has shifted toward technology. Managers find themselves using technology daily. Examples include the systems and applications used in a restaurant or catering environment. No longer is a stand-alone cash register or paper seating chart enough. Now, enterprise, meaning company wide, systems have been put in place to take advantage of data collection and collaboration across different locations. On the lodging side, properties are now managed by entire systems that track the status and charges of specific spaces and allocate costs and supplies accordingly, all the while interfacing with the outside world via cloud technology. From apps, to fitness tracking and games, to in-room technology, there is much to consider. If you are not "up to date" they could go elsewhere. The use of the emerging technologies plays a large role in this edition of *Technology Strategies for the Hospitality Industry*.

Audience

If you are a current hospitality management student or a hospitality professional wishing to better your MIS knowledge, you can use this textbook. With an eleven-chapter layout and specific emphasis on aligning technology to business strategy, this text presents both specific and conceptual themes.

New Layout and Unique Features

This text is a collaboration among authors who have been there. Further, the living world of hospitality technology is incorporated via interviews at the beginning of each chapter with leaders in our industry. Take a look at the beginning of each chapter to see if you recognize anyone. Through these interviews, we take a look at hospitality technology from two main vantage points. From Par to Oracle, we first seek to understand *Technology Strategies for the Hospitality Industry* from a vendor's perspective. Second, we look at these systems and applications from the view of those who purchase and use it every day in hospitality, be they a general manager or a director of technology for a specific property. Through these two views, the reader is able to fully capture the function and use of technology in the hospitality industry.

Entrepreneurial

Regardless of the economy, the drive and execution of innovative ideas play a vital part in our industry and are presented throughout the book. From the ability to make a restaurant reservation over the Internet through companies such as OpenTable (Priceline, Inc.) to new smartphone applications and augmented reality, new technologies are giving more capability to both managers and customers.

Layout

After the opening interview, the subject matter is detailed in the chapter itself, with a case study and learning activity at the end. After reading the chapter, we recommend that you reread the interview with your newly gained knowledge.

Chapter 1 welcomes you to the world of hospitality information technology and introduces the topic of competitive advantage. These two themes set the tone for the rest of the book, while presenting to the reader what career and business opportunities are available through technology understanding and usage. Rounding out the fundamentals section, in Chapter 2 we have a description of computing essentials and networks, requisite knowledge for the next section.

Chapter 3 begins with a detailed discussion of e-commerce and digital marketing. Next, Chapters 4 and 5 cover operational-specific applications for both the F&B and lodging sides. Chapter 6 is our expanded chapter on meeting and event technology. Chapter 7 is our most detailed chapter and is a thorough analysis of the global distribution system (GDS), where and through which much of our customer data originates and travels. Chapters 8 and 9 round out the text with a discussion of databases and customer relationship management (CRM) (Chapter 8) and the efficient usage of information through such systems as executive information systems (Chapter 9). Chapter 10 is a new chapter on augmented and virtual reality (AR/VR). Finally, we close our text with a chapter on technology investment (Chapter 11) and an appendix with a sample request for proposal (RFP) that may also be used in the investment discussion. Enjoy!

FOREWORD

We no longer live in a business environment where the effective use of technology provides a strategic advantage; we are now faced with the reality that relevant technology knowledge is only a start. This is truly the case in the hospitality industry, where customer expectations for accessibility of information and transaction ease driven organizations to continue to innovate and implement new technologies to stay ahead of their competitors. The hotel industry, for one, has evolved over the years to the point where a myriad of challengers exists, not only competing against other hotel chains for the room nights or meeting revenue, but also with the Internet booking channels like Expedia, Travelocity, and Booking.com. These companies exist as a channel for consumers to leverage. While they sell inventory in the hotels and provide that as a service, they also take a large percentage of the profitability from the brands by providing a more visible and often seamless booking experience to the consumer. From the emergence of new brands appealing to the changing tastes of a millennial customer to competition for search-engine dominance on the Web to get consumers to your direct site and not through an intermediary, the industry will continue to look at solutions that technology can bring to bear that allow them to remain in control of the costs, their guests, and ultimately their continued existence.

Given today's tech-heavy climate and the need to create efficiency through the prudent use of technology, this book will help the reader make sense of the growing use of technology in the hospitality industry across all aspects of the business. We are exposed to the existence as soon as we begin our search online for a hotel, are reminded at the time of check-in, see further evidence in the guest room, meeting rooms and public areas, and cannot ignore the technology prevalent in the restaurant and bar. Truly, the hotel has become an integrated ecosystem of technologies all generating data, providing real-time access to information, and allowing the hotelier the means to manage the business factually.

Like many industries, hospitality has benefited tremendously from the growth and proliferation of cloud-based technology solutions and the removal of premise-based processing. In the past, every location required a dedicated computer (often per application) in order to manage the application, the data, and any interfaces created that allowed data to be shared with other on-site or off-site applications. The architecture was problematic and led to challenges around keeping the applications updated, problem-free, and operational at all times. Technology has now evolved to the point where most if not all hospitality systems actually support a SaaS (Software as a Service) model permitting less demands in terms of hardware and maintenance issues on premise and making heavy use of connectivity to the Internet as the backbone of the new technology estate.

The hospitality industry is a complex ecosystem of collaborative products and services each designed to provide further value to the guest. Each offering requires core access to fundamental data to understand who the guest is, what they might want or value in terms of the product offerings, and the capabilities to ensure that the services are properly presented, charged for, captured, and paid for in order to complete the transaction. Whether we are looking at a spa system that understands the previous stay information for a loyal guest or a golf management system looking at handicaps to select proper scheduling of playing partners, the applications rely on a system of "co-operative intelligence" in order to provide relevance to the guest and address their wants and needs.

The design and content of this book is intended to provide the reader with a better understanding of the current state of hospitality technology, as well as a view to where the industry is headed. From chapters that speak to the need for a coherent well-thought-out e-commerce strategy to the emerging use of new technologies such as augmented and virtual reality to market properties around the world to potential consumers in their homes, the industry continues to evolve dynamically, leveraging the emergence of new tech to its benefit.

At the core of the hospitality-technology stack is data: it is the lifeblood of all systems and properly collected, managed, and evaluated, can be the difference between operational success and failure. Historically, hotel systems existed in silos with each product (reservations, point-of-sale, property management, spa, golf, meeting scheduling, etc.) having its own data stored often in different formats that couldn't easily be shared with other systems. The result was a disjointed environment that did not meet the business needs of the hotelier but more importantly was a major disservice to the guest whose expectations of a holistic experience was seldom met. The hotels or resorts that were able to meet the guests' expectations often did so with heavy doses or labor and manual manipulation of data to create the experience for the guest at the expense of heavy labor costs. With increased pressure on wages, the industry has recognized that this process isn't sustainable and has challenged the technology providers to knock down the walls and create integration that allows data to move in and out of collaborative systems in order to achieve the same guest experience without the heavy manual touch. The growth and standardization of industry-grade databases such as Oracle and SQL allow the ability for systems at the most granular level to share information, and the emergence of integration tools like web services and standard APIs (application program interface) means that data sharing can occur in the cloud on an enterprise level rather than at the property or micro level.

Today's hospitality consumer has high expectations: much like abilities in their consumer-technology world, they expect to be able to find anything, book anytime, and pay using any number of options. They expect that the pricing that is displayed for them is the best price, and that if it does not meet their needs they will either be offered other choices or they will move on. The percentage of reservations being made online continues to dramatically increase, and as reported in 2017 by the research performed by Smart Insights, 60% of leisure and 41% of business travelers make their travel arrangements via the Internet. Not only does this statistic continue to trend up, but guests are much more savvy about what they want (and what they don't) and will be active in the creation and review of comment sites like Trip Advisor and Yelp before they book. It is reported by Tnooz that 95% of consumers read reviews before booking. What this means for the hotelier is that the management of their product, services, message, and customer sentiment now extend out beyond the property or the chain out to the World Wide Web. Managing this message and ensuring that guests who have had bad experiences (and are happy to post about them) can be identified and resolved in a timely basis may actually have more business impact than a guest dispute that occurs on property. While good news may travel fast as the old adage states, the new reality is that bad news goes viral.

While technology has done much to change the day-to-day operations in the hospitality industry, it must be viewed through the lens of providing better information for the hotelier to manage their business. Technology in and of itself is irrelevant without a plan, a purpose, and proper business operations to support it. The book speaks to the importance of identifying the requirements that technology can address, the manner in which applications can be sourced and selected, and key principles to follow when implementing solutions to maximize their chance for success. As has been said many times, technology solutions often fail because of a reluctance of those asked to support them to change, so the humanistic side of technology and its adoption is critical when such initiatives are contemplated.

I hope you can take advantage of the eleven chapters provided by this book; it can serve as your guide to the dynamic world of hospitality technology. Whether you are embarking on a technical career or more on the operations side of the business, the content will be equally applicable and will provide you the basis for understanding the climate, appreciating the challenges, and moving forward with your career aspirations. While I hope you can leverage the knowledge provided, remember that at the core of the business, it is hospitality and the existence of it that will drive the industry now and for all time. People who don't love the opportunity to serve others to provide the ultimate guest experience need not apply.

Enjoy.

Toby W. Malbec
Managing Director
ConStrata Technology Consulting

BIOGRAPHIES AND ACKNOWLEDGMENTS

Peter Nyheim, Ph.D. is the Principal at BizEnglish, a technology agency focusing on English-speaking clientele. Prior to BizEnglish, Dr. Nyheim taught at Penn State University and Drexel University.

Dr. Nyheim earned a B.A. in Government from Lehigh University, an MBA from Drexel University in Information Systems and a Ph.D. in Work Force Education from Penn State University.

Leading this charge a third time has been quite an endeavor and aside from my contributing authors, publisher, and interviewees, many deserve praise. I would like to thank all the many companies, colleagues, and individuals who helped with this project. Take a look inside the book to see them all!

Paul Lawler
University of Hawai'i at Mānoa

Dongsoo Lee
Arkansas Tech University

Zhenxing Mao
California State Polytechnic University, Pomona

Glenn Rinsky
Jefferson State Community College

Diane Withrow
Cape Fear Community College

CHAPTER 1

Introduction and Competitive Advantage

Chapter Objective

- At the end of this chapter students will gain an understanding of the technology they will use in their career and competitive advantage.

Learning Objectives

- Gain an overview of IT within a career path
- Understand the importance of IT
- Understand your personal strengths and weaknesses

- Gain an understanding of developing a business strategy
- Understand what sets you apart
- Obtain a long-lasting strategy

Chapter Introduction

Interview

Laura Habina is assistant director of revenue management at the InterContinental New York Barclay.

1. What do you do now?

With news of the Waldorf Astoria New York closing for renovations, I was fortunate to have the time and resources in order to plan out the next best step for myself and my career. In January 2017, I accepted a position as the assistant director of revenue at the InterContinental New York Barclay, a part of the IHG portfolio. I work on a team of three at the newly renovated property, collaborating, developing, and implementing both short- and long-term strategies to achieve and exceed the $70 million rooms' budget all the while gaining share versus our competitive set in an extremely dynamic and unpredictable New York City market. I focus on strategies for both Transient and Group rooms revenues and ensure that the entire organization is focused on our goals from each step of implementation and execution: from sales to events, to housekeeping and front office.

2. What technology do you use in your everyday life?

We have a corporate propriety system where we manage our inventory and rate plans. This system syncs with our property management system (PMS), OPERA, which is used across multiple different hotel brands around the world. In a world that is constantly evolving, we have migrated our key systems to a web-based platform, so we are able to constantly access our data in real time and make strategy adjustments from a laptop, tablet, or smartphone. Subscribing to market and competitive data warehouses is vital in my everyday life. With assistance from STR (Smith Travel Research) as well as TravelClick, I have all different technologies and resources to help make better decisions to drive revenue.

3. What is a typical day for you?

The best part about working on property at a hotel in New York City is that no two days are the same. My mornings generally begin with reviewing all the night audit reports from my overnight manager and then diving into my daily report that provides me a snapshot of where we stand for the next 365 days. It's vital to understand where our mix of business stands and how our revenues are pacing versus ourselves, our completive set, and our market, so we can make necessary adjustments to capture demand and pick up room revenue where we need to. While the majority of my day is spent monitoring price points and inventory, I also spend my day coordinating with my front office team to ensure the day's strategy is carried out as well as working with my sales team to provide the most optimal rates for both the client and the hotel in order to win the business from our competitors and achieve our internal goals.

4. What resources do you use to keep current?

I am constantly reviewing STR data and publications as well as TravelClick's "Demand and Rate 360" to stay current to my immediate competitors in the New York City market. CBRE Hotels is also a good resource I use to gain more insight about domestic market conditions and trends, as well as to stay informed on overall forecast predictions for future years with PKF publications. I enjoy keeping current with LinkedIn for hospitality updates and news and seeing what my colleagues are reading and posting. There are so many developments and announcements in the hospitality industry, so it's great to see what people are passionate about in their network in the world of hospitality.

5. What technologies would you recommend that future managers study?

I would recommend that future managers study and take note of the changing platforms and applications when it comes to hospitality. More and more hotels are integrating technology into the operations process, so it's important to understand the functionality of these kiosks, programs, booking apps, in-room technology, and so on to help guests throughout their entire experience. Every company is different when it comes to what technologies are relevant to its everyday operation, but the important thing is to understand that technology is always evolving so we must evolve as well.

6. What other advice do you have for future managers?

My advice for future managers is to make the most of your time, both professionally and personally. Try new experiences and challenge yourself. You never know where life may take you, but being open and willing to try new things may open the door for something truly incredible that you never thought of.

1. Overview

Laura provides some great insight here for our opening chapter and its career focus. At the start of each new academic term, the number of students enrolled in our classes seeking careers in hospitality information technology (IT) is generally small. Yet, after comparing IT salaries to those for traditional positions in hospitality operations (e.g., management, sales, and human resources), one may want to rethink his/her career path. Money aside, the reality is that for most careers, IT is an integral and necessary component. Thanks to the convergence of various forms of technology (e.g., computers, software, and cloud technology), the rise in electronic business (e-business), and a growing number of enterprise-wide technology initiatives, technology is a critical aspect of almost any job (see Table 1-1), disrupting functional silos and creating the need for boundary spanners. Simply put, IT is changing everything—from guest expectations and needs to industry structure to how we perform our jobs and what skills we will need to be successful. In fact, it is changing the very nature of how services are delivered. Consequently, IT is inescapable and must be a core skill for any aspiring hospitality manager or executive. Management guru Peter Drucker often stated that everyone in the firm is responsible for marketing the firm and ensuring customer satisfaction. In a similar vein, because of the confluence of business process, competitiveness, and technology, everyone in today's organization, by default, must be responsible for IT and think and act like a **chief information officer** (CIO). Congratulations, you have just joined the IT team—whether you like it or not!

It's true. Take marketing, for example. It is tough to be a great marketer without IT. In today's high-tech era, IT is a prerequisite to marketing and must go hand in hand. One cannot make marketing decisions in a vacuum without in-depth knowledge about the capabilities and limitations of IT. Global distribution, supply chain management, customer relationship management (CRM), electronic commerce (e-commerce), digital marketing, social media, customer segmentation, revenue management, and so on are all underpinned by IT applications. Thus, a good marketer, by default, must be well versed in IT.

The same could be said for every other discipline, including human resources, finance and accounting, management, and operations. You can't make decisions about the business without using IT (or information generated from IT systems) and without factoring in IT considerations. Front desk managers must be intimately familiar with property management system (PMS), revenue (yield) management, central reservations system (CRS), review sites, call accounting and the private branch exchange (PBX), voice messaging, guest locking systems, mobile concierge systems, energy management systems, and more. Similarly, restaurant managers must be proficient in point-of-sale (POS) technology, inventory management systems, menu engineering, mobile applications, and the like, and all managers must be intimately familiar with the risks of using technology in business and appropriate ways (including policies, procedures, and training) to safeguard against these risks.

How can a hospitality executive determine how to maximize value for the firm if he or she is faced with resource constraints and must decide between, say, a new cloud-based sales and catering system and the renovation and re-theming of a restaurant outlet? How can one possibly estimate cash flows, assess risks, assign risk premiums, and calculate returns on investment (ROI) without fully comprehending IT? It would be rather difficult to evaluate the pros and cons, quantify the benefits, and understand the strategic opportunities associated with each option to make a well-informed business decision without having a solid grasp of IT. From your perspective as an aspiring manager or executive, how can you lead others, make hiring decisions, and mentor and develop people without understanding the technological future of the industry?

TABLE 1-1

IT Is Important to Every Hospitality Position

Position	Brief Description of Duties	IT Knowledge Requirements
General Manager (GM)	Responsible for overseeing the entire operation.	• Operational systems, business intelligence, and reports to manage, control, and direct the business • Technology to track and communicate with customers, suppliers, employees, regional and corporate management, and owners • Balanced scorecard • Big picture knowledge related to all aspects of the business and systems used throughout the business in order to make decisions and determine how best to allocate resources • Microsoft Office/Google Apps
Director of Finance (Controller)	Responsible for the accounting and financial aspects of the operation. Establishes and manages budgets, maintains the books, prepares financial reports, acquires funding for capital projects, and controls against theft and waste.	• Spreadsheets • Data analytics • Business intelligence tools • Balanced scorecard • Project management software • Back-office accounting system • Security surveillance and audit trails • Time and attendance • Payroll • Microsoft Office/Google Apps
Director of Rooms Operations	Responsible for all guest service functions in a hotel, including front desk, reservations, bell staff, housekeeping, concierge, and telephone operators.	• Property management system • Reservation system • Revenue management system • Distribution and channel management • Customer relationship management and loyalty program • Telephone and call accounting systems • Guest lock system • Guest response system • Concierge system • In-room guest amenities (e.g., movies, high-speed Internet access, mini bars, and guest safes) • Inventory systems • Microsoft Office/Google Apps
Revenue Manager	Responsible for setting rates, restrictions, and selling strategies for hotel rooms and managing room inventory allocated to the various distribution channels used by the hotel.	• Revenue management system • Reservation system • Distribution and channel management • Property management system • Sales and catering system • Business intelligence • Microsoft Office/Google Apps

Position	Brief Description of Duties	IT Knowledge Requirements
Director of Sales and Marketing	Oversees the sales and marketing activities of the operation and its advertising and promotion materials; is typically responsible for group business (i.e., corporate accounts, reservations involving 10 or more guestrooms, meetings, and conventions).	• Sales and catering system • Lead generation and tracking databases • Sales force automation • Customer relationship management and loyalty program • Web site and e-commerce • Reservation system • Content management system • Social media • Reputation management • Distribution and channel management • Revenue management system • Meeting room layout and design software • Microsoft Office/Google Apps
Food and Beverage Director	Oversees all food and beverage operations. Manages day-to-day operations, purchasing, and inventory management.	• Point-of-sale technology • Inventory management • Recipe management • Purchasing and receiving system • Table management • Restaurant reservations • Labor forecasting and scheduling • Menu engineering • Microsoft Office/Google Apps
Director of Human Resources	Responsible for all aspects of staffing and team building. Duties include hiring and termination decisions, benefits administration, payroll, policy compliance, training, promotions, special programs, and succession planning.	• Human resources information system • Labor forecasting and scheduling • Time and attendance • Payroll • Benefits • Online training • Intranet • Microsoft Office/Google Apps
Director of Security	Oversees the security operations for the organization to ensure the safety of guests and workers alike.	• Access control systems and guest locking system • Surveillance systems • Fire alarm system • Biometrics • Microsoft Office/Google Apps
Director of Engineering	Oversees the facility, maintenance, and equipment.	• Heating, ventilation, and air conditioning (HVAC) system • Energy management system • Preventative maintenance system • Work order management system • Microsoft Office/Google Apps
Director of Housekeeping	Oversees the cleanliness of the facility, including all public space, administrative offices, and guestrooms.	• Property management system • Labor forecasting and scheduling • Inventory systems • Microsoft Office/Google Apps

Position	Brief Description of Duties	IT Knowledge Requirements
IT Manager	Oversees, maintains, and secures the various computer systems used throughout the organization; provides support to end users; and assists with the selection, procurement, and implementation of computer applications and hardware.	• Operating systems • Hardware platforms • Programming languages • Network and communications architecture (both wired and wireless) • Project management software • Electronic mail (email) server • Systems security • Antivirus and malware detection tools • Backup and recovery • Database/Big data administration • Report writer tools • Analytics • Social media • Technology trends • All systems used throughout the business • Microsoft Office/Google Apps

Just think about this question for a moment. Many are quick to say that they don't need to become proficient in a particular area because they can hire someone else to handle those responsibilities or because they can outsource those functions. Generally speaking, this type of thinking is short-sighted, and when it comes to IT, it can be outright dangerous—especially considering the stakes involved. IT tends to rank among the top expense categories of most firms. It also tends to be one of the most pervasive and enabling—or confining—resources in the firm. Therefore, every manager or executive must strive to understand how to use IT, see its strategic potential, and recognize its limitations so as not to be bamboozled by it, led astray, or be constrained by the limitations of the firm's IT infrastructure. While hiring experts or outsourcing may be a viable approach and help reduce the amount of expertise you must have in this area, it does not completely absolve you from having proficiency and a solid understanding of what technology can and cannot do and what questions to ask. Like anything, understanding and using IT require investment (of both time and money), commitment, and diligence. Your knowledge in this area will reduce your dependence on others and improve your ability to ask the *right* questions so you can properly lead your firm.

2. Welcome to the World of IT!

The discussion in the previous section suggests a very clear message. IT is one of the greatest forces driving change in almost any industry, especially the hospitality industry—so get used to IT! Unfortunately, human bandwidth, that is, people's ability to grasp IT and understand how to effectively use it and apply it in business, is one of the greatest barriers to a firm's ability to successfully adopt IT and realize its many benefits. The IT wave will likely continue for the foreseeable future for several reasons. First, the pace of change and the expected number of technological advances continue to grow at alarming rates. Second, the technological demands of guests continue to rise. This is especially true of the Millennial Generation (Gen Y) and Generation Z, which have practically been reared on technology. Third, the competitive environment is growing in intensity with increased investment in and emphasis on IT. Fourth, labor issues continue to plague the industry. Both the cost of labor and the scarcity of people willing and able to fill industry positions require greater focus on technology as a viable alternative to run the business and service guests. For these reasons,

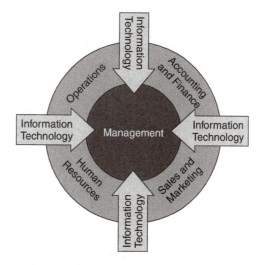

FIGURE 1-1

IT pervasiveness creates the need for boundary spanners and IT-savvy individuals.

IT is quickly becoming one of the most important skills industry managers and leaders need to possess and one of the most important competitive methods a hospitality firm can exploit to gain advantage in an increasingly competitive business. These advantages come in many forms including, but not limited to, differentiation, efficiency (economies of scale), resource capabilities, cost reduction, and information asymmetry. Despite their diversity, these advantages all have one thing in common; they are all enabled by IT. Thus, whether you are interested in pursuing a career in IT or not makes little difference. The underlying premise is the same; no matter what you choose to do as a profession, you need to become proficient in IT at the personal, intraorganizational, and interorganizational levels.

By default, your career will involve IT. IT transcends today's organizations by crossing and blurring all traditional departmental, organizational, and geographic boundaries. This is especially true with large-scale initiatives such as e-business, enterprise resource planning (ERP), CRM, and analytics. The illustration in Figure 1-1 helps bring this reality to life. IT-related decisions require input from multiple perspectives within the organization since IT is pervasive throughout the firm's **value chain**, all of the primary and support activities of the firm required to produce products and services that generate revenues and drive profits. Consequently, if the organization is to exploit IT for competitive advantage, business leaders, regardless of the discipline (e.g., management, marketing, finance, accounting) they represent, must (1) focus on enterprise-wide solutions, (2) be able to serve as **boundary spanners** (people who can cross multiple disciplines or areas of knowledge), and (3) become technologically savvy. Decisions involving IT cannot be made in a vacuum, and because of their reach, cost, and strategic implications, they should *not* be delegated to others. They require commitment from the top, insight from all aspects of the business, and the involvement of those possessing specific expertise in IT.

3. Managing Your Career

Unquestionably, this is an exciting time to pursue an IT career within the context of the hospitality industry, and our chapter interview gave us some good advice. Hospitality and tourism are among the largest and fastest growing employers worldwide and they offer a rich, yet diverse, set of possibilities. IT is among the fastest growing areas of employment and one of the economy's great contributors, a trend expected to continue well into the future. The intersection of these great industries offers much excitement, opportunity, and new careers for those who seek and would like to take advantage of them. Are you interested?

Moving forward, IT will continue to be one of the greatest forces driving transformation in almost any industry, including hospitality. Consequently, everything will continue to change—from how we work and learn to how we transact business with our guests and employees to the technological amenities and infrastructure found in our establishments. Moreover, technology will redefine the very nature of what constitutes good service and how services are delivered. With the rise in e-business, self-service, and mobile technologies, these changes have only become more pronounced and more commonplace—moving the industry to new heights technologically while expanding the globalization of the hospitality industry. Certainly for those seeking careers in this industry, exciting opportunities abound, and because of IT, many new career possibilities have surfaced.

To excel at your career, you need to have passion and enjoy what you do. You also need to continue to develop yourself and your skills. Learning should be a lifelong journey and a regular part of your job. The hospitality industry has become so complex and continues to change at a rapid pace. Thus, you, too, need to change, adapt, and stay current with all aspects of the business—and especially with IT. One of the nice things about IT is that there is a built-in mechanism or incentive that forces you to stay current if you want to stay employed—the very desire to stay marketable and relevant.

Remember that career paths for most people seldom resemble straight lines. They often take many twists and turns, but these twists and turns are largely up to you and often offer many wonderful developmental opportunities that can lead to new, exciting, and very different career opportunities than what you may have initially thought possible. It is your responsibility and obligation to yourself to manage your own career. While others can help you with this important task, no one can do this for you as well as you can do it for yourself. After all, you know yourself best, particularly your interests, goals, and what motivates you and gives you personal satisfaction.

At this point in your career, one of the best things you can do is to conduct a self-assessment or **SWOT (strengths, weaknesses, opportunities, and threats) analysis**. Determine what you like and what you don't and inventory your skills and core competencies. Be sure to think about what you would like to do long-term and what skills will be required to achieve your goals. Where are you strong, and where is there room for improvement? What skills are you lacking, or which ones need further development? How prepared are you for the digital economy? What are the job opportunities like presently, and where will they be in the next five, ten, or fifteen years? In essence, you want to create your own personal balance sheet that identifies your assets (strengths) and liabilities (weaknesses) relative to the marketplace you will enter. Then, just as you would do if you were managing a firm's balance sheet, figure out how to improve your assets through value creation (adding something for which people are willing to pay that wasn't there before and will provide a noticeable advantage) while reducing, and hopefully eliminating, your liabilities. Look for jobs that will serve as springboards to new opportunities and help you progress and achieve your ultimate career dreams. Each position you take should help you acquire new skills and serve as a stepping-stone or springboard to the position you ultimately desire. When it comes time to interviewing for a job, be prepared to address with conviction the question, "What value do you bring to the table?"

4. Strategy

After having aligned your IT needs and your career, next in importance is its strategic use. IT is an important resource for any firm. In today's era, it is hard to imagine how any business, especially a hospitality business, could operate without the assistance of IT. IT applications are seen throughout an entire firm—integrated with almost every business discipline and process, a useful resource for decision making, and increasingly a key ingredient in driving business value. As such, IT must be viewed holistically with the business in mind and be a topic of discussion in nearly every business decision, particularly those involving business strategy, marketing and distribution, operations, and future growth planning. Also, all business leaders should have some proficiency working with IT and an understanding of how to use it effectively to solve business problems, serve business needs, and create new opportunities. As such, the IT function should be represented at the executive-suite level with the chief information officer (CIO) occupying a seat at the decision-making table with visible support and participation from all top-level executives. These factors will ensure that IT is factored into decisions early on and for the right reasons—to create business value and advantages.

Within the hospitality industry, IT represents one of the largest areas of capital expenditure. To some, IT might be viewed as a rather large expense, but it should be viewed as a strategic opportunity. In reality, IT is both a support tool and a strategic enabler. IT should never be used for the sake of IT itself or just because it is the latest and greatest. Instead, IT should be used purposefully with the end business goals in mind. It should be used to solve business problems. If not used correctly, IT can become nothing more than an unwanted expense, a source of frustration, or an inhibitor to change, but when used correctly, many exciting possibilities can result—from service enhancements and product differentiation to new revenue streams. Moving forward, hospitality executives must continually look toward the strategic opportunities technology offers and use technology as a **competitive method**—or as a tool—to differentiate and create **competitive advantage**. Thriving in today's competitive world is all about doing things better, faster, cheaper, and differently than anyone else.

The creation of competitive advantage must involve multiple aspects of the firm coming together. In this chapter, we want to explore the use of IT for creating—or at least contributing to—competitive advantage in a hospitality firm. If you look at history across the general business landscape, you can find many great companies that have creatively and strategically deployed IT to create competitive advantage. Some of the many examples include American Airlines and its reservation system, SABRE; FedEx and its shipping and package tracking software, PowerShip; Wal-Mart and its supply chain management technology; Hertz and its system for driving directions and use of mobile technology to support quick car returns; and Dell Computer's self-ordering system for customized personal computers. More recent technology innovations include McDonald's kitchen production and management system to support efficient and low-cost operations, Marriott's reservations and revenue management systems to achieve rate premiums and higher occupancy rates than industry averages, Mandarin Oriental's in-room guest technology to create memorable guest experiences, Southwest Airline's Ding! application to push special promotions to customers and sell distressed (i.e., last-minute) inventory, Harrah's customer relationship management (CRM) to personalize services and promotions, InterContinental Hotel Groups' use of mobile technologies to enable and support guest services for people on the move, or Uber and Airbnb's app and Web site. These are just a sampling of some of the many creative and successful applications showing how technology can drive competitive advantage and differentiation. They illustrate how crucial technology has become in driving the competitive and very dynamic landscape. The magnitude of these initiatives also suggests the need for a great deal of vision, competencies, and capital resources to make things happen through IT.

Our challenge as hospitality managers is to find new opportunities—just as these exemplar companies did—in which IT can be used to solve business problems, create better service experiences, provide cost and/or informational advantages, and create distinction in the marketplace. Ultimately, technology should be used to lower cost structure, increase revenues and market share, create unique value propositions for guests, and generate unprecedented returns for investors or shareholders. Certainly, these sound daunting—and they are! Creating competitive advantage requires creative, out-of-the-box thinking. Like Apple's former CEO, Steve Jobs, one must think differently. This requires seeing the future first, taking some calculated risks, and doing things that no one else has attempted. To do so requires dedication, determination, focus, and consistent allocation of resources. Sometimes, one can stumble from time to time, but if one learns from his or her mistakes, progress can be made. If creating competitive advantage were so easy, then every manager would have already thought of all the great ideas possible, and every company would have implemented them by now. Creating competitive advantage requires you to see things that others cannot or do not see and then act on these opportunities to make them happen, but it does not stop there. Once the competitive advantage has been created, the challenge shifts to sustaining that competitive advantage or destroying it and either reinventing it or replacing it with something else before anyone else has time to copy it and catch up to your lead. There is no resting on your laurels. This is a complex and never-ending game. Therefore, you, as a manager, must be prepared to play aggressively, think quickly and creatively, and be in the race for the long haul. Are you ready? Will you think differently, and act quickly?

5. Achieving Competitive Advantage

Competitive advantage sounds really awesome, but what does it mean? Understanding this concept is vital to the success of future hospitality leaders, especially given the competitive and volatile nature of the hospitality industry, the high stakes of competition, and the growing trend toward commoditization—where products blur and become indistinguishable from and, therefore, interchangeable with one another. In simplistic terms, competitive advantage is derived from one or more unique capabilities of the firm and brings value to the firm. These capabilities set one firm apart from others within the industry and within its competitive set. These single out the firm for some reason, making it *different* from others competing in the same space. Typically, this differentiation comes from the firm's resources and capabilities, is established as part of the firm's strategy, is reinforced by the firm's culture and mission statement, and is supported by the firm's budget. Competitive advantage results from doing things faster, better, cheaper, or different than anyone else. It can be measured in many ways; for example, in terms of product or service quality, market share, brand recognition, customer loyalty, employee loyalty, profitability, and cost structure.

Traditional sources of competitive advantage come from gaining leadership positions in one or more of four arenas: price and quality, timing and know-how, stronghold creation, and deep pockets (D'Aveni, 1994). To properly put things in perspective, consider that everyone (i.e., employees, customers, investors, or franchisees) has a choice in today's competitive marketplace. Oftentimes, this choice can be made between multiple competing, yet similar, offerings. With information being so readily available, these people can do their homework and make more informed choices. They can be picky and extremely demanding. Are you positioned well to win their attention and to get them to select your company's offerings? What makes your firm a better choice over other options in the marketplace? What is the deciding factor, the thing that really makes the difference? This is what competitive advantage is all about.

IT provides competitive advantage if it helps a firm reduce the firm's cost structure, generate profits, make better and faster decisions, or differentiate its products and services. Competitive advantage results when a firm gains an advantage (typically in the form of economic rents, increased market share, or information asymmetries) over its competitors by exploiting its strengths relative to those of its competitors (Ohmae, 1992). In this context, competitive advantage from IT results when the technology itself helps a firm in achieving economies of scale, reducing costs, differentiating the firm's products and services, creating barriers to entry, building **switching costs** (things that lock in or bind a consumer to a product or company—discussed more in Chapter 3 under subscriptions), changing the basis of competition, adding customer value, altering the balance of power with suppliers, providing first-mover effects, or generating new products (see also Applegate, McFarlan, and McKenney, 1996; Hitt and Brynjolfsson, 1996; D'Aveni, 1994; Bakos and Treacy, 1986; Clemons and Kimbrough, 1986; Porter and Millar, 1985; Cash and Konsynski, 1985; McFarlan, 1984; Ives and Learmonth, 1984; Parsons, 1983).

Based on Porter's teachings, a series of questions can be raised (see Figure 1-2) to help evaluate the strategic potential and ultimate competitive advantage that can be derived from a technology-based initiative. This list is not exhaustive, but it is representative of the types of considerations one should have. It is suggested that these questions be raised often when defining strategy and setting priorities involving IT.

Resource-Based View of the Firm

The assessment of competitive advantage is an important step in the IT investment decision-making process, and internal efficiency can provide one source of competitive

- Can IT create entry barriers to keep out potential new competitors? If so, how?
- Can IT create switching costs to lock in customers and make it difficult or undesirable for them to seek out other alternatives?
- Can IT help the firm understand its customers better, use information to provide unique experiences and customer service, and build lasting relationships that lead to loyalty and more spending?
- Can IT be used to lower the firm's cost structure, streamline operations, or to create economies of scale?
- Can IT be used to create new business opportunities and revenue streams?
- Can IT be used to differentiate the firm's products and service offerings? If so, how?
- Can IT be used to improve product or service quality or ensure consistency?
- Can IT be used to build better alliances or strategic partnerships to help the firm gain access to new markets or access to resources and skills it does not presently have?
- Can IT be used to provide an edge in dealing with suppliers or enable better negotiating leverage?
- Can IT change the nature of competition and the dynamics within the industry, shifting them in the firm's favor?
- Can IT help the firm sustain its competitive advantage in the market place?
- Can IT better equip employees to be more productive and capable, perhaps by providing information to them or providing faster access to information to help them do a better job and outperform the competition?
- Can IT help to provide informational advantages, namely more and better information than what suppliers or competitors may have to make faster decisions, negotiate better prices, and so on?
- Can IT help a firm do more with less?
- Can IT help to create a "wow" experience that is memorable and will be recounted to others?
- Is IT aligned with the strategic objectives of the firm?
- How can IT be better used to help the firm achieve the firm's strategies?

FIGURE 1-2

Key questions to ask of all IT projects.

advantage (Sethi and King, 1994). According to Sethi and King (1994), the two prevailing approaches to assessing competitive advantage are the following:

1. **Outcome approach**—This approach places great emphasis on competitive efficiency, business value, and management productivity, and uses such measures as revenue growth rate, ROI, return on assets, profits, and net worth. It takes a macro-level perspective by focusing on aggregate measures that address performance of the firm.

2. **Trait approach**—This approach identifies specific attributes of an IT application that are known to contribute to competitive advantage. These are reflected in concepts like competitive forces, strategic thrusts, value activities, and the customer resource life cycle. This approach takes on a more micro-level view since the focus is on an individual IT application and the role it plays in enhancing the firm's competitive advantage.

To assess competitive advantage derived from a single IT application, Sethi and King (1994) define a construct called Competitive Advantage Provided by an Information Technology Application (CAPITA). **CAPITA** is defined by five dimensions: efficiency (the extent to which an IT application allows a firm to produce products and services at prices lower than its competitors), functionality (the extent to which an IT application provides the functions and capabilities required by users), threat (the impact of an IT application on the balance of power between suppliers and buyers), preemptiveness (early adoption of an IT application to usurp the market), and synergy (the degree of integration between an IT application and the firm's goals, strategies, and environment).

Because of the commodity-like nature of IT, Cho (1996) presented an alternative view of competitive advantage grounded in theory pertaining to the **resource-based view** of the firm as studied by Clemons and Row (1991) and Mata, Fuerst, and Barney (1995). Using this framework, Cho suggested that a company achieves competitive advantage through the culmination and convergence of a series of events, resources, experiences, and underlying management processes. Alternatively stated, competitive advantage is the result of not only how a firm competes (or plays the game) but also the assets it has in which to play or compete. The competitive advantage is derived collectively from a variety of firm assets that make up its resources and capabilities. These include its people (and their skills and expertise), financial assets, IT portfolio and infrastructure, corporate culture, portfolio of products and services, competitive methods, strategic alliances, and so on. There is no one contributing factor but a series of ingredients or idiosyncratic resources that when combined provide a competitive edge in the marketplace. Plimpton (1990) termed this hidden or **tacit** competitive edge as the *X Factor*. It's like a secret ingredient in a recipe. For many organizations, the integration of software applications and IT with the organizational structure and its staff provides the source of competitive advantage (Adcock et al., 1993). Because of its tacit nature, the competitive advantage and its contributing factors are difficult to identify and, therefore, hard to duplicate. The resulting competitive advantage can then be sustained for as long as it remains inimitable and not obsolete, a period that is becoming shorter all the time in today's hypercompetitive marketplace.

Finding sources of competitive advantage that are unique and inimitable is important, especially in the service industry where barriers to entry tend to be relatively low and because service concepts can be easily copied. One of the reasons so many Internet firms failed in the Dot.Com era is because many Internet entrepreneurs underestimated the ease and speed in which their concepts could be copied. Thus, their concepts became undifferentiated and indistinguishable among their competitors, and competition grew at a much faster rate than what was anticipated. A small customer base at the time (recall that Internet access was not as prevalent and that the number of users was a much smaller percentage of the overall population as it is today) was diluted. Customers spent their time shopping for the best price, causing everyone's profitability to fall. Therefore, barriers should be erected whenever possible, and sources of competitive advantage should be embedded in the organization and should comprise the firm's unique factors (or what is known as idiosyncratic resources). This will create tacit competitive advantage. Finally, firms should protect their competitive advantage and discourage employees from talking with outsiders regarding the sources of competitive advantage. Doing these things will make it harder for others to copy, and allow firms to prolong their advantages.

Past Examples of Competitive Advantage Derived from IT

Throughout the hospitality industry, there are many examples where firms are creatively using IT to create competitive advantage. The following are some examples seen across the hotel industry in the context of global distribution systems (GDSs) but whose reach goes beyond to include service delivery and customer relationship management (CRM). Although described in the context of GDS, the examples of competitive advantage derived through (1) economies of scale, (2) functionality, (3) accuracy of information, and (4) proprietary technology are readily transferable to other technology applications and areas of the hospitality industry.

1. **Economies of scale** have been among the most significant sources of competitive advantage derived from GDSs. Building a GDS is a costly, time-consuming, and difficult venture. It requires great expertise, both technical and operational. Not all companies have the resources, expertise, and wherewithal to develop a GDS. Moreover, the costs have exceeded the reach of many organizations. In chains and affiliate organizations that provide reservation systems technology and services to their member hotels, the incremental cost to add new hotels is pretty minimal relative to the core investment required to build the system. As such, the initial investment and fixed costs can be allocated over a wider base, thereby providing greater economic efficiencies and decreasing the participation cost for each hotel in the network. These efficiencies appeal to franchisees that seek access to global distribution channels but lack the capital and expertise to develop their own. Ef-

ficiencies and economies of scale lead to lower deployment costs, operating costs, and transaction fees. Hence, a GDS is a primary selection criterion for companies interested in affiliating with a franchisor or a management firm. As the franchise network and number of hotels under a single umbrella grow, so do market penetration and market share. Size then becomes an important factor that can be leveraged to gain additional economies and clout with external entities.

2. Another source of competitive advantage comes from the functionality of the GDS, its links to external systems, and its flexibility to adapt to an ever-changing business environment. For the hospitality industry in particular, this means having the ability to control inventory and rates (including booking rules, restrictions, and selling strategies), to distribute this information seamlessly and in real time to a multitude of access points (e.g., travel agents, airline GDSs, reservation call centers, sister properties or products, other member hotels), and to generate instant confirmations continues to separate the capabilities of competing hotels. Access and links to external systems extends the reach of the hotel GDS, thereby attracting a broader audience from all over the world.

Functional advantages also include ease of use and the GDSs' role in supporting the selling process (i.e., the conversion of inquiries to bookings at the best possible rates). These advantages are typically measured in terms of the number of room-nights or revenue generated by the GDS, occupancy, REVPAR (revenue per available room), REVPOR (revenue per occupied room), and guest loyalty. An example of a temporary competitive advantage resulting from GDS functionality is Marriott International. At a time when the industry was in recession, Marriott turned to strategic and disciplined discounting as a means to increase occupancy. Borrowing pricing strategies from the airline industry, Marriott created a twenty-one-day advance purchase promotion. In order to receive these low rates, a guest was required to meet certain conditions and comply with certain rules or restrictions (called "fences") (Hanks, Noland, and Cross, 1992). In order to enforce these fences, Marriott's Automated Reservation System for Hotel Accommodations (MARSHA) needed to contain sophisticated functionality to manage room inventory and to monitor customer purchase patterns. Since many competing chains lacked similar functionality at the time, they had difficulty in copying Marriott's promotion. Thus, Marriott enjoyed a competitive advantage until such time that other chains could modify their reservations systems to accommodate the same type of practice. Recognizing the short-lived nature of its competitive advantage, Marriott continued to develop its MARSHA reservation system and enhance its integration with its hotel property management and demand forecasting revenue management systems to develop more sophisticated pricing strategies that allowed higher rate premiums and occupancy percentages than industry competitors. Thus, Marriott managed to stay ahead and outperform its competition. A key lesson for all to take away is the need to continue to improve or develop new competitive advantages because they seldom last. More than likely, they will be short lived before someone figures out how to copy or build a better solution as seen in newer OTA models or even social networks.

Flexibility is another important consideration. GDSs must be able to effectively adapt to changing market needs at a moment's notice. Cycle times are too short to tolerate long lead times. Because of the systemic nature of a GDS environment, a change in one area (which could be either functional or technical) will most likely constitute a domino effect. For example, many hotel companies are looking to deploy mobile applications (mobile apps) to support reservation inquiries and bookings, guest profiles, loyalty account balances, online check-in, keyless room entry, and more for guests on the go via their smartphones. The development and implementation of mobile applications require a great deal of thought to systems enhancements to many core systems (including GDS, PMS, and the hotel's Web site), usability (i.e., user interface design), platform considerations (i.e., hardware and operating systems), system interfaces, security, the guest experience, and the overall service delivery process. Mobile apps represent just one of many areas that could be used to illustrate the need for flexibility in design and programmability of the information systems and interfaces comprising the GDS to accommodate new business needs and guest expectations. In a hypercompetitive environment, changes like this will become more common, more frequent, and more necessary for one's competitiveness. They will be driven by new consumer trends, more capable technologies, advances in mobility and the Internet, and competitor moves. Like in the Marriott example previously cited, companies that can capitalize on these functional advantages can gain competitive advantage as long as other firms cannot easily copy or acquire the functionality.

3. A third source of competitive advantage is less tangible. It relates to the accuracy of the information (i.e., content) and the hotel's ability to track the guest. From a guest's perspective, a hotel's ability to meet his or her expectations and provide the correct room type, features, amenities, and services requested at the time of reservation distinguishes the hotel from its competitors. Regardless of what channels are used to book a reservation, each guest should find convenience, hassle-free service, and reliable information. The distribution channel should convey a sense of confidence to the guest that the information being shared is indeed accurate and current and that all of his or her requests for services (i.e., location, room type, features, and amenities) will be honored upon arrival. This confidence and convenience, in turn, builds guest loyalty. From the hotel's perspective, tracking the guest plays an important role in guest recognition and delivering customized services. Since each guest interaction represents an opportunity to learn more about a guest, data collection, storage, and retrieval are critical to building strong relationships, creating unique and personalized experiences, and developing customer switching costs. Being able to mine the reservations database will be a new source of value and advantage.

4. Another form of competitive advantage comes as the result of proprietary technologies or patents, which create barriers to entry or duplicate capabilities. Although patents present challenges, patents are common throughout the software industry, because they represent intellectual capital. Their presence in hotel GDSs is less common. Hyatt Hotels and Radisson Hotels are two companies that currently enjoy patents for functional features contained in their GDSs. Hyatt (U.S. Patent 5,404,291) patented an inventory control process and revenue maximization routine used by its SPIRIT CRS. Radisson's patent (U.S. Patent 5,483,444) protects the company's innovative "Look to Book" program and "World of Winners" sweepstakes program, which provide incentives to travel agents and others who provide electronic bookings at Radisson hotels. Under the "Look to Book" program, agents are awarded points or credits, which can later be redeemed for prizes, for each reservation booked. The "World of Winners" sweepstakes program randomly provides prizes or rewards to booking agents. The technology implemented by Radisson administers this program over a diverse network, where multiple computer systems and travel agencies are involved.

Although these sources of competitive advantage continue to remain viable, they are not sufficient in today's hypercompetitive world, especially since hotel products are becoming more commodity-like. In the future, as the concept of branding erodes, hotels will need to find new sources of competitive advantage. This text builds on these past examples and looks at new evolving ones.

6. Sustainability

There is great debate as to whether or not competitive advantage—from IT or some other source—can be sustained. In other words, how long can a firm enjoy competitive advantage? What is its life expectancy? While there are no easy answers to these questions and while the answers would be context-dependent, there is consensus among management gurus and industry leaders that competitive advantage is not, by itself, sustainable for long periods of time. Some forms of competitive advantage (e.g., ones that involve patents or steep learning curves) can provide periods of sustainability. However, in all cases, competitive advantage can be lost or become obsolete with time. This is especially true with IT since it becomes obsolete so quickly. Moreover, as IT becomes more affordable, more standardized, and more easily copied, what once only the big chains could afford is now accessible by small chains and independents, albeit at slightly higher costs. Just consider how software as a service (SaaS) and cloud computing (where browser-based computers access computer programs housed remotely via the Internet) are making software functionality available and affordable to the masses.

It is possible that, in some cases, competitive advantage can be sustained over periods of time, particularly if it is not easily copied, if it alters industry structure, or if it has some protective parameters such as a noncompete contract or a patent, but in most cases, competitive advantage will be short lived. Therefore, hospitality leaders should always be thinking about their next competitive move or next big thing. Porter (1985, pp. 171–172) suggests four tests of desirable technological change that can lead to periods of **sustainable competitive advantage**:

1. The technological change lowers costs or enhances differentiation and provides a sustainable (i.e., inimitable) technological advantage.
2. The technological change shifts cost or uniqueness drivers in favor of a firm.
3. Pioneering the technological change translates into first-mover advantages besides those inherent in the technology itself.
4. The technological change improves overall industry structure.

Copeland and McKenney (1988) noted that economies of scale and experience (i.e., the learning-curve phenomenon) are important but insufficient in establishing long-term success and competitive advantage; management foresight and attitudes also play vital roles and are necessary to building lasting advantages. Hopper (1990) agreed that sustainability of competitive advantage from IT is difficult, if not impossible, to achieve. He further observed that once the competitive advantage is lost, the industry's sophistication (i.e., the minimum stakes needed to compete and maintain competitive parity) becomes greater. This, in turn, increases the costs of doing business and the complexity of competition for all players in the entire industry (Weill, 1991). We see this today. The hospitality industry is capital intensive due in part to the sophistication of technology and the number of systems required to operate a business to maintain parity with competitors.

For illustrative purposes, consider property management and point-of-sale systems. At one time, the earlier adopters of these technologies enjoyed competitive advantages. Over time, however, as these systems became more affordable and commonplace, the advantages were minimized, and these systems changed from ones that provided strategic advantage to ones of competitive parity. Today, if an operation does not have these core systems, it is at a noticeable competitive disadvantage.

To prolong competitive advantage, Hopper (1990) recommended shifting the focus of IT to *how* IT is used rather than on the tools themselves. Assume that whatever technology is being used, it can be easily acquired and implemented by a competitor. Therefore, the competitive advantage will come, not from the technology itself, but how the technology is used, what it can do, and how it enables employees to perform their jobs. Hopper (1990) predicted that competitive advantage will be derived from the information collected and shared throughout the organization. Technology can always be purchased, but this is not necessarily the case when referring to knowledge (Copeland and McKenney, 1988). Therefore, competitive advantage will be a function of the ability of a firm's workforce to creatively exploit the capabilities of IT to create new products and services that sell well, to personalize products and services, and to create memorable experiences that wow guests while charging premium prices. Competitive advantage will come in the form of (1) innovations that result from a firm's ability to effectively leverage its unique resources, (2) competitive asymmetry or differences between firms as a result of their unique resources, and (3) the ability to preempt competitive responses and, thereby, maintain technological superiority (Cho, 1996; Clemons and Row, 1991; Feeny and Ives, 1990; Segars and Grover, 1995).

To achieve sustainable competitive advantage, most scholars and industry leaders agree that a firm must continuously invest in its resources and capabilities to build core competencies and a culture that encourage learning, innovation, and risk taking so that new advantages can be created. The following chapters in the book offer examples of new innovations in technology that can be used strategically. Deep pockets, know-how, and technology are however not enough to ensure long-lasting advantages. In fact, D'Aveni (1994) advised firms to continually seek ways to destroy their competitive advantages (creative destruction) and create new ones before the competition does this for them. He even recommended multipronged approaches (sequential thrusts) to make it more difficult for competitors to react with counter responses. Successful firms continuously innovate and reinvent themselves. In doing so, these leaders stay out in front while others are several steps behind trying to play catch up with some previous initiative. Which ones will you choose? How will you use them strategically? Read on and welcome!

7. Summary

As professors and industry professionals, we are often asked what skills are required to succeed in the hospitality industry. There are five principal areas we always advise our students to consider, regardless of specific career focus. These include (1) developing business acumen and leadership skills, (2) establishing a strong-technical skills foundation (i.e., financial and statistics, communications, and interpersonal), (3) becoming technologically savvy, (4) understanding the art of service management (the craft elements of the business), and (5) being socially and ethically responsible. The industry is highly complex and extremely competitive. Customers and investors are becoming increasingly more demanding. Keeping pace with the demands and making sound business decisions to respond accordingly require strategic thinking, strong analytical and financial skills, and a keen sense as to where the business is heading. Leadership, interpersonal, and communication skills are also essential since we are in a people business. Remember, human resources are our most important strategic assets. We need good, capable, and caring people to accomplish what we do. The thesis of this chapter focused on the technology aspects and why you must master these to be a successful business professional and industry leader. Because the hospitality business is service oriented, the customer or guest must take center stage in all that we do and plan. In order to create unique, memorable experiences, we must also understand the dynamics of service management and how to blend high tech with high touch to provide the right information at the right time to the right people to create the right experience or service as required by the guest at any given circumstance. We are solution providers. As such, it is up to us to make what is seemingly impossible possible—and with ease. In the end, we, as leaders and business professionals, need to know how to use the many business tools (technology or otherwise) available to us to flawlessly execute our service mission in an ethical and socially responsible manner and with an eye toward profits and shareholder value—every time and with every guest. To do this, we need to be well rounded and understand as many aspects of the business we can to know how to lead and direct. Your skills assessment and career planning are vital to your future and making sure you are well prepared, so get started on these immediately.

Next one needs to actively seek ways to gain competitive advantage through IT. It is not enough to be first to market. For example, Marriott International was the first hotel company to implement in-room checkout in conjunction with the now defunct Spectradyne. Unfortunately, it failed to develop this technological amenity under terms of exclusivity with its vendor. Consequently, it was not long before this functionality started to appear in its competitors. Now, it is an industry standard. Alternatively, Carlson Hospitality, parent of Radisson, has sought patents to protect some of its technology initiatives and give the company some time advantages, however slight. Everything that can be done to create an uneven playing field in your favor (so long as it is legal and ethical) should be actively explored. Let's learn from these experiences and see what new sustained competitive advantages we can find in the following chapters.

Please remember that IT itself is seldom the source of competitive advantage because it can be easily acquired and copied. Rather, it is how IT is implemented and used within a firm (i.e., what people do with it) that leads to competitive advantage. The degree to which competitive advantage can be attained will be a function of how well IT is integrated within the firm, from the culture to the business processes to the systems themselves. The specific competitive advantages derived will be based on how a firm chooses to allocate its resources to implement IT, its overall effectiveness in doing so (e.g., its ability to cost-effectively harness the capabilities provided by the IT tools and applications), its portfolio of resources and capabilities, and the employees' willingness to embrace the technology itself. Integration of all of these points is needed for success. Good Luck!

8. CASE STUDY AND LEARNING ACTIVITY

Case Study

Let's talk with Laura again from the beginning of the chapter:

1. Can you tell me about your background?

I have always enjoyed taking care of people. At my favorite job in high school, I worked in a studio kitchen where I learned basic culinary skills, easy (and delicious) recipes, and safe food-handling procedures. We frequently hosted private events during the evenings in the kitchen, where we helped people create their own meals and provided demonstrations for more advanced items for customers to take home. The idea of people taking care of other people, and providing that unforgettable experience sparked my love for hospitality. So, by being a native of the Pennsylvania and having an interest in hospitality, there was no other option then to apply to the Hospitality Management School at Pennsylvania State University. During my time there, I became intrigued in the strategic and analytical side of the business, and pursued a career path where I could combine my love for the two worlds and that is how I got into the world of revenue management.

I graduated from Penn State and accepted a position with the Waldorf Astoria New York in their Management Development program with a concentration in revenue maximization. During my nearly four years at the Waldorf Astoria, I spent my first two years in operations; I learned the ropes of front office, housekeeping, and group services. My last two years, I worked as a revenue analyst and was then promoted to revenue manager. As revenue manger, I was on a team of three individuals with a primary responsibility in group sales and catering revenues while also contributing to the overall transient room's strategy.

2. Where do you see your career path heading?

My hopes are to eventually move up into a more regional leadership role within IHG or another large hotel brand to have more exposure to other big cities outside of New York City. I enjoy working collaboratively. I feel that it's best to always bounce ideas off different people to have the best thought-out and creative strategy. By being in this position, I would be able to work with different minds and work with them to implement their strategies to achieve their individual and companywide goals.

Learning Activity

1. What are the key learnings you take away from this story? How can you apply them to your own career planning?

2. Scan industry job postings from a variety of online and offline sources in search for hospitality managerial positions, IT and non-IT alike. What positions are available? For each position, list and discuss the stated qualifications, skills, job duties, and IT expertise required to perform the job. Which positions are most appealing to you and why?

3. Interview a hospitality business professional in the area of the industry that interests you most and find out in what ways IT affects his or her job and abilities to effectively manage and compete in today's complex and challenging world. What advice can this person offer you in terms of developing your skills and preparing yourself for a future industry career?

4. Define and develop what you would consider to be the ideal career path for you. What steps will you need to take to achieve your goals?

5. Debate with a group of friends or classmates the chapter's thesis that IT is an essential part of every hospitality business professional's career. Do you agree with the chapter's premise? Why or why not? What evidence can you provide to support your position? How would you counter the opposing view?

9. Key Terms

Boundary spanners
CAPITA
Chief information officer
Chief technology officer

Competitive advantage
Competitive method
Economies of scale
Resource-based view

Sustainable competitive advantage
SWOT analysis
Tacit
Value chain

10. Chapter Questions

1. Identify at least three examples of hospitality businesses that rely heavily upon technology. For each example, discuss how technology is used, why it is used, and the benefits it affords each organization.

2. What does it mean to be a boundary spanner?

3. What are the different career options available within the hospitality industry for those wishing to explore a career involving IT? How do these options and the skills required vary across industry segments?

4. How would you advise someone interested in pursuing a career in (a) hospitality IT and (b) hospitality management? For each, what steps should he or she take to prepare? What schooling and coursework would you recommend? What types of work experience or jobs would you advise? What skills should be developed and why?

5. Define what the hospitality industry might be like in twenty years. How will business be conducted? What roles will technology play? What will be the hot issues keeping managers awake at night? How will you prepare for these?

CHAPTER 2

Computing Basics and Networks

Chapter Objective

- At the end of this chapter students will gain an understanding on how computing devices operate and how data travels.

Learning Objectives

- What are some common IT questions
- Gain an understanding of basic computing functions
- What are some basic components
- Understand how they function and basic types
- How do they work and why are they important
- Understand how your local network functions

- How does data move over longer distances
- Understand protocols and addressing
- Explain how Web pages work
- How does data move over long distances without wiring
- What are some current and future trends
- Understand the main dangers if data is not secure

Chapter Introduction

Interview

Jennifer Jones is a well-regarded hospitality technology consultant.

1. Can you tell me about your background?

My first job out of college really set the foundation for my career path in IT, but more specifically, hospitality technology. I worked for a software provider for a well-known property management system (PMS) as an implementation specialist. Not only did that help me learn the back-end configuration of the system as well as training it, it taught me how to conduct the "orchestra" of a well-planned implementation.

My experience grew as I ventured into sales and catering applications, adding the knowledge of how systems interface by mapping data and understanding the different methods of integrations. I was employed by a start-up technology company and it gave me the ability to work side by side with product management and development teams to apply customer enhancement requests into an evolving product line, which allowed me to adopt the processes around software development, quality assurance, user acceptance testing, and software releases. Another few years were spent focusing on digital signage in the hotel and casino industry consulting with clients on design aspects as well as obtaining experience in hardware and enterprise deployments.

After spending almost ten years on the hospitality applications side of technology, I decided to take my systems knowledge over to the consulting side of the world working for a firm that specialized in technology consulting in the hotel industry for luxury resorts, mostly new construction and renovations. While applying all of the project management skills I had learned from previous software implementations, this allowed me to conduct several technology projects at once for new hotel openings. Strong vendor relationships and management of those teams were the key component to being successful to keep costs in check as well as meet demanding timelines. Learning the infrastructure of the hotel became increasingly important, as one needed to make sure that a proper backbone was in place along with sufficient cabling to ensure a hotel could support all of the technology being built into it.

After working for several organizations where I acquired a wealth of knowledge around hospitality-specific applications and developed enriched relationships with hoteliers, technologists and vendors, I became an entrepreneur and sole-proprietor of an IT consulting firm that I own and manage myself. In my business, I help clients solve business problems with innovative technology solutions. I will sit with clients and gather business requirements needed for new technology. Sometimes, we are able to help recommend process changes that allow them to be more efficient in their operations but most importantly, enhance the guest experience. Running your own organization is not for the faint of heart, but it has given me the insight and the skill set needed to operate all aspects of business that a successful organization needs.

2. How about security?

In today's world, one of the most important aspects of security is around credit cards (Chapter 4) and how we protect our guests' data as well as transmit it in a secure fashion. Countries outside of the United States, such as Canada, are more advanced in some of these areas, especially around EMV compliancy utilizing Chip and Pin.

Tokenization of guest credit cards is the first important pillar to achieve. Hotels and restaurants need to make sure that they are no longer storing guest credit card numbers in any databases (on-premise or cloud). Simply encrypting the card is no longer enough as a data breach can easily pull out raw credit card information. Organizations need to make sure that their vendor's technologies can support it.

Secondly, hotels and restaurants must implement updated payment devices that support point-to-point encryption (known as P2PE) to ensure that the submission of the credit card data during the guest transaction to get the token is secure. This requires certification from your vendor application along with the payment gateway and processor.

The final pillar to EMV compliancy requires businesses to no longer swipe credit cards and instead implement card readers that accept credit cards with chip technology. These specially injected readers are tailored to individual merchant locations and allow merchants to achieve the highest level of credit card security and alleviate themselves of any fraud liability.

Another security risk is around the continuous problem with phishing emails and how they can cause mayhem on our organization's networks. Training employees on PCI and how to recognize these phishing schemes and hackers on company email is extremely important. Opening the wrong email or attachment, although it appears to be from a legitimate contact, could allow ransomware to be placed on your network, which could paralyze the use of systems or access to data until a significant payment is made, usually in an untraceable cryptocurrency, like Bitcoin.

3. **What new innovations are you most excited about?**

For many hotels and restaurants, especially those who do not have large IT departments, the introduction of cloud-based technologies is a huge benefit as it helps keep a light IT footprint at our properties. This has helped shift the maintenance and responsibilities of our systems over to our vendors in which we typically pay for in monthly software as a service subscriptions.

Robotics has already been introduced in hotels to provide properties labor savings. When guests request towels, snacks, etc., simply load them into a robot, who effortlessly delivers them up the elevator right to the guestroom door. You will also begin to see more restaurants utilize drones, allowing for quicker delivery times and reducing pollutants in our air from taking delivery vehicles off our roads.

From both the guest and staff perspective, voice-generated applications will begin to emerge more as this technology has already found a comfortable space inside most consumers' homes. Imagine a PMS application in which an agent can check a guest in without a keyboard, mouse, or tablet and instead by talking to the application. Guests could find a restaurant or book a table without searching an app on their phone.

Facial recognition will be utilized for access into various platforms for staff and can also allow us to better recognize our loyal guests.

4. **What resources do you use to keep current?**

There are many industry associations I make sure to be a part of such as Hospitality Financial and Technology Professionals (HFTP) and Hospitality Technology Next Generation (HTNG). Both organizations offer certifications from both the professional and vendor sides. They also provide workshops and discussion threads you can attend and follow to share ideas on business innovations and discuss problems with your peers.

I always attend trade shows such as HITEC (organized by HFTP) and regional chapter meetings. There are several annual conferences that the associations discussed here hold as well as the individual vendor conferences that are held specifically about their application. In either environment, you can meet with vendors to learn more about specific products, receive education from classes given by industry colleagues, and learn from veteran users of specific applications.

I subscribe to several industry online blogs and trade magazines. Hospitality Upgrade has always been a great resource of news as well as providing a good place for me to research innovative technologies. Social media sites such as LinkedIn are helpful to see what is trending or pose a question to colleagues.

5. **What technologies would you recommend that future managers study?**

Managers should focus on making partnerships with vendors who can support mobile-friendly technologies. Vendors can adopt this trend either by providing functionality within their applications or should offer APIs that allow you to develop your own integrations to third-party systems that can achieve these needs. From mobile guestroom keys to mobile check-in, guests can decide if they even need to stop at the front desk. Guests can use their phones to message the front desk to ask a question, housekeepers can expeditiously update room statuses, or a guest can enter their name on the restaurant's waitlist before even leaving home.

The future is about enhancing the guest experience and providing as much of a personalized experience as you can, whether it be for a hotel stay or a visit to a restaurant. An investment should be made not only into capturing all the data you can about a guest, but being able to do something with the "Big Data" (Chapter 8). Managers will need to understand how to aggregate data across several platforms. Marketing technologists will need to know how to use this data to tailor the interactions you have with your guests during the entire customer journey. This artificial intelligence, or "AI," will allow us to target marketing efforts on recommendations based on our guest's preferences and historical purchasing patterns.

6. **What other advice do you have for future managers?**

Think out of the box. You don't have to pick from off-the-shelf technologies all the time. Take risks where you can and be innovative. Successes come with failures. Make sure to cultivate important relationships and not to burn bridges. We're in the hospitality business because we're hospitable. We like to assist anyone where and when we can. Reach out to alumni and faculty and establish mentors. They will want to help you. One day, you can pay it forward to the next class in our ever-important industry.

1. Overview

Jenn has provided a great overview of the importance of technology and network understanding in our industry. Now we need to establish a foundation. This chapter will cover the basics of computing and networks.

Before you can make accurate and timely decisions, you first need to know and understand the foundation. What is a computer or computing device? What are some different types? How does it work? Does it think as I do? What's under that cover? How does the data travel from place to place? These and others are questions that anyone new to technology may have. Let's start with a system.

2. System

Before you learn about computing devices, you must first understand the system behind them. Just what is a system? You see this word all the time with regard to computing: management information systems, systems analysis, the systems department, and so on. Simply put, a **system** is a way of doing things. Right now you may be writing notes about what you are reading in the margin of the book or highlighting your text on your e-reader. Perhaps you read a definition twice, or say it out loud to help you remember it. Whatever the case, you have your own system. One of the first endeavors hotel managers make when they start a new job is to evaluate the old system of their particular department (how was it done before?) and to adopt their own system (i.e., having more front desk clerks on duty at certain hours). That is how they handle busy periods, which is "a way of doing things." So in order to take the fear out of the word system, and hopefully computers as a whole, think of computers as a part of *your* way of doing things.

You might already have an ideal way of doing things, so how does a computer fit into your system? First off, a computer needs data, which is simply raw facts made up of words, numbers, etc. Data is input into the system, processed, and transformed, by you, into information (Figure 2-1). Here is a simple example: Assume you bought a stock for $10 and sold it for $15, generating a profit of $5 or a 50 percent return. A computer can do the operation 15–10 or 5/10 and give you an answer, but it is up to you to interpret the answer as good or bad. For example, you might ask, "How does this compare to other stocks?" Information is simply data to which people have given meaning and shape.

How does this apply to someone in hospitality management? Well, besides the obvious systems, such as managing rooms or seats and food and beverage consumption (which will be covered later), managers often use computers to handle their budgets. You input all the numbers and tell the computer what to add, subtract, divide, and so on, and the computer supplies a number. It is the manager's duty to interpret that number. In other words, you give the data shape and meaning, turning it into information. Maybe the number will tell the manager that she or he is over budget when it comes to labor and, therefore, needs to schedule fewer people during certain shifts. The manager is using the data and the system and, with a computer application, is getting information to make a managerial decision. This is a prime example of how computers are used in the hospitality industry to help managers make accurate and timely decisions.

The raw facts in the definition of data come in a specific form. This form is known as **binary code**. *Bi* comes from the Latin word for two. In binary code, the data can be presented in two options: a 1 or a 0. It makes words or letters by stringing together these 0s and 1s in a particular order. The order 01000001 represents the character A in Figure 2-2. This binary code is how a computer counts, whereas our own counting system is in base 10 (see Table 2-1).

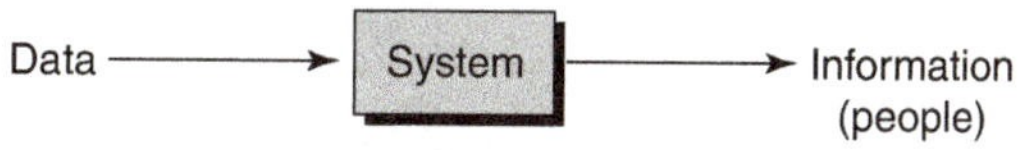

Data ──────▶ System ──────▶ Information
                                    (people)

FIGURE 2-1

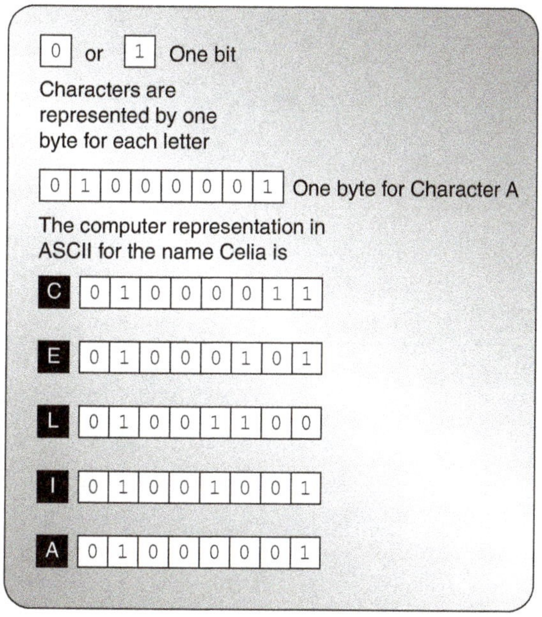

0 or 1 One bit

Characters are
represented by one
byte for each letter

0 1 0 0 0 0 0 1 One byte for Character A

The computer representation in
ASCII for the name Celia is

C 0 1 0 0 0 0 1 1

E 0 1 0 0 0 1 0 1

L 0 1 0 0 1 1 0 0

I 0 1 0 0 1 0 0 1

A 0 1 0 0 0 0 0 1

FIGURE 2-2

Bits can either be a 1 or a 0. Eight bits make up a byte
or a standard character. The word *CELIA* is made up of
the depicted bytes.

In the decimal system, you go up to ten digits and start over. Binary counting is a little different. Look at Table 2-1. Can you see the pattern? Start with a 0, and from the left, each new number is where a 0 from the previous number is replaced with a 1. Can you see how the 1s seem to be moving to the left? When all 1s have replaced the 0s, a new number is started with a 1 in the beginning and more 0s than in the last set. These 0s and 1s are known as bits.

Bits, short for binary digits, make up the smallest form of data storage. Put eight of them together and you get what is known as a **byte**. A byte represents one standard character or number. Again, the letter A is represented by the following bits: 01000001. The next vowel, E, is represented by its unique combination of 1s and 0s: 01000101.

Bits and bytes make up the beginning of data storage and measurement. They are followed by **kilobytes, megabytes, gigabytes,** and **terabytes** and **petabytes, exabytes, zettabytes,** and **yottabytes**. Remember that eight bits make up a byte. The number 1024 is the one to remember.

1024 bytes = 1 kilobyte
1024 kilobytes = 1 megabyte
1024 megabytes = 1 gigabyte
1024 gigabytes = 1 terabyte
1024 terabytes = 1 petabyte
1024 petabytes = 1 exabyte
1024 exabytes = 1 zetabyte
1024 zetabytes = 1 yottabyte

To understand how a computer "sees" whether a bit is a 1 or a 0, you must first understand how a bit travels. Remember electricity and Ben Franklin? Electricity is actually defined as "the class of physical phenomena arising from the existence and interactions

TABLE 2-1
Base 10 versus Binary Counting

Base 10				
1	11	21	91	101
2	12	22	92	102
3	13	23	93	103
4	14	24	94	104
5	15	25	95	105
6	16	26	96	106
7	17	27	97	107
8	18	28	98	108
9	19	29	99	109
10	20	30	100	110

Binary
0
1
10
11
100
101
111
1000
1001
1011
1111
100000

of electronic charge." Therefore, **electricity** is a phenomenon and **voltage** measures its potential. If you vary these two in a consistent manner, then you have a **signal**.

A signal can travel down a wire or even through the air. Signals come in two general categories: analog and digital. **Analog** signals travel as a wave that has many points or states as seen in Figure 2-3. It has a high point in B and a low point in D with points A, C, and E in-between.

A **digital** signal does not have points in between such as A, C, and E. It only has high and low points and varies instantaneously with no points in between. These high and low points are called high states and low states, which are just voltage levels. Look at Figure 2-4.

In a digital signal there are only two states. The high voltage level represents a 1 and a low voltage level represents a 0, which is precisely how a computer identifies bits.

Remember when the television signals went digital? Most likely not, but they did. Chances are that you used cable that was already digital and so were not affected. However, many still used the old "rabbit ear antennas" that received analog signals, and had to replace them with new equipment that received digital signals. Analog signals are older than the digital signals that computing devices use. Analog lines are found today in old phone lines generally running from your house to the nearest phone company building. From there, the majority of carriers use digital signals. It is important to know that analog signals are used for data requiring continuous states such as voice and video and that the two types of signals can be used in conjunction with one another for greater efficiency. In daily usage, an analog signal can be converted into a data signal whereby it can be "cleaned up" and then converted back into an analog signal with no background noise.

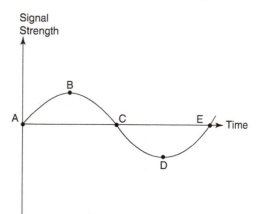

FIGURE 2-3

Sine waves have many levels. Here the sine wave has a high point B, a low point D, and points A, C, and E at the beginning, middle, and end.

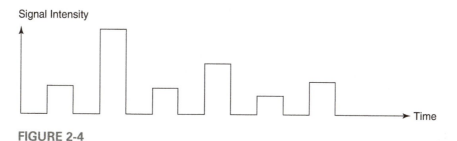

FIGURE 2-4

In contrast to sine waves, digital signals have just a high and a low point.

3. Hardware

Let's introduce or review some basic terms that any manager needs to understand. **Hardware** is something physical you can touch and feel such as your computer screen. If you take off a cover of a computer, you would see a green board with circuitry and extensions. This is known as a printed circuit board (PCB) or a motherboard. This is the foundation of the computer where all of the connections take place. On this foundation sits the **central processing unit (CPU)**. This is the brain of the computer. Laptop and netbook manufacturers continue to shrink the motherboard for advanced portability. Attached to the motherboard is memory. **RAM** stands for *random access memory* and is where your applications such as word processing or spreadsheets run when they are used locally. Some RAM is temporary, meaning that once you turn your computer off the data is erased like a blackboard. That is why you need to save your work. There are many different types of RAM for different hardware units. Getting the best type before purchasing and making sure you have enough can speed up your device. Next, the **hard drive** is the part sealed in an airtight metal container. This is to prevent any dirt or other particles from entering and corrupting the data. This disk drive is where local data is stored and retrieved. Disks are divided into sectors and tracks, with the **operating system (OS)**, keeping track of which sector contains what data. The hard disk also contains an area that is used for memory known as a **cache.** This part of the disk works with RAM in storing and retrieving frequently used data such as Web pages or files. For the most part, smartphones and other handheld devices use different types of memory in place of a hard drive. A common term in the **smartphone** and tablet lexicon is the **SIM card** which stands for **subscriber identity module.** Found on this transferable card are common identifiers such as the phone number and personal contacts among others and carrier-specific information.

4. Software

Next is software. Software is the detailed instructions that control the operation of a computer system. "A software program is a series of statements or instructions to the computer. The process of writing or coding programs is termed programming, and the individuals who specialize in this task are called programmers" (Laudon and Laudon, 2015, p. 75). Software comes in two basic categories: application software and system software. "Application software, or applications, are the programs written for or by users to apply a computer to a specific task" (Laudon and Laudon, 2009, p. 173). The "off-the-shelf" productivity software such as word processing, spreadsheets, or specific programs written in languages such as Java, Python, C++, Pearl, and Ruby are examples of application software. Application software is needed because the hardware understands only its own "machine language," or binary numbers. Application software is written in words and then translated into machine language by a compiler or interpreter. Putting it together, a programmer writes words of code; the code is sent through a compiler or interpreter that translates it into machine code—those 1s and 0s that computers understand—as illustrated in Figure 2-5.

Other examples of common "out-of-the-box" application software include multimedia presentation, contact management, browsers, publishing, and so on. Think of an industry, and chances are it has software that is standard to it. Out-of-the-box software is convenient because thousands of common tasks have already been automated and can be accessed by pointing and clicking. **Application Protocol Interfaces (API)**, as mentioned in the interview, allow software to communicate with one another. The two main versions in our industry are the property management system (PMS) and the point-of-sale (POS) system, which will be covered later.

5. Networks

Now let's look at how data goes from place to place in networks. The prevalence of networks in the hospitality industry may surprise you. A guest making a room reservation on their phone, a meeting planner virtually touring a potential property for a large meeting, or simply uploading a video are all examples of networks in use in the industry today. How often you interact with networks, when studied in detail, demonstrates not only their ubiquity as pointed out by Jenn in our interview, but also their importance in communication as well as in revenue generation.

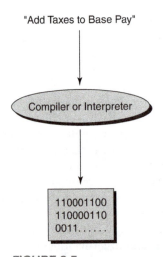

FIGURE 2-5

Through the use of a compiler or interpreter, familiar words are translated into machine code.

Additionally, with the ever-increasing availability of real-time information to management and staff, not to mention customer expectations of communication at the property level, network knowledge is vital to remain competitive.

The terms **networks** and **networking** refer to the broad subject of managing computer networks and the information on them. "A network is a transmission system that connects two or more applications running on different computers" (Panko, 2008, p. 1). Networking is a detailed subject matter. To management, however, there are three primary interest areas.

Security, Performance, and Reliability

Is it safe, fast, and running are three questions that beg for the answer "yes." Ensuring that the network is protected from unauthorized users while available to authorized users seems logical. In reality, it is a daily challenge. Hacking of a company's Web page or theft of customer data are often nightly news items. New regulations by the credit card companies actually mandate a certain level of security to thwart any such occurrences. Speed is also important. Slow networks not only lessen communication ability but can also drive guests toward your competitors. If you encounter a Web page or app that is loading slowly, how long does it take you before you move on to another? There are just too many options, and "fast" is what the customer expects regarding technology. Finally, any system that doesn't function properly or "goes down" is not an option. It has become too much of a worldwide lifeline. Let's start with small networks.

6. Small Networks

If you operate in an office or school setting and your computer can communicate with other computers or computing devices, you are most likely using a **local area network (LAN)**. Like all advances in technology, LANs provide a business need. Specifically, they do the following:

1. Allow resources to be shared. For example, instead of everyone having a printer, which would be cost-prohibitive, the resource is shared by multiple end-users.
2. Allow data and information to be shared. Through networks, and unrestricted by geography, all managers can have access to "real-time" company information.

Obviously networks are all about sharing. On the back of a computer you will find openings with multiple pins or sockets. These are known as ports. "A **port** is the combination of a connector plug and internal electronics ..." (Panko, 2008, p. 39). Ports include serial, parallel, and the newer more interoperable united serial bus (USB). Ports are used mostly for local communication with **peripherals** such as scanners. In networks, computers need another important device. All stations on a network, such as computers, printers, and kiosks, which are ease-of-use touch screens, are known in networking terms as nodes. In order for nodes to join a network, a network interface card is needed. **Network interface cards (NICs)** provide network access and addressing information. An expansion slot can be seen on the rear or side of most computers. This is where an NIC can be inserted. Each and every NIC has a unique 48-bit address (known as the MAC address) that the manufacturer assigns. This unique addressing allows for efficient sending and receiving of data. With an NIC, your computer is given a new name and joins a larger community.

Just as storage has its own measurement in bytes, data transfer rates have their own form of measurement in bits per second (bps). These bits are the same as found in binary code. Remember that storage is measured in bytes and data transfer rate, or speed, is measured in bits. When your network communicates with another network such as the Internet, a **router** is used that routes the data.

What these fast-moving bits travel through from computing device to computing device are known as mediums:

1. Twisted pair copper wires. Copper is a great material for signals to travel on. The phone line in an older house (if not using cable or fiber) contains two pairs of

copper wires (four wires in total) twisted together and known in networking terms as RJ-11. Each pair represents a line. In many LANs, a larger form of twisted pair is used. It is known as RJ-45 (often known as Ethernet) and contains four pairs of twisted copper wires. The wires are twisted in such a manner that points on the twist can block interference from the other pairs of wires.

2. **Coaxial cable.** If you have cable television, this is the local medium involved. LANs can also utilize this copper core medium. Coaxial cable contains one heavy copper wire that is heavily insulated by three different layers to prevent interference.

3. **Fiber optics.** This is a medium consisting of very thin (think of a strand of your hair) and expensive glass fibers covered by a protective layer. Here, instead of an electromagnetic signal, pulses of light are used. A flash of light indicates the 1 bit. Absence of light indicates the 0 bit. Fiber optic technology is very reliable and unsusceptible to electromagnetic interference. Fiber optic cable has been around enough that it is being seen more at the local business and residential level. Its speed and reliability makes it ideal for the larger networks discussed in the next section.

4. **Wireless.** To be fair, wireless is not a medium but rather a broadcast technology. It is not bound by wires in between points. At the LAN level, wireless technology enables users to operate digitally without being tied to a desk. It is not perfect. Brick walls can be a major obstacle. For that reason, multiple access points, which transmit and receive data for the nodes on the network, are used. Access points at the local level vary in appearance from small cones to plates and are in charge of moving the data across the wireless spectrum.

5. Other wireless technologies found at the local level include **Bluetooth** and **near field communication (NFC)**. Bluetooth is used at the very local level (10 meters or less typically) and can aid in such tasks of wirelessly syncing your smartphone calendar with the one on your computer. NFC is even closer (very close or touching) where syncing (i.e., photos) is also often the purpose. We will continue our discussion of wireless in the section, "Large Wireless Networks."

Networks are not just hardware. Just as the OS runs the show in a desktop computer, another system software is the boss here. A **network operating system (NOS)** is a system software that routes communications on the network and manages network resources. A NOS commonly resides on a server. A **server** from a hardware perspective is simply a more expensive computer with lots of memory, hard disk space, and a fast CPU (to name a few items) that provides shared resources to the network. The NOS is the boss of the LAN. Because network outage can result in lost revenue and decreased employee productivity and because security is always a concern, often a redundant or backup NOS server is used in case the primary server fails. Additionally, backup power supplies such as a generator or off-site power supply arrangements made with a third party are a good idea in case the electricity should fail. This is of particular concern for international properties, where infrastructure can be unreliable.

A network server is just one example of a server. Servers can be dedicated to specific tasks in large organizations. Three other servers play a crucial role in LANs and networks at large.

1. A file server is a computer and a storage device dedicated to storing files. Any authorized person on the network can store files on the server. File servers often contain commonly used templates and data for day-to-day activities. An expense report used by management is an example of a file stored in a file server.

2. A print server is a computer that manages one or more printers. Hospitality organizations may use a large number of printers as well as make them available to guests. A large number of printers in use require a dedicated server.

3. A database server is a system that processes database queries. Most hotel systems are server based where a search engine is integrated into the system to handle simple and complex queries. We will look at databases more closely in Chapter 8.

In the hospitality world one common piece of networking equipment is also found—the **private branch exchange (PBX)**. The PBX has long been a part of the hotel industry. For example, a hotel with five hundred rooms that all contain phones needs a connection to the phone company. However, purchasing or leasing five hundred phone lines plus staff lines would be cost-prohibitive, particularly since at any one time only 30 percent or less of the phone lines are utilized (or less since we all have our own phones). Enter the PBX. The PBX is used to direct incoming calls to the larger organizational setting. An incoming call goes to the PBX, with say fifty ports, and is directed to the specific location such as a hotel room. An outgoing call is done in reverse. With phone lines already in place in many organizations, PBXs can also be used in lieu of LANs although this is less and less the case. Older analog PBX systems are being replaced with newer digital ones. The PBX's interface with the telephone network introduces our next network topic, large networks.

7. Large Networks

To understand large networks as well as the evolution of small networks, you need to understand telecommunications. **Telecommunications** is simply long-distance communications. This long-distance communication involves a network you already use, the telephone system.

Alexander Graham Bell accomplished the first voice transmission in 1876. Many years later a nationwide phone network was established and controlled by one company, American Telephone and Telegraph (AT&T) until its breakup in 1984. From there, other companies such as MCI and Sprint entered the picture in competition with AT&T for the long-distance telephone market. Since a 1996 deregulation act, in theory, companies from different industries such as cable companies, broadcasters, and phone companies have been allowed to compete in each other's markets.

With the adoption of digital signals, large networks can reap the benefits. The first type of larger networks is the **wide area network (WAN)**. A WAN is a network of larger geography than a LAN, ranging from a couple of miles to the entire world. An emerging network is the metropolitan area network (MAN) for a metropolitan area or in and around a city network. With hospitality organizations having multiple sites or properties, connectivity and collaboration are needed. This functionality was first enabled by WANs.

Different network services are available in WAN utilization on the mediums discussed earlier. Basically these services or technologies speed up data transmission over long distances. Their transfer rate is dependent on bandwidth. **Bandwidth** is the difference between the highest and lowest point of a signal. It is this available area in between where the data flows on a channel.

8. The Internet

Perhaps the most well-known network is the Internet. Internet access, particularly wireless, is almost totally expected by guests, with pricing always an issue. From smartphones to fit bands, the Internet is used by many devices and in different ways. The Internet, a network that no one owns outright, links multiple networks and users around the globe.

The Internet has its own protocol that is quickly becoming the dominant small and large network protocol worldwide. This protocol, known as **TCP/IP (transmission control protocol/Internet protocol)**, was established by the department of defense in the 1970s. The Internet's foundations lie with the U.S. military. The thought process is that a decentralized network would make any nuclear attack upon the network less significant because network control and storage are not in one place. If the server at your location goes down, it has almost no impact on the Internet at large. With this spread out network in mind, the military came up with the TCP/IP protocol to ensure common practices in communication. TCP/IP has layers that govern data flow through the software and hardware of the sending and receiving computing devices.

Today the Internet has been embraced by multiple organizations, with quasi-governmental organizations overseeing its operation and address allocation. When you use the Internet, you access it through an Internet service provider (ISP), which has its own servers and IP addresses (provided to them) to be given to customers. IP addresses provide the location of a node or network. An IP address is a static address. For example, 198.4.159.10 is the IP address of *www.prenhall.com*, the publishers of this book.

In contrast, a dynamic address may be assigned by an ISP to a user accessing the Internet via an ISP for a short time. It is the ISP through a **domain name server (DNS)** that assigns letters—which are easier to remember (e.g., Prenhall.com)—to numerical IP addresses, although both may be used.

9. The World Wide Web

The **World Wide Web** is the most recognizable communication tool on the Internet. The *Web* and the *Internet* are terms often used interchangeably, which is incorrect. The Web is *part of* the Internet. The Web likewise uses the TCP/IP protocol. A **uniform resource locator (URL)** uses the aforementioned DNS server to point to Web resources and addresses such as *www.psu.edu*. A URL is a Web address. The Web also uses specific formats. **Hypertext markup language (HTML)** is one format of the Web that provides formatting and presentation functionality as well as navigation and search capabilities. Hypertext signifies that the text when clicked will take you to another location on the Web. **Extensible markup language (XML)** is a newer form of formatting and presentation on the Web with greater emphasis on the meaning of the data. XML allows businesses to interact via the Web with a common understanding of what the data represents. Incorporating these and other functionalities is the vital piece of software used to surf the net. Applications such as Chrome, Internet Explorer, Firefox, or Safari, which are known as browsers, open the door to browser-based Internet communication.

10. Large Wireless Networks

Because of their mobile nature, wireless networks are on the rise. Wireless transmissions are electromagnetic signals sent through the air. Common wireless transmissions include satellites, and cellular and personal communication services (PCS).

The word *microwave* causes most to think of the type of oven. When an electromagnetic signal passes through water it is disrupted and generates heat as a by-product. The good-microwave ovens send electromagnetic signals that end up heating water molecules, giving us warm food and drink. The bad-satellite television in rainy Seattle can be problematic since water droplets can upset reception. Microwave usage in networks is highly efficient. In conjunction with satellites that redirect the data to a new location, wireless transmission can move large amounts of data over remote places such as oceans and deserts, making it ideal for distant sites.

Cellular technology uses geographic areas that are divided into "cells." Each cell has an antenna or tower to receive a signal transmitted by a cell phone that passes it off to an available channel in the next cell all the way to the end point. Because many antennas and towers are needed to hand off the phone call, coverage can be scarce in remote areas.

For obvious reasons, the Web has embraced wireless technology as well. Specifically for the hospitality industry, the technology can be used to pinpoint a potential customer's location and provide that customer information about nearby restaurants, hotels, stadiums, and so on.

11. Forward-Looking Issues in Hospitality

From a management perspective, and to some degree from a guest perspective, new uses of the Internet are giving hospitality organizations more options. **Cloud computing** is one such offering where companies such as Amazon, IBM, Google, and Microsoft are providing processing power, storage, and applications on their servers, which can be accessed via the Internet. With cloud computing we are also seeing newer "edge" devices that can provide much of the data processing rather than waiting on the cloud. Hospitality technology-specific vendors are also increasing in offering their applications over the Internet rather than on-site. What was once known as an application service provider (ASP), where generic software was made available over the Internet, has developed into a more customized application tailored to a specific company's needs by the vendor but likewise stored and managed by the vendor on their servers and accessed over the Internet. This is known as **software as a service (SaaS)**.

Drones are also seeing more usage in hospitality. What were once only cameras in the sky are quickly becoming service delivery options with a whole host of research and development in the works. The Internet of things or newer devices accessing the Internet is increasing. Imagine a restaurant refrigerator ordering milk on its own. Care must be taken in our industry with more and more devices coming "online." As we saw in the interview, voice is also gaining popularity in searches. We will look at searches in more detail in the next chapter.

12. Security

Security issues are a great concern when using networks and the Internet. Current mandates regarding credit card security will be looked at in Chapter 4. Meeting this need, newer classes of networks using Internet technology have sprung up, providing businesses with a secure way of conducting transactions in such a public environment. Currently, ISPs and organizations utilize **virtual private networks (VPNs)**. A VPN provides a secure connection to different sites of an enterprise over the Internet. Specific protocols are used that wrap data transfer, inhibiting penetration from unauthorized users. With innovations such as this, secure transmissions are further enabled. Now companies can offer telecommuting options to their workers. This allows off-site workers comparable access to the same data and network speeds while at home or away from the office. VPN's effectiveness has led to it also becoming a standard for internal or company networks.

The degree of access, if at all, given to others using a network calls for difficult decisions. Granting and restricting access to Internet resources is done by software known as a firewall. **Firewalls** prohibit unauthorized users from accessing Internet resources through user verification and passwords. Advanced firewalls also **monitor** Internet intrusions and attacks. A popular form of attack is a *denial of service attack* where routers and other devices on the Internet are co-opted and form what is known as a **botnet** and are directed to a specific Web site. The volume overwhelms a Web server and prohibits other users from accessing its resources, rendering it useless.

The Internet of things has progressed to the point where real world devices are controlled by virtual means. This unfortunately places people at risk of real world injury, if cyber criminals decide to use these networks to disrupt or attack critical infrastructure. Cyber-crimes will result in physical injury as denial of service attacks increase. Many unsecured devices are giving criminals the chance to disrupt huge online Web sites and the American economy as a result. Recently, the largest DDos attack in history disrupted the Internet, pulling down major sites like Twitter, Netflix, and CNN. The difference with this attack was that it was executed by a botnet made up of devices like digital cameras and DVR players.

Botnets make up these DDos attacks. A DDos attack is when a cyber criminal or organization directs an overload of Web site traffic to your online property, which causes it to crash. Typically called a distributed denial of service attack, these block online shopping by causing your servers to crash and disrupting your sales process.

Because your consumers can no longer access your site, or products and services—they simply go to a competitor, while you scramble to fix the problem. According to RivalHost, DDos attacks have increased 2.5 times over the last three years and are set to keep rising.

The costs involved when cyber criminals execute DDos attacks on a brand are extremely high. Virgin Blue, the airline, lost $20 million in revenue due to a DDos attack in 2010. All e-commerce hospitality brands need to be aware and fully prepared to combat these cyber-attacks.

Botnets may also spread viruses, **worms**, **Trojan horses**, and **spyware**. **Viruses** are malicious pieces of software. Worms, Trojan horses, and spyware work a little differently. While a virus needs an end-user to activate it (unknowingly), say opening an attachment that ends in .exe (Don't do it!), a worm does not. Worms exploit information on your computer (e.g., email addresses) and spread themselves without human interaction. Trojan horses are phony software that appear to do one thing but once installed do another, such as deleting files, whereas spyware can record passwords and key strokes. Be careful what you install and click online!

Due to the Internet's designed public nature, oftentimes the Web server is put out in front and separated from other network resources. The area between the Web server and the rest of the network is given a military-sounding name, the demilitarized zone (DMZ). Use of firewalls and placement of servers often dictate how remote workers can and cannot access company resources such as files and emails.

Firewalls play an important role in network protection. Good network administrators will update their firewalls daily against the malicious pieces of software. Firewalls must be used. It is often surprising to organizations that use advanced firewalls with monitoring capabilities how often an attempted or successful intrusion happens on their network. Larger organizations can see thousands of attempts daily; yes, daily.

Communication between different networks has its own security issues, particularly when the Internet is used for such privileged data as credit card numbers. In addition to the methods used by VPNs, scrambling of messages, known as **encryption**, is often necessary to keep transmissions private. Encryption involves a mathematical operation that assigns different values to a key. Given the discussion of eight bits representing a specific key, encryption assigns more 1s and 0s algorithmically to each key to mask the actual keys used, and thereby the entire message. The number of additional 1s and 0s used represents the strength of the encryption method used. Common cost-effective encryption methods used today are 128 bits. Luckily, there comes a point where it is cost-prohibitive to attempt to crack higher encryption methods. It simply takes too much processing power and time. Unfortunately, technological advances in encryption are also taking place in the nefarious encryption cracking software realm.

Security issues are more local than one might think. Studies show that most breaches or thefts of company data are done internally. A locked door and restricted access can solve many problems. On the other hand, external threats are often at a lower level than you may think. They are enabled by telephone tricks where one party calls another and tricks that party into giving access information. This is an example of **social engineering**. A problem in the hotel industry is when a hacker calls a hotel room and claims to be from the front desk. Managerial procedures are needed. Oftentimes, hackers, or those who penetrate a network, use social engineering methods to get in the door of a network and wreak havoc on Web sites or illegally obtain data. For these reasons, network administrators concern themselves daily with a host of issues. The first issue deals with user authentication. Currently, user identifications and passwords are commonly used. Other tools include rights and permissions of data. For example, a housekeeper is not given access to sales data, nor is a member of the wait staff given client home phone numbers. By restricting who has access, many problems can be avoided. Having proper policies in place can also aid in network security. Letting employees know about current phishing emails is a common one. **Phishing** is broadly defined as fake emails that trick the user into providing information such as social security or bank account numbers. **Spear phishing** is tailored for one individual and looks very real. In the age of employee empowerment, data access must be studied constantly by all levels of management. Advanced network software development has created **network behavior analysis (NBA)** software that analyzes a network for irregularities.

Advanced identification technology such as iris (eye) and fingerprint scanning along with facial recognition take away many of the vulnerabilities of password and user IDs. Costs have dropped to a degree that fingerprint technology is becoming more common as a password replacement.

While smartphones have enabled much more personalized access by both management and the guest, security must be applied here as well. Proprietary corporate property may reside on many smartphones, so passwords at a minimum are needed. Aside from the aforementioned content regarding security, smartphone security software is available, giving the administrator many options on what can be done with both the corporate phone and guest access.

13. Summary

Management, in any form, requires understanding. Since technology plays such an active role in daily operations and future planning, understanding technology is critical. On this road to discovery, you have found out that computers work much the way that other things do—via a system. Data goes into a system, which (and with the aid of people) turns it into useable information. When data moves in digital signals, a computing device will read the high and low points of this signal, giving you a binary code. From the motherboard to RAM, you have seen where these binary digits travel and are stored. In conjunction with this hardware, different software is used to manipulate the data and generate information without having to understand machine code. Whether a generic smartphone application or an industry application, it is quality software that provides the value in the management of information.

Network understanding is now also a required tool for any hospitality manager. We use it daily and so do our guests. From small networks, found in a restaurant, to larger global hotel communication systems, network knowledge is a must. When a network goes down or is not used properly, lost revenue and unhappy customers can result. Growing in importance by the day is network security. Up-to-date firewall software and data encryption are a good start, particularly when considering that customers' personal information and credit card numbers make up much of the network data. A true security strategy including employee policy and procedures, which is tested often, serves as a true complement to any hardware or software. No matter what organization you are in, networks require constant attention.

14. CASE STUDY AND LEARNING ACTIVITY

Case Study

Julie is the assistant general manager for a local independent hotel. She was recently hired due to her technological expertise. The owners of the hotel wished to increase their property's network security. Other hotels in the area were the victims of security breaches, and the owners feared that they would be next.

Julie knew from her training and past experience that what was needed first was a situational analysis to find points of vulnerability. She wanted to handle the major problem spots first before she dug into the more technical matters and relatively quickly identified some potential hazards. She compiled a list of the first ten vulnerable points she encountered and turned it over to the owners that morning.

Vulnerabilities

1. Front desk staff is giving out too much information over the telephone
2. The room holding the network servers is unlocked
3. The computer system does not require users to change their passwords often enough
4. Both guests and employees use the same network
5. Employee and guest smartphones can access the hotel's wireless network
6. Firewall software requires manual updates

7. No employee network policy currently exists
8. Software installation is allowed on all computers
9. Business center computers do not require passwords
10. She was able to access the hotel's wireless from across the street

After receiving the list, the owners told Julie that a competing hotel a couple of blocks away just had their network hacked and were unsure of the damage. Since this was the fifth hotel in their area to be breached this week, they were worried that they might be next. They wanted her to act fast. Julie was by no means done with her audit and was sure that she would find many more points of vulnerability, but she believed that these were most of the "big ones." She knew that network security was both an art and a science, but she needed to start somewhere to secure the operation.

Learning Activity

1. What should Julie do first?
2. Why should she do this first?
3. List in order your next nine priorities and justify your answers.
4. Apart from these ten, can you think of other possible vulnerable points?

15. Key Terms

Application Protocol Interfaces (API)
Analog
Bandwidth
Binary code

Bit
Bluetooth
Near field communication (NFC)
Botnet

Byte
Cache
Cellular
Cloud computing

CPU
Digital
Domain name server (DNS)
Electricity
Encryption
Exabytes
Extensible markup language (XML)
Firewalls
Gigabyte
Hard Drive
Hardware
Hypertext markup language (HTML)
Kilobyte
Local area network (LAN)
Megabyte
Monitor

Network behavior analysis (NBA)
Networks and networking
Network interface cards (NICs)
Network operating system (NOS)
Operating System
Peripherals
Petabyte
Phishing
Private branch exchange (PBX)
Port
RAM
Router
Server
Signal
Smartphone
Spear phishing

Social engineering
Software as a service (SaaS)
Subscriber Identity Module
System
TCP/IP (transmission control
    protocol/Internet protocol)
Telecommunications
Terabyte
Uniform resource locator (URL)
Virus
Virtual private networks (VPNs)
Voltage
Wide area network (WAN)
Worms, Trojan horses, and spyware
Yottabytes
Zettabytes

16. Chapter Questions

1. How do people fit into the definition of information?
2. How is data counted?
3. What is a virus?
4. What are some examples of smartphone OSs?
5. What is binary code?

CHAPTER 3

E-Commerce and Digital Marketing in Practice

Chapter Objective

- At the end of this chapter students will be able to understand digital marketing and e-commerce in hospitality and tourism.

Learning Objectives

- Learn the many channels of customer interaction
- Gain an understanding of the basic e-commerce technologies
- What is it and how is it applied
- What are the technologies used in e-commerce security

Chapter Introduction

Interview

Catherine Krugler is the General Manager of Bedford and Co. in New York City.

1. **Can you tell me about your background?**
   a. After graduating with a degree in Hospitality Management from Penn State University in 2009, I moved to New York City and took a job with Darden. During my 1½ years with Darden, I managed at two different Olive Garden locations focusing on FOH at both locations. I then joined Shake Shack, at the Theater District location. I spent five years working with Shake Shack, three years as general manager. After Shake Shack, I spent a year working with The Westin at Grand Central. Most recently I've taken over an independent restaurant, Bedford and Co.

2. **In your current project, how are you using digital media to grow your customer base?**
   a. Working at Bedford and Co. is exciting since we are truly a small business that is relatively new. Being open less than two years has meant that we've needed to build our guest base from the ground up. Knowing that technology is where most diners are turning to get information about restaurants and make dining decisions, we've needed to focus our energy on our digital media campaigns to make sure we are found when potential guests are looking. Being a small business means that a lot of these campaigns are run internally, as we do not have the resources to have this all outsourced.
   b. Social media is extremely important these days: Instagram, Facebook, and Twitter are all daily focuses of mine for business purposes. These platforms have algorithms that determine your visibility; the more you use their platform the more visible you are on it. In order to maximize visibility, multiple users usually need access to accounts so that we are able to constantly post (Facebook live, Instagram stories). Giving access to a few users puts your brand in jeopardy, if someone who has access does not clearly understand the goals. We have a company that has arranged daily posts on these main platforms, but once a day posts are not enough; they are just the bare minimum. So additionally, I'll post to our stories, boost posts so they are sponsored advertisements, or I'll offer a deal to someone who mentions said post. For example, "Screenshot this post and get a free glass of prosecco Friday night."
   c. You then need to think about the different restaurant specific platforms where diners look for information. Yelp, OpenTable, various food publications, bloggers, and influencers. Yelp being the most successful dining information platform, we have decided to participate in their advertising program. Their advertising program has a few different aspects that are beneficial for restaurants: (1). No other restaurant will be featured on our page. (2). We can be featured on other restaurant pages (that are not paying for advertising). (3). They feature your restaurant in specific search queries.
   d. Finally, there are so many platforms where your business information is listed and reviews are left; you can also post and engage guests on these platforms such as Google Business, Trip Advisor, and some others mentioned above. Every time there is a change in business operating hours these sites need to be updated. Also diners are leaving valuable feedback on these platforms, so we monitor these daily/weekly and engage with guests that leave feedback.
   e. We also have a database of emails from guests that have made reservations, hosted events, or requested to be on our email list that we send biweekly emails to. These emails can be anything from a small reminder that we do bottomless brunch to we are completely changing our wine list and have great bottles on sale now.

3. **What are some things not to do that could turn off your customers?**
   a. Overloading them with information that they don't want. We have different email lists that we use to share information and send targeted emails to.
   b. Share incorrect information. With your business information being posted on a number of different sites it is extremely important to make sure the information is consistent and accurate.

4. **How do you keep them engaged?**
   a. To keep them engaged we not only try to interact back when they interact with our social media, but we also post interactive posts. For example, on Instagram you can host a poll that your viewers can participate in. Also, when a guest posts a picture of something at our restaurant we try to repost it, which makes people feel really connected and special.

5. How do you keep current?

   a. We've identified a number of businesses that we admire and follow their lead. We also look to a social media company for insight, as well as read the blogs and publications to see what is popular. We do have a PR team that guides us seasonally and keeps us updated in advance of any opportunities to get our restaurant out there.

6. Any advice for future managers?

   a. Nothing is as important as the in-person interactions. Guests still make their decisions based on loyalty and connection. No matter where you are working, during service, the guests in your business are the most important.

1. Overview

Catherine introduces us to some real-world examples on how managers can manage digital marketing successfully. As she stated, the virtual world allows hospitality consumers to begin the buying cycle long before any action-steps are taken toward organizing, booking, or paying for their travel experiences.

Consumers pre-experience the trips and travels they most desire from any number of growing touch points—including desktop computers, mobile phones, smart watches, and tablets using the Internet as a tool for research, discovery, and planning.

Once online, consumers select which channel they would prefer to use, to engage with their chosen brand. This might be on a brand Web site, a social media page, or on a mobile app. These multi-channel experiences pose a number of significant problems for brands—namely the unification and creation of a seamless brand presence across many different platforms.

It only becomes an omni-channel experience for the customer, when they are able to quickly and easily identify and engage with their chosen hospitality brand wherever that brand crops up online. Omni-channel also refers to the integration of the virtual world with real-world technologies—especially as they relate to cross-device attribution.

For a hospitality brand, being able to market effectively to consumers by creating a strong, seamless, and easy to access brand presence fully utilizing modern technology is the most direct, sustainable, and growth-orientated path to long-term, customer retention.

Omni-channel marketing involves the ability to target consumers across multiple devices, on multiple platforms to secure sales. The hospitality brand collects data and infuses future digital strategy and marketing content with insight, amplifying the reach and conversion of each platform, technology, and marketing message.

Understanding consumer behavior across these many channels and devices is key to launching and managing a seamless brand experience that functions efficiently.

Advertising

Perhaps the obvious, if not the most complex aspect of e-commerce and digital marketing, is advertising. Everyday usage of the Internet yields a barrage of advertisements for a great number of products and services.

Ads are presented in many ways, such as native ads (ads that appear to be a part of the content that the user is consuming) or retargeting ads (ads that seem to follow you all over the net, displaying items based upon your past browsing habits). Newer online attempts are the many videos that are preceded by an advertisement (i.e., YouTube).

According to *BrianCliette.com* the growth of social networks has led to the development of social media advertising in all of the major social networking sites, that is, Facebook, Twitter, Instagram, Pinterest, and LinkedIn allow advertisers to create ads to target their site's users.

Whatever your view of advertising online, companies in the advertising business are financially dependent on making sure that their advertisements are being seen. Currently, advertising revenues are suffering, with some estimates stating that only some 2 percent of online ads are actually clicked on. With advertising-blocking software becoming more available, this particular business model has many challenges ahead.

Auctioning

The Internet created a market that brings sellers and buyers together instantly. The auction format of e-commerce is likely to become increasingly popular. Sites like *Expedia.com* continue to grow exponentially since they enhance efficiency while maximizing the return for the buyer and seller.

Many companies that conduct auctions take a percentage of the revenues from auction-driven transactions. These third parties, or clearing companies, usually charge the seller a commission fee based on a percentage of the total revenue generated at auction. This is exactly what eBay does.

Mobile Commerce

According to *BrianCliette.com*, smartphone penetration is still steeply on the rise and the best medium for delivering a seamless omni-channel experience to consumers.

In other words, a consumer's mobile phone is easily the most accessible device for stepping into the hospitality buying cycle that exists in the world today.

Mobile commerce is fast becoming an imposing force in the race for total customer acquisition, retention, and repeat conversion. Just look at the business strategy of *Booking.com* (owned by Priceline)—a company that has focused on mobile delivery and hyper-personalization through big data (Chapter 8).

They are twice as large as their next biggest competitor, and continue to dominate the hospitality booking landscape with their outstanding omni-channel experiences through mobile apps and tools.

Business and leisure travelers enjoy the convenience, trust, and content created by the brand, which helps them make good decisions throughout the buying cycle. The anytime/anywhere experience that mobile phones offer consumers is particularly attractive in the travel and hospitality niche.

The fast-paced environment often calls for changes, additions, security, and above all—something brands can offer consumers—instant and easy amendments during travel.

Mobile commerce also opens up new methods of delivering key messages, shopping, and ensuring repeat sales. Just look at the hyper convenience of Flipkart, India's online marketplace. Users can upload photos of fashion items to find similar products, instead of using general text search.

It appears mobile commerce is the leading form of commerce that large hospitality brands are pursuing in omni-channel marketing.

Social Commerce

Social commerce continues to escalate in importance in the hospitality niche. According to Schieber Research, buying on social platforms is growing at quite a rate—in terms of retail and referral traffic it's outpacing all other online channels.

For the hospitality niche, the ability to sell via social media platforms like Facebook, Pinterest, and YouTube is going to become increasingly important. So while the direct "buy now" buttons may not be producing the ROI (return on investment) that marketers expected them too, we can't underestimate the critical nature of social commerce as it relates to the buying paths flowing to owned brand media and platforms.

From a broader perspective, as we saw in the interview, social commerce also includes messaging apps, email, and content used for customer attraction on social sites. Whether direct or indirect, it's clear that selling through social sites will become a key avenue for hospitality brands—especially as innovation in digital technology allows more people regular access to these online platforms.

User-Generated Content

Considered among the highest value forms of content used in digital strategy today, user-generated content or UGC adds authenticity to any online brand presence. The only form of content more persuasive than high-conversion brand content is UGC—created by unpaid fans, brand advocates, and consumers that want to reach out and be part of the story you tell online.

UGC is a smart way for hospitality brands to lighten the content burden on their various creative teams, and a strong method of stimulating trust and familiarity with consumers. UGC content can act as marketing research, giving your brand valuable feedback on new products, new directions, or concerns that need to be discussed.

It's also promotional in that it proves your brand cares about consumers and actively fosters a two-way conversation with individuals that use your products and services as Catherine stated. One of the most classic examples of this was when Starbucks launched a Web site where ongoing conversations could happen with their audience.

In terms of omni-channel marketing, UGC is also extremely cost-effective, because it is offered freely—and as Starbucks has proven, the information gathered from an audience can actually earn the brand using UGC a fortune if the data is correctly fed into other growth and marketing initiatives.

2. E-Commerce Technologies

Overview of E-Commerce Technologies

Understanding the new and dynamic options available for hospitality brands in the realm of e-commerce technology is essential to online success. These e-commerce technologies are evolving all the time, improving the way brands sell and resell to consumers on multiple platforms.

Technology is making it ultra-simple to attract, retain, and convert hospitality consumers repeatedly in ways that they find simple, convenient, and helpful. E-wallets and one-click checkouts are making online spending the preferred way to book travel experiences without the hassle of calling, going to a set location, or even having to enter personal details into a system.

Data collection systems, transaction processing, Internet marketing, and supply chain management are just some of the technologies integral to sustaining a profitable hospitality brand online today. With cross-channel integration several of these e-commerce technologies can be knitted together concurrently to form a powerful system for sourcing and selling to consumers.

As the backbone for any competent hospitality brand looking to make an online impact, knowing which technologies to choose and focus on will mean the difference between profit and loss.

Servers

In e-commerce, servers (not your waiter or waitress, but computers) play an important role. The first type is the **Web server**, which primarily stores Web pages, tracks usage known as "hits," and provides the requested Web pages to the end user.

It is the server software and additional functionality of the server (faster processor, more memory, and hard disk space) that enable the server to perform its many tasks.

Dictating the size of the server is the amount of expected traffic it is to handle. In high-traffic organizations, redundant servers are employed. For business transactions, **e-commerce server** software is used to handle everything from online reservations to purchasing.

It is this software running on the server that provides links to payment systems such as credit card interfaces and includes storefront listings such as availability, price, and shipping information. Additionally, this software links to other systems and provides the user with the shopping cart utility seen on many Web sites.

E-Commerce Web Apps and Tools

Your Web store and how it sells to your consumers depends on the Web apps and tools you will choose for your brand's online presence. According to the Monteray Hotel Web site revamp, something as drastic as revitalizing your Web site presence increases conversions and reaches new customer segments in a way that immediately improves your bottom line.

A big part of this is the assembly of your e-commerce applications and tools, and how they will work together as a coherent strategy for converting and retaining your attracted traffic. Powerful hospitality brands want to improve their online bookings, their event submissions, and increase how often their existing customers stay and spend at their locations.

The best way to approach this is through the strategic selection of a smart content management system (CMS) and a responsive Web site streamlined to sell, using the best e-commerce technology.

Conversion Rate Optimization

Every action or interaction on your Web site that your consumer performs is a win for your hospitality brand. Conversion rate optimization is the process or set of systems required to help you improve how many site visitors decide to act on your various prompts and messages.

A high-conversion brand Web site is incrementally and substantially more profitable than a high-traffic Web site with low-conversion rates.

Analytics

Everything on the Internet can be captured and recorded in the form of data. Analytics is a system for finding, understanding, and using important data and the patterns that will give your brand insight into how best to improve conversions and sales across the board.

The science of analyzing data online is something all hospitality brands need to invest in early, in order to have a fully functional and profitable online presence. Analytics is discussed in later in this and in other chapters as well.

UGC (Pixlee, Curalate)

Web apps and tools that help your brand secure quality UGC from your audience are increasingly in demand. Brands like Pixlee and Curalate assist you in converting your social media audiences into content creators and brand advocates.

Selling with fan or advocate-created content on social platforms is incredibly effective. These tools are invaluable for a competent UGC campaign.

Social Sharing

To get your brand message out online, the act of social sharing needs to be taken into account when creating your content. Referring back to the interview, getting hospitality consumers to share your content across social media increases reach, amplifies the spread of your message, and attracts more people to your brand.

The W Hotels Chain, for example, launched a geofilter campaign to encourage social sharing among Millennials—a key target demographic—by joining forces with Snapchat and overlaying images with phrases like "wish you were here" to create demand.

Browser Notifications (Pushfire, Pushcrew)

Browser notifications are an often overlooked, but powerful method of attracting consumers back to your Web site and other media. Used correctly these push notifications work in any browser, on any device, and improve click through rates and engagement in real-time online.

Companies like Pushfire and Pushcrew give you a simple method of accessing and utilizing these notifications, which can be rolled out to your segmented, tracked audience.

Email Subscriptions

Email subscriptions are a critical asset for any hospitality brand to nurture, as these lists will become part of a system of strategies for repeatedly attracting and converting existing consumers. The ability to email your list at any time helps your marketing team amplify all messages, strategies, and conversions.

All a subscription requires is an email sign up page and permission from your consumer to become part of your list. Integrating quality email strategy into your marketing mix is an essential modern day practice. Caution is also needed not to overdo do it and end up in the user's junk mail folder.

Social Buy Buttons

To weaponize social feedback systems and encourage social sharing and purchasing behaviors in your consumer base, social buy buttons are becoming increasingly important. They allow your consumer to buy directly from the platform they are on, conveniently using a simple, direct buy button.

Pinterest is most famous for their social buy buttons, which allows site users to click a "buy it" button on a pin, and purchase the item they like straight from the mobile app.

Live Chat

Live chat and multi-channel assistance offers consumers a reliable, convenient, and instant method of acquiring the answers to questions they need, to complete planning and make the purchase. Replacing in-store representatives, integrating with new technologies that allow a certain degree of automation, and VR or AR (Chapter 10) demonstration makes live chat a powerful strategy.

Live chat helps overcome the barriers to purchase, by being available to the consumer at anytime, anywhere, and it connects consumers to hospitality brands for improved communication.

Dynamic Landing Pages

A strong landing page is one of your brands key conversion assets, because it convinces your target demographic to buy or act on your message. A dynamic landing page is tailor-made to structurally suit each of your buying segments, according to what they want—and what they searched for.

These customized experiences amplify your landing page conversion rates because they show the individual consumer exactly what they are looking for, using media that will work best.

Content Management and E-Commerce Platforms

All high-conversion Web sites are CMSs that support the creation, modification, and updating required to receive ongoing returns from digital content. Your CMS lets you manage the content on your Web site in a logical and simple way.

It's important that you understand how various e-commerce platforms impact your digital marketing initiatives, because each platform has its own functionality and unique features. That means each e-commerce CMS will look different in the front-end that is visible to your consumer base, and will function differently in the back-end where your team organizes and manages content.

There are many ways to compare and contrast e-commerce platforms for your brand, and arguments can be made for pricing, ease of use, and marketing impact. The most popular CMSs are Magento, Shopify, and Big Commerce.

Many large brands choose to pursue the custom development route, like Airbnb did, which can be very rewarding but will require a large team and strong financial investment. In terms of scale, smaller hospitality brands do well with easy systems like Shopify, while Magento and Big Commerce are common content systems driving larger brands.

Social Media

Social media continues to be a dominant factor in digital marketing, with each social platform creating their own unique ways to help you sell or find referrals, online. According to Schieber Research, Facebook has 52 percent of the market share, and is a leading platform for brands.

Each social media platform has a role to play in the digital shopping experience for the consumer. In the hospitality industry, this is particularly true. Traveling inspires content creation and stimulates the use of social media for connection and sharing and to support new experiences.

These Internet-based applications gather large in-built audiences around your brand, which—much like your email list—can then be repeatedly integrated into the buying process and converted for sales. A strong social media presence continues to increase in significance for a wide range of online strategies, including SEO, direct selling, customer experience management, and market research.

A brand with a powerful social network spread across several prominent social media platforms is likely to sell much more now and in the future using digital marketing content and strategies.

Subscriptions (Starbucks, Cratejoy)

A subscription model is a superb method of sustaining ongoing sales online. Many brands are reformulating and choosing to become subscriber-based companies, in order to sustain online value with an existing consumer base and spread that value throughout their online presence to their many product offerings.

The subscription model ties a consumer into an ongoing contract with a brand, often with automatic monthly or annual payments. Brands work hard to secure a subscription, which pays off because consumers only have to complete their details once to become members. Media providers like Netflix and HBO have made the online subscription model highly profitable.

Companies like Starbucks and Cratejoy have instituted subscription models with great success. Starbucks allows regular coffee lovers to subscribe and enjoy perks and exclusive incentives for being a member with their Starbucks Reserve program.

Cratejoy connects people to what they love most, and subscribers can choose from a number of "boxes" brimming with items that will enrich their lives. It's not as easy to back out of a subscription, so they are relatively reliable and secure.

Subscriptions are very convenient, especially when it comes to making repeat purchases for items you will need on an ongoing basis. Your brand is able to plan ahead and there is a stable revenue stream that can be focused on for growth and development.

Loyalty Programs

Loyalty programs have become a popular omni-channel marketing device to attract and retain consumers. These programs are designed to reward subscription or exclusive customers for buying frequently from a hospitality brand.

Loyalty programs are incentive-based and offer consumers access to special deals, discounts and free items that infrequent consumers cannot have. Best of all, brands can access buying behavior and data on their loyal customers that helps them streamline marketing efforts.

According to Schieber Research, loyalty programs have increased in importance over the last few years. Using methods like retargeting and remarketing, email, and inbound marketing—brands actively pursue converting existing consumers with tailor-made offers based on previous interest.

A great example of this is Graze, a service that has an online subscription model and offers healthy snacks to consumers via email during sports events. The emails contain exclusive customized details based on the subscribers past buying history. Using predictive analytics and tracking AI software continues to help brands offer the right products to select consumers at the right time.

Inbound Marketing

Inbound marketing focuses on attraction as opposed to interruption—the preferred marketing style of the nineties. Using engaging digital content and relevant social interactions, this form of marketing takes the shape of a magnet—pulling consumers toward its messages instead of thrusting unwanted messages upon them.

Another word for inbound is pull, and this form of marketing quickly replaced the old forms that once existed before the Internet and social media. Inbound marketing also heavily focuses on the individual, their unique wants and pain points to amplify success in converting them to loyal customers.

Using a collection of modern digital marketing strategies like blogging, content marketing, search engine optimization, and social media marketing—brands are able to better understand and deploy content for their consumer's omni-channel experiences.

Each platform becomes a touch point for attracting new leads and converting existing consumers into repeat buyers. These individuals are always "inbound"—hence the name.

Affiliate Marketing

The Internet's oldest and still one of its most effective methods of performance-orientated marketing is by using marketers affiliated with the brand to sell their products and services. Back in the nineties, affiliate marketing was the original method of creating passive income, as large brands sought to create revenue sharing programs to help move more of what they were selling.

Before social media and content marketing, affiliate marketing was the go-to online sales tactic for gaining reach and visibility. Hospitality brands would allow affiliates with their own marketing tactics to sign up to promote their offerings for a set percentage or fee per sale.

Today affiliate marketing is basically the same; it still operates based on commission and is mostly open to anyone who wants to try their hand at selling online. For brands, it makes sense to have an affiliate marketing program in place, because it will attract skilled marketers who will help them reach their sales targets. With an attractive enough commission, high volumes always sell.

According to BI Intelligence, these programs are now mainstream and widely used by major retailers and publishers. Affiliate marketing makes up as much as 16 percent of U.S. e-commerce orders according to Custora, beating social commerce and display advertising in its effectiveness.

Internet of Things (IOT)—Smart Speakers, Smart Everything

Where is the Internet and how do people access it? These are the questions that drive the concepts behind the Internet of Things (IoT). As we touched on in the previous chapter, think of it as the ever-increasing global network of interconnected devices that collect, store, exchange, and allow us access to data.

As more and more physical devices, buildings, electronics, and smart wearables become connected, the Internet is gradually being pulled into the real world. At the same time, it is affording us the opportunity to track, measure, and analyze the data generated from engaging with the Internet.

Connectivity with smart devices helps us better understand and manage the world around us. In the hospitality niche, the IoT relates to the smart devices that will assist you in connecting with, tracking and marketing to your ideal consumers.

Data is power, and with the IoT comes the ability to understand your consumers on such a minute level that customization and reaching individuals at the right time with the right offering is now a reality. Every hospitality brand should consider utilizing and colonizing a part of the IoT to secure valuable data that can be used in short- and long-term digital marketing strategy.

Messaging Apps and Chatbots

One of the key omni-channel strategies online right now involves messaging apps and chatbots, which are discussed in other chapters as well. Over the last few years messaging apps like WhatsApp and Wechat have secured billions of users all over the world, and as any good marketer knows—where there is an audience, there is marketing potential.

Now, these messaging apps are an important service tool during the online purchasing process. In terms of strategic value, they assist during all three stages—presale, during, and postsale. With any person-to-person communication there is an instant improvement in customer service. Combine this with the development of chatbots and the IoT, and it's a data goldmine.

Chinese retailer *JD.com* now allows Wechat users to shop on their Web site through the chat app, with payments being managed by the Wechat payment feature. At the same time, many of the best in class hotels and airlines are using messaging apps to reserve accommodation through social media platforms like Twitter.

Stayful, for example, offers a #tweetstay feature that signals the company to find you a hotel room and to negotiate a better price for you—all with one tweet. Convenience and functionality on this level will only improve sales and communication between brands and consumers.

3. Digital Marketing

Introduction to the Topic of Digital Marketing and Its Impact on Hospitality

When a hospitality brand markets online using digital technologies and online strategy— this is considered digital marketing. As seen in the interview, most often it involves a large collection of components, platforms, assets, and content messages assembled under a distinct strategy in order to generate ROI.

These strategies and tactics can be extensive, complex, and overwhelming for many brands, and understanding where to invest and maximize marketing spend is key to launching and managing an ongoing online presence that generates sales.

Digital marketing has significantly impacted the hospitality space, making critical features like bookings, accommodation selection, and loyalty rewards delivery instant and easy for the consumer. According Statistics Brain, online travel sales nearly doubled between 2007 and 2012, and 57 percent of all bookings are now made online.[1]

As the hospitality industry continues to innovate, so will marketing practices like SEO, search engine marketing, paid advertising, email and content marketing, reputation management, and Web analytics—which means that staying ahead of trends is key if you want to enhance your ability to sell online.

According to Forrester, 60 percent of guests use social media during the buying process. Google has said that 19 percent of hotel searches are done on mobile. Experts are urging the hospitality niche to adopt digital marketing as an ongoing omni-channel experience, or risk being left behind as real world and virtual integration narrows, and consumers flock to brands they love best online.[2]

SEO

Getting found online utilizes search engine optimization (SEO) techniques. SEO is defined as the set of Internet tools used to increase one's page ranking in search engine results. If your business does not show up on the first couple of pages when someone enters the keywords "Philadelphia Barbeque Restaurant" you may never be found by that potential customer.

[1]Internet Travel and Hotel Booking Statistics, http://www.statisticbrain.com/internet-travel-hotel-booking-statistics/

[2]Defining a Hotel Digital Marketing Strategy, http://www.guestcentric.com/defining-a-hotel-digital-marketing-strategy/

SEO companies exist and charge for getting your Web site found. Three SEO tricks that you can do yourself are the following: (1) make sure that potential keywords that a user might type into Google or Bing appear on your actual Web page, even more than once, with the more common ones in bold (i.e., Philadelphia Barbeque); (2) put all the keywords in the meta-tags; (3) place those relevant links (i.e., other well-known barbeque-related sites) on your page; and (4) update your site often with well-presented information that your customer wants. This is typically a blog or video.

We are seeing increased usage of the third trick between two companies who may have reciprocal links, which are nothing more than links set up on each other's Web page and commissions paid in resulting sales. In our example, imagine the barbeque restaurant having a link to a barbeque sauce Web site, which in turn has a link on its Web site back to the Philadelphia Barbeque Restaurant.

Finally, if nothing else, any hospitality entity should utilize the various alert functionalities provided by a search engine Web site such as Google and Bing. Simply plug in your search terms and your email, and the search engine will do the work for you and send you an email when you want it with the results.

SEM

The path to purchase online often begins with search, and there is no greater spot for your search terms than in the top positions on a search engine like Google. SEM, or search engine marketing, is how hospitality brands attract Web traffic using paid ads.

It's different from SEO in that that it uses alternative methods of attracting Web visitors to your site directly from the search engine itself, as opposed to your brand Web site. This doesn't mean that SEO doesn't often fall under the umbrella term of SEM.

There are two main kinds of SEM, organic and paid. Typically, SEO is organic SEM, while paid SEM involves paid search advertising and other forms of search engine–based advertising. These include cost per click (CPC), cost per thousand impressions (CPM), and pay-per-click advertising (PPC).

The three major search engines that SEM applies to are Google, Bing, and Yahoo—though it is widely accepted that good practices on Google will translate through to the other search engines as well. There are many different types of search ads, including pay per call, contextual, display, and behavioral targeting ads.

If your brand is particularly accomplished at achieving the top bids for your targeted search terms, you can attract a lot of useful traffic to your Web site directly from search engines themselves.

Paid Advertising

Online, paid advertising refers to any subset of advertising that you have to pay for—most commonly from an ad network or space that you "rent" from an owner. If you want your organic advertising campaigns to be successful, they need to be balanced with a strategic paid advertising plan so that you can strengthen the impact and reach of your message.

Along with driving additional traffic to your core Web site properties, these ads are also highly targeted which means attracting exactly the right buyer at the right moment of purchase. Couple this with the beneficial SEO impact and you have yourself a well-rounded traffic attraction system.

It takes hospitality brands a while before they learn how to utilize each ad format and platform correctly, and with a fair return on investment. These ads often lead to high-conversion landing pages, which means that the sourced consumer lands immediately on one of your most persuasive and powerful online sales tools.

Sometimes, the right paid advertising strategy coupled with high-impact, dynamic landing pages is enough to kick off any promotion and see positive returns. It is very important to note, however, that unlike organic traffic, paid traffic vanishes when your investment in it stops.

Media Buying

Media buying can be described as a management process in the ad industry. A media agency, for example, will be responsible for the negotiation of the placement and the price of the advert being promoted online.

Good media buyers secure prominent online real estate where your hospitality ads can be displayed for high-conversion rates at an affordable price, for high ROI for you. This can take place on Web sites, in videos, in ad networks like YouTube and on other social media sites.

On the flip side of this, a media buyer can also secure relevant content for a network, platform or brand collaboration.

Pay-Per-Click—PPC

PPC or pay-per-click advertising is a model that has a fee structure based on clicks. When a consumer clicks on one of your ads, you will pay the ad network or platform an agreed upon fee.

Those blue ads at the top of Google are PPC ads (i.e., which are part Google advertising platform know as "Google Adwords"), and are meant to attract the most amount of clicks for the related search result. As the advertiser you will have to bid on a keyword, set a price and enter the auction. Then, Google determines your relevance and displays the ad.

Cost per Action—CPA

In paid advertising, CPA or cost per action refers to a sales-related action that an advert prompts. The risk is lower for advertisers because you only have to pay if you get that sale or lead, depending on how you set it up.

Most often these actions are related to things like email sign ups, downloading something, or registering for an ongoing relationship with that brand.

Shopping Ads

One of Google's ad offerings includes a product called shopping ads. These are meant to be paid promotional ads placed in prominent spots on Google. They appear on multiple devices and can show up in search, on YouTube, and in image suggestions.

They are commonly media-rich and are clearly marked as sponsored. A subtype of PPC marketing, these shopping campaigns can be useful to product-orientated hospitality marketers.

Pay per View—PPV

Strictly speaking, PPV or pay-per-view is when a TV service provider offers a pay-for-TV service to subscribers. Viewers are able to buy events to watch, and advertisers flock to sponsor the events ordered because of the built-in viewing rates.

More recently PPV has been used to describe online events that are attracting subscribers. Because it's a subscriber service, advertising on the platform or at the events can be extremely beneficial to a hospitality brand.

Paid Social Advertising

Paid social advertising is a vital marketing practice when building and attracting an audience to your brand. These social adverts appear on social networking sites like Facebook, Twitter, YouTube, and Instagram, and they're a great way to guarantee that your content is seen by relevant parties.

Many of these social ads follow a PPC model, or unique platform models meant to amplify their effectiveness on your chosen social site.

Native Ads

Native advertising is a very effective method of delivering a sponsored message in the form of content that the platform audience is used to consuming. This paid media often appears as sponsored advertorials, in-feed native ads on social platforms, and recommendation widgets.

All native ads are designed to look and feel like they could be organic content, which makes them especially attractive to readers and viewers.

Mobile Ads

Mobile advertising focuses on advertisements that are created for impact on mobile phones or smart devices. It includes a wide range of subsets, each as promising as the other if you are considering making your omni-channel campaign mobile first.

Everything from banner ads to videos, text messages, push notifications, apps, native ads, and interstitial ads that convert on mobile, fit into this category.

Retargeting

Some marketers say retargeting and remarketing are the same. Some disagree. In this context retargeting is a method of advertising that brings consumers back to your Web site after their first visit. Browser cookies are dropped on your consumer's Web site and your ads follow them around the Internet, delivering your message until they feel compelled to return.

Have you ever wondered why you keep seeing the same ads on different Web sites? That is retargeting at work, with the brand hoping you'll return to be converted.

Email Marketing

Email marketing remains one of the best online marketing methods, if you want your consumers to return to your Web site or buy from you again. In the hospitality industry, emails are particularly valuable because consumers are happy to give hotel and travel brands their email details.

Permission-based email marketing is therefore simpler in this niche, as you'll be sending your consumers all sorts of important details via email anyway. This opens up many opportunities to convert them repeatedly during their holiday or stay, and then at a future time.

Having a well-thought out email marketing strategy can tie into many other strategies including your social media strategy, your ad campaigns, your blog strategy, and your loyalty program. Consumers can be offered services such as the facility to purchase show tickets, dining, and event experiences via email.

The bulk of any quality email campaign can be automated, which keeps it low cost and easy to execute for marketing teams. It remains one of the finest content delivery methods in the virtual world today and you can relate value directly to the size and conversion potential of your list.

Reputation Management (Hotel-Focused Reputation Management)

One scathing review gone viral can cripple a hotel's online presence and income until the scandal blows over. We're living in the era of peer reviews and testimonials, endorsements, and ratings. This is exactly why correctly managing your hotel's online reputation is key to a strong omni-channel campaign. Reputations take years to build and can be destroyed in moments on the Internet.

As a wise man once said, "Your reputation is your revenue," and in the competitive hospitality industry it's easy for a few bad reviews or online rumors to cut your profits in half. Ignore reputation management online and you'll be facing some sort of crisis soon enough. That's why reputation management companies exist, because it's so important to revenue flow.

As a hospitality brand you need to make sure that positive sentiment is spread far and wide, while negative sentiment is controlled or buried—depending on the damage it causes. Part of this is customer experience management; another part is being active about the reviews you receive.

It takes nothing for a disgruntled customer having a bad day to say the worst things about your hotel's restaurant online. If you don't have the infrastructure in place to take immediate action and fix the problem, it will progressively lessen your perceived value as a brand.

Content Marketing

Content marketing refers to how your brand will communicate its core message online through content that tells a series of stories. This type of marketing focuses on the online materials that need to be created in order to communicate with your target demographics on different platforms.

The goal of content marketing is always to attract and retain an audience, which makes it an effective and supportive digital sales strategy. The ability to create targeted stories that impact your various marketing segments will help your brand grow exponentially online.

Far from just being a random crop of videos, images, and text—content marketing attempts to differentiate your brand stylistically, aesthetically, and tonally from competing hospitality brands. There are many excellent brands in hospitality that are using content marketing well.

Loews Hotel group ran an incredible "Travel for Real" campaign that appeared in print and online. It focused on UGC on Instagram that created a PR splash in their niche. Guests created over 35,000 posts and the hotel group chose the best of them for their ad campaign, which was very successful.

Video Marketing

Video marketing is fast becoming the content medium of choice for savvy marketers who want to see high returns on their marketing spend. In the hospitality industry, you're selling an experience more than anything else—and these experiences can be created and shared using video.

From Web site explainer videos to tutorials and educational materials, to social videos meant to engage your audience and inspire interaction—video is to the Internet now what television was to the world in the eighties and nineties.

Videos have been found to have very high engagement potential, and they tend to attract the most comments and sales conversions. Recently with the rise in live video, even more video-centric marketing methods are taking the social media space by storm.

Hospitality brands would be wise to invest in video marketing strategies for their audience—it's great for SEO and personalizes the company. Many unknown hotels have benefited by putting themselves on YouTube and operating as a destination channel for holiday experiences.

Plus, according to Forbes, 80 percent of people surveyed responded that they would choose video over text content when required to consume information.[3]

Podcasting

Creating a series of episodes for your hospitality brand centered on easy-listening—is another up and coming, yet relatively unused marketing method online. Podcast audiences are increasing, and good podcasts are gaining huge footholds for brands using them.

Audio broadcasting on the Internet is like having your own brand radio station—only you get to control what the content of the conversation is about. In the hospitality industry, this means **podcasting** is a form of content marketing that indirectly promotes your offerings without ever pushing direct sales on your listeners.

Hotels like the Marriott International, InterContinental Hotels, and the Freepoint Hotel are all dedicating themselves to creating hotel-centric podcasts for their audiences. These podcasts speak about life at the hotel, and help visitors get a better feel for the culture of the brand and the people that work there. This is a very effective marketing tool.[4]

---

[3]Michael Humphrey, *What You Need to Know about Social Video Marketing in 2017,* https://www.forbes.com/sites/michaelhumphrey/2017/07/10/what-you-need-to-know-about-social-video-marketing-in-2017/#378be18660c6

[4]Deanna Ting, *Hotel Podcasts Really Want to Be the Next Big Thing in Content Marketing,* https://skift.com/2017/04/26/hotel-podcasts-really-want-to-be-the-next-big-thing-in-content-marketing/

Conversion Optimization

In digital marketing, conversion optimization refers to your brand's ability to improve or increase various key performance indicators and metrics on your Web site and other online properties. Often, when part of a digital strategy, conversion optimization is incremental—fed by the data collection and interpretation performed by the marketing team.

Your hospitality brand may have an excellent traffic attraction system, but a very low-conversion rate on your Web site's landing page. In this instance, it means that your brand needs to focus on conversion optimization—or the act of converting more of your traffic into active buyers. With the right conversion rates, even lower traffic levels can result in more sales.

Web Analytics

Web analytics can be seen as your ability as a brand to understand the behavior of your Web site visitors and use the data you collect from their interactions and presence. Simply defined as toolsets for "website analysis"—Web analytics can comprise of a number of different tools and methods for attempting to influence the behavior of the consumers engaging on your online properties.

Analyzing behavior is done so that you can improve your conversions and increase sales. Analytics empowers you to do this by helping you make sense of the data flowing to and from your sites. Google Analytics, CrazyEgg, and Optimizely are some of the tools used to improve conversions.

4. Security

"Cybercriminals aren't content with the status quo. As the value of some forms of data falls, they are casting their nets wider and improving their tactics. No system is 100 percent secure, but too many organizations are making it easy for them" (reference "Verizon's Data Breach Investigations Report 2017").

Security of Your Electronic Transactions

In any e-commerce transaction, data security must be a prime concern. Just as bank robbery has not gone away, nor will data breaches. Locally, consumers have come to accept the risks of using credit cards in places like hotel lobbies and restaurants because they can see, touch, or consume certain products and make judgments about that specific environment.

On the Internet, without those physical cues, it is much more difficult to assess the safety of a business. Also, because serious security threats have emerged, becoming aware of the risks of **Internet-based transactions (IBTs)** and acquiring the proper technology solutions (cell and smartphones too!) that overcome those risks is imperative. According to Verizon, the major risks associated with e-commerce and its security include the following:

1. **Spoofing**—The low cost associated with Web site design and ease of copying existing pages make it all too easy to create illegitimate sites that appear to be published by established organizations. These sites set up professional-looking storefronts that mimic legitimate businesses in an effort to obtain credit card and other information.
2. **Unauthorized Action**—A competitor or disgruntled customer can alter your Web site so that it refuses service to potential clients or malfunctions.
3. **Unauthorized Disclosure**—When transaction information is transmitted, hackers can intercept the transmissions to obtain your customers' sensitive information.
4. **Data Alteration**—The content of a transaction can be intercepted and altered en route, either maliciously or accidentally. User names, credit card numbers, and dollar amounts sent are all vulnerable to such alteration. (VeriSign, 2017)

From an end user or customer perspective, we find that they have four main concerns when doing business online:

- 73 percent of online shoppers cite identity theft as a major concern.
- 97 percent of online shoppers are concerned about others illegally accessing their transactional information or online accounts.
- 95 percent of online shoppers are concerned about phishing.
- 83 percent of consumers want more assurance that their information is secure.

Securing Your Web Site

A secure online transaction is the goal of every consumer. A proven, low-cost solution to secure online transactions is a **server ID**. Server ID technology is used by virtually all of the Fortune 500 companies on the Web and all of the top forty e-commerce sites. Server IDs work to make online transactions secure. A server ID, also known as a digital certificate, is the electronic equivalent of a business license. Server IDs are issued by a trusted third party, called a **certification authority (CA)**. The CA that issues a server ID is vouching for your right to use your company name and Web address. Before issuing a server ID, a CA reviews your credentials, such as your organization's Dun & Bradstreet number and/or articles of incorporation, and completes a thorough background checking process to ensure that your organization is what it claims to be and is not claiming a false identity. Only then will a CA issue your organization a server ID. This ID provides the ultimate in credibility for your online business, which is so critical for users of hospitality resources.

Message Security

Another security concern is the actual message or content being transmitted. Message security is handled by a high-layer protocol and is aided by encryption. This technology is known as SSL. **Secure sockets layer (SSL)** technology is the industry-standard protocol for secure, Web-based communications.

Web servers are now configured to work with a server ID, with the server automatically activating SSL. The result is the creation of a secure communications channel between your server and your customer's browser.

Any hospitality-based Web site can communicate securely with any customer who uses Chrome, Firefox, Microsoft Internet Explorer, or popular email programs.

Once activated by, and in conjunction with your server ID, SSL immediately begins providing you with the following components of secure online transactions:

- **Authentication**. Your customers can verify that the Web site belongs to you and not an impostor. This bolsters their confidence in submitting confidential information.
- **Message Privacy**. SSL encrypts all information exchanged between your Web server and customers, such as credit card numbers and other personal data, using a unique session key.

To securely transmit the session key to the consumer, your server encrypts it, with each session key used only once during a single session.

Message Integrity

When a message is sent, the sending and receiving computers each generate a code based on the message content. If even a single character in the message content is altered en route, the receiving computer will generate a different code, and then alert the recipient that the message is not legitimate. With message integrity, both parties involved in the transaction know that what they are seeing is exactly what the other party has sent (VeriSign, 2017).

These and other features provided by SSL are no longer sufficient to many customers, who are often put at ease by seeing an actual logo of a well-known certification authority such as VeriSign or Thawte. We will look at other data security measures for on-site credit card transactions in Chapter 4.

Hospitality units that can manage and process e-commerce transactions gain a competitive edge by reaching a worldwide audience, at very low cost. But the Web poses a unique set of trust issues that hotel, restaurant, and travel groups must address at the outset to minimize risk. Customers submit information and purchase goods or services via the Web only when they are confident that their personal information, such as credit card numbers and financial data, is secure. The solution for hospitality companies that are serious about e-commerce is to implement a complete e-commerce trust infrastructure for all endpoints, and not just computers.

E-Commerce Security Trends

The security of your e-commerce platforms is a key priority for your brand to move forward. Each year a number of critical reports are released detailing the latest e-commerce security trends that will impact brands across the world.

Weak passwords and email attachments are still the most common methods that allow cybercriminals into your online properties. Make no mistake, there is an escalating threat in the security of all owned properties online, and staying ahead of these attacks is very important.

According to IBM, now we are seeing hunt attacks, in which organizations proactively scour their networks looking for threats, as opposed to previous years where automated threat alerts would tell them of an impending issue. As hacking becomes more sophisticated, so will the countermeasures you put in place to protect your online presence, media and identity.

E-commerce security trends are always evolving, and last year over a billion credentials were stolen from various platforms, social sites, and e-commerce brands. Social attacks, phishing, and cyber espionage are also on the rise; therefore, being informed and prepared is essential. Security is talked about in numerous parts of the book. Let's take a look at some important statistics in the e-commerce realm: 95 percent of phishing attacks that led to a breach were followed by some sort of software installation ("Verizon's Data Breach Investigations Report 2017").

Growth in Cyber Crimes

Cybercrimes continue to grow as the criminal element online becomes more sophisticated and catches up to modern technology. There are quite literally dozens of ways your brand could be exploited, hacked, and victimized by these unscrupulous criminals.

According to Verizon's Data Breach Investigation Report, outsiders perpetrated 75 percent of attacks, while organized crime perpetrated 51 percent. The majority of theft occurred because of weak or stolen passwords, and 73 percent of breaches were financially motivated. Other motivations include corporate espionage, social justice, and identity theft.

Ransomware, Malware, and Adware

Sixty-one percent of the data breach victims in this year's Verizon's Data Breach Investigations Report are businesses with fewer than 1,000 employees ("Verizon's Data Breach Investigations Report 2017").

Ransomware, Malware, and Adware are types of malicious software or cryptoviruses that execute an unlawful act on an unsuspecting cyber victim. Ransomeware involves a threat to publish personal data or block access to critical data in return for ransom.

Malware actively disrupts or damages computer systems or data within computer systems, and Adware or Spyware automatically displays advertising materials most commonly in the form of unwanted pop-ups.

According to that same investigations report, Ransomware has become the fifth most common form of data breach, up from its rank as the twenty-second most common form of malware in 2013. These threats come from online browsing and email and are generally the most common types of cyber attacks.

Exploiting Social Commerce

According to IBM, cyber security will impact social commerce, as providers try and strike the correct balance between protecting their brand reputations, using consumer data, and working cooperatively with government institutions.

Criminals will also use social platforms to spread fake news about major data breaches to manipulate stock prices for financial gain. Much social trust will be destroyed as these people move from blocking data, exposing it and deleting it, to changing it for criminal benefit using social media as the delivery tool.

Zero-Day Exploits

A **zero-day** vulnerability refers to a hole in software that is unknown to the vendor. This security hole is then exploited by hackers before the vendor becomes aware of the breach and hurries to fix it—this exploit is called a zero-day attack (http://www.pctools.com/security-news/zero-day-vulnerability/).

Zero-day exploits will escalate as criminals find vulnerabilities in software, and use them for identity or information theft. All a hacker has to do is write an exploit code and release it. Too often brands and developers go for years without realizing that a vulnerability in the software has caused an ongoing attack or leak.

IBM predicts that even with the existence of brand bug bounties encouraging hackers to find these vulnerabilities for financial reward, zero-day exploit value on the dark web will far exceed whatever these companies are willing to pay—so there is a lot of incentive for criminals in this sector.

Fake Reviews

Fake reviews online are not only unethical, they are part of a much more sinister set of cybercrimes that are actively harming online businesses and consumers every day. In order to sell a product, hackers and cyber criminals create fake reviews from thousands of people—for example, endorsing a product as the best thing they've ever used.

Some of these reviews are so sophisticated that you can't tell they are fake. Because reviews make people buy things, these fake reviews could con people into buying a product that is usually quite bad. Being educated about these threats is critical—they destroy brand trust and consumer loyalty, and put money in the hands of criminals.

In 2013, Samsung was fined for astroturfing, or pretending messages were coming from consumers instead of their own business. They hired a large number of writers to create and distribute positive reviews about their products on forums. It was ruled as extremely illegal by Taiwan's Fair Trade Commission.

5. Summary

Omni-channel marketing uses various social platforms, content pieces, digital technologies, and owned online destinations to collect data to inform and advance your digital marketing practices, which in turn fuel hospitality e-commerce sales and bookings.

In Section one, we introduced omni-channel marketing and how hospitality brands need to embrace data-driven practices online in order to sustain a seamless brand narrative. We also discussed elements of omni-channel marketing, including advertising, auctioning, mobile commerce, social commerce, and UGC.

In Section two, we reviewed the role of e-commerce technologies in digital marketing, and spoke about the importance of cross-channel integration, and how it works to create a system for online selling. We explored various e-commerce technologies—including servers, nine types

of Web apps and tools, CMS, social media, subscriptions, loyalty programs, inbound marketing, affiliate marketing, IoT, messaging apps, and chatbots. Examples were given throughout.

In Section three, digital marketing was introduced and its impact on the hospitality industry was reviewed. Then, specific components of digital marketing were defined including SEO, SEM, nine types of paid advertising, email marketing, reputation management, content marketing, video marketing, podcasting, conversion optimization, and Web analytics.

In Section four, we discussed the relevance of security in an omni-channel strategy, and reviewed electronic transaction security, Web site security, message security, and different e-commerce security trends that hospitality brands should be aware of moving forward.

6. CASE STUDY AND LEARNING ACTIVITY

Through social media, businesses small and large are finding new ways to interact with their current and potential customers. Brian Cliette was hired by a large restaurant chain to help with its Web 2.0 strategy. Brian was fresh out of college with a hospitality management degree and found that his youth worked to his advantage.

The problem that the company had was that social media was new and unknown to many of the senior executives who were the decision makers, and they did not completely trust the ideas that they were hearing from their consultants who were also senior-level people. It very much seemed a younger person's game. Brian remembered the last thing his boss said to him before he accepted the offer, "I didn't have Snapchat in college nor did we have Facebook." He knew social media was much more than Facebook and was actually the general term covering all UGC on the Internet. What an opportunity! He was in charge of social media strategy.

He remembered from his hospitality management classes that he needed to think broadly at first and then target his initiatives. He also had heard many times that there was a point where customers feel that a company can overdo it (constant emails, texts, etc.) and disengage. His new company was a quickly growing fast food chain with a wide menu that attracted customers of all types. Each restaurant's marketing was done at corporate headquarters, which supported fifty restaurants on the east coast. On average, each restaurant served three hundred people a day and provided both lunch and dinner. Only 10 percent of the customers belonged to the company's loyalty program that entitled them to certain discounts. A fair amount of data was captured, including email addresses of these customers. Many did not join due to privacy concerns. Anecdotal evidence from the on-site managers estimated that well over half of their customers frequented the restaurants more than once a week. Brian began thinking of all of the many social networking systems he could utilize, such as Facebook, Snapchat, Twitter, Instagram, smartphones, and YouTube.

Learning Activity

1. What parts of social media marketing should Brian use and how?
2. In your mind, which is the most effective and why?
3. Which is the least effective and why?
4. How can social media be used effectively internally for employees?
5. What problems could one encounter in any social media endeavor?

7. Chapter Questions

1. What is a business model?
2. Describe the difference between B2B and B2C e-commerce.
3. What are some other e-commerce business models?
4. What is a blog?
5. How is a Web server used in e-commerce?
6. How is an e-commerce server used?
7. What does collaborative filtering software do?
8. What are cookies?
9. What is SEO?
10. What are a few of the differences between SEM and SEO?
11. How is SSL used in e-commerce security?
12. Why is UGC Important?
13. How can hotels use chatbots to better serve guests?
14. What is meant by omni-channel marketing? How is this different from social media marketing?

8. Key Terms

Authentication
Certification authority
Data alteration
Social commerce
E-commerce server

Internet-based transactions (IBTs)
Message integrity
Message privacy
Podcasting
Secure sockets layer (SSL)

Server ID
Spoofing
Unauthorized action
Unauthorized disclosure
Zero-day

CHAPTER 4

Restaurant Management Systems

Chapter Objective

- At the end of this chapter students will gain an understanding of the technology used in restaurants.

Learning Objectives

- Define a restaurant management system
- What are the core technologies used in restaurants
- What are some different types of direct customer ordering

- What are the strengths and weaknesses of each restaurant technology system
- Understand the new ways of payment and future advances

Chapter Introduction

Interview

Elizabeth King is a well-known information technology consultant.

1. Hi, Elizabeth, would you mind sharing a little bit of your background?

I have almost forty years of business experience in retail and food service environments. I have been managing people for thirty-nine of those years. About twenty-five of those years have been in IT organizations for large companies like Macy's, Eckerd Drug Company, Rite Aid, IBM, and Starbucks. I have about twelve years of experience in human resources in departments that were accountable for leveraging technology for efficiency and for a better employee experience. This experience was at Starbucks. I also have a year of IT consulting experience and currently, a year of HR consulting experience.

I am a graduate of Penn State University, with a degree in Political Science. I serve on the advisory boards of the College of Information Sciences and Technology and the Entrepreneurial and Innovation Hospitality Management Allies.

2. Have you seen some common pain points in restaurant technology?

The two largest issues (pain points) in restaurant technology are an appropriate labor scheduling system that has the features/functions needed for a large-scale restaurant chain and the marriage of mobile order and pay with the operational efficiency that makes the customer experience for mobile order and non-mobile order appropriate.

With regard to labor scheduling, the current packages are either too monolithic and therefore lack flexibility or are flexible but lack the effectiveness of managing labor in a large chain. Sustainability and smooth operations of the data bases and application do not effectively meet current chain needs.

With mobile order and pay, the challenge is moving the clogs at the cash register to clogs at the distribution points. Starbucks continues to add technology to try to reduce problems of incomplete orders etc., but the challenge of the clogs at the espresso machines continue to be an issue.

3. How can managers successfully use all of the new data that they have at their disposal?

Most organizations are working with business intelligence (Chapter 9) or big data (Chapter 8) systems to provide operational data that is actionable to their managers. It is almost impossible to use all the data today unless it is structured into usable reports or alerts that point a manager to problems. In chains or individual restaurants that are not able to do this, then the most important data are those data points that impact bonusable goals, revenue, waste and underutilized labor, and products.

4. What new technologies are you most excited about?

I am most excited about the potential for mobile order and pay technology though I think the impact may have more to do with better design of the product production in a restaurant. I also think that social media and how best to harness it for revenue generation and customer interactions is still an under-utilized resource. I also think there is a lot of potential for improving the operations of restaurants as the "internet of things" allows for much quicker and perhaps even real-time resolution of in-store issues that can effect the successful operations of the unit, the customer experience, and the employee experience.

5. How do you keep current?

I spend a lot of time reading articles in Fast Company, Restaurant Magazines, and most importantly visiting restaurants and observing what is being done. I am fortunate to be on a number of advisory boards at Penn State that allow for sharing of new products, updates to existing technology, and most importantly how those are being deployed. I also spend time reviewing news articles and even quarterly shareholder reports from companies that are developing and installing restaurant technology.

6. What advice do you have for new and future managers?

Learn about being a servant leader and follow that model. You will only be successful if you know how to maximize the contributions of your team. If you don't like the idea of managing and leading people, then find career options that do not require that. Great leaders have a passion for their people and without that passion success is not possible.

Also, start to develop your network of colleagues and mentors that allow you to have people to talk to when things are going well and when they aren't. You need people to bounce ideas off of and provide you with feedback.

Make sure your LinkedIn profile is up to date and remains up to date. This is the best way for people to find you as both you and they migrate to new opportunities! You will get the most out of these relationships if you invest in them, so invest!

1. Overview

Elizabeth provides a great snapshot of restaurant technology in use. Newer systems such as the ones coming online need to work with and access the data from some common systems found in foodservice. **Restaurant management systems (RMSs)** are the crucial technology components that enable a single outlet or enterprise to better serve its customers and aid employees with food and beverage transactions and controls. Everyday examples of their application range from quick food to fine dining. When you place an order in a fast-food restaurant, the machine being used by the person in front of you is part of the RMS. The same is true when you make a reservation online for a five-star restaurant. These are just two instances of RMSs in use today. This chapter's objective is to acquaint you with the many elements of an RMS and show how, through its use, current and future restaurant technology can enable management to operate a more profitable and efficient business. Restaurants are fast-moving and dynamic environments and are seeing more technology every day. Like many parts of the hospitality industry, using it effectively can be challenging. Knowledge of the core offerings is needed first.

2. Restaurant Management System (RMS) Components

The size and scope of RMSs vary among organizations. There are five main offerings:

- The point-of-sale (POS) system
- The kitchen management system
- Inventory and production management systems
- Reservations and table management
- Reporting and analytics

Restaurant operators are constantly looking for ways to better understand their customers in order to serve them better. They also need a centralized system to carry out the business at hand. Many now use the POS system. By definition, a **POS** is either a stand-alone machine or a network of input and output devices used by restaurant employees to accomplish their daily activities including food and beverage orders, transmission of tasks to the kitchen and other remote areas, guest-check settlement, credit card transaction processing, and charge posting to folios (Figure 4-1). As mentioned earlier, a POS system looks much like an **electronic cash register (ECR)**. In fact, earlier POS systems were known as ECRs. Many restaurants have just a POS system in their technology solution. Others utilize handhelds and other advancements. Whichever the case, it is these systems that collect and disseminate information about the guest and guest orders for the establishment. The POS is the main component in RMSs.

Other POS Functionality

Aside from its basic task of order handling, a POS system also provides additional functionality.

Decreased Service Time

One of the benefits of technology is the increased speed found in communication. In a restaurant setting, both dine in and take out, a POS system allows for quicker communication among all points involved. If set up correctly, an order placed at a POS station, a handheld component, or a tablet at the table, will also be seen in the kitchen, the bar, offices, the host stand, and any other necessary areas. In other words, everyone has the needed information. Newer advancements in mobile apps and tablet technology allow quicker order processing, with each order being transmitted in real time to the applicable area. Imagine a large table with ten customers. With portable or table technology each order is seen, by say, the kitchen, as it is taken in real time without having to wait for the whole table's order to be completed and then inputted afterwards at a POS station, allowing the kitchen more lead time. For this and other reasons, operators are embracing these newer technologies.

Recalling from Chapter 2, the concept of software as a service (SaaS) is being embraced by many in the foodservice sector as well. POS transactions and data can be remotely hosted by a vendor and provided to scaled-down POS terminals (known as thin clients), when needed, usually over a wide area network. While some see efficiencies and cost savings in this model, others see problems in security and potential down networks. Expect more debate and advancements in this arena. Another example of operators embracing SaaS is through their enterprise management, where POS data from various outlets can be accessed through online browser-based software in almost real time. Actual transactions are not handled here. Rather, this online software offered by a number of vendors provides crucial management data, such as sales of a specific food or sales made by a server, by poling the various POS data, again in almost real time. With this data, accessed from anywhere where the Internet is available, and the ever-expanding offerings of these enterprise systems, management is capable of making more timely decisions.

Order Accuracy

With a POS system, miscommunications are minimized. Each order has a specific field assigned to it that is used by all. For example, a hamburger may have the field "HMBGR" or simply "Hamburger." Rather than input the field, a server chooses from a list of fields provided by the POS system. With this common language, all involved in the service of food and beverage are communicating with the same vocabulary and presentation methods, thereby eliminating common handwritten and oral miscommunications. Advancements in

FIGURE 4-1

Point-of-sale systems such as this from the MICROS (now part of Oracle) Corporation aid servers and managers in a growing number of ways. Because of their proximity to food and beverages, POS systems are often built to be more resistant to spills and other mistreatment than other pieces of technology.

(Source: Courtesy of Oracle/Micros, Inc.)

conversational ordering, where the specific words of the customer's order (Can I get my hamburger bun lightly toasted?) is also being accepted by newer POS systems.

Security of Cash Transactions and Internal Auditing Functions

Many restaurants are temporarily responsible for handling cash and credit cards and now, mobile payments. POS systems must be able to accommodate these and common customer-desired functionalities such as split checks as one example. To minimize risk and help coordinate with other security software or video, a POS system records all orders and transactions, including gift cards, to each employee's assigned identification number on the POS system. It is up to the employee to make sure that his or her financial totals match those recorded by the POS. If a discrepancy occurs, a POS system utilizes an auditing function that allows management, through report generation, to dissect and retrace a particular employee's transactions during the shift(s) in question.

Reduced Training Burden

The hospitality industry has a great deal of employee turnover. Training can become difficult with so much staff coming and going. POS design takes this factor into account. With familiar graphical user interfaces, touchscreen function buttons, and help commands, a waitperson is not left in the dark. Newer offerings in hospitality offer training through gamification, where a new hire plays a game to learn the software. Various levels and modules exist, making training more of a game, and hopefully more fun.

Labor Scheduling and Performance Control

As talked about in our interview, this continues to be a pain point. Newer POSs may offer a labor-scheduling function replacing spreadsheet planning. However, more efficient labor scheduling is accomplished through separate software with advanced versions containing Web and mobile interfaces. With these Web and mobile interfaces, team members may see their schedules and, with a click of management approval, switch shifts. Labor scheduling offerings such as these are seen throughout the industry and can be very helpful in larger properties. Additionally, through report generation, a proper POS can aid management in employee performance appraisals. How much product is sold by each server and when along with other performance controls are controlled and accessed via this function.

Analytics

Lastly, what are the most profitable items? When are they being sold? Which items are not selling? How are customers paying? How has the weather affected our sales? These and many other questions can be answered by the sales reporting functionality of the POS. Due to the importance of understanding sales, other third-party vendors have targeted this aspect of the POS in their product offerings. Now, there are numerous software options for the manager who desires better food and beverage sales intelligence including Web behavioral monitoring.

The Kitchen Management System

Kitchen Management System (KMS)

The kitchen management system (KMS) is concerned with displaying and tracking food orders. Think of a computer monitor in a kitchen that displays the orders and type (eat in vs. take out or delivery), it's assigned server, and the time elapsed, among other details. With a KMS, a kitchen can become more efficient and quicker with paging systems or other mobile technology incorporated, which alert a server when an order is ready—to make sure that the soup is served hot! Additionally, a KMS may be connected to the customer technology. A KMS also allows back-of-the-house management access to data to be used for staff-training purposes, such as turn-out times or order of production. Finally, with food safety a growing concern, newer KMS offerings contain a log of such things as time and temperature (to name a few!) of kitchen activity that can serve as another training tool and also a cloud-based log of what happened on a particular day, if needed for legal purposes.

Inventory and Production Management

To remain competitive, management can no longer reevaluate inventory and menu items on a monthly basis. Through known technologies such as bar codes and RFID, inventory can be tracked. How establishments use technology to manage their inventory and menu items differs among locations. In some, the POS is used. In others, it is tracked by a system that may or may not connect to the POS. Newer offerings may include a vendor interface, supply chain integration and other online ordering capabilities. Whatever the case, inventory and menu systems are primarily concerned with three themes:

- Inventory levels and consumption
- Purchasing
- Theft

Inventory Levels and Consumption

In assuming a new role in food and beverage, a new manager is given (it is hoped) a detailed report of how much inventory of each product is to be kept on hand. This level is known as *par stock*. With a networked RMS, item removal and action can be tracked. From there, the RMS can also track consumption volume, rate, and sales price. Common inventory-level functions also include the crucial **"snapshot by day"** operation summarizing all inventory actions for that period.

Purchasing

Restaurants are also concerned with a number of factors surrounding the purchasing of products for their site(s). Dates of purchases and delivery, quantity, and purchase price must be logged and tracked for safety and business reasons. Alerts may be set up to prevent dated food and beverage products from being served. However, people determine the final outcome since some items, such as fish and vegetables, are not easily tracked and managed by technology. As with the sales report generation in the POS, business intelligence plays a major role as well. Those food costs are just too important to the bottom line and promotions not to be tracked and managed by the advancements in RMS technology.

Theft

Often called shrinkage, theft is a problem. Controlling shrinkage significantly adds to a restaurant's bottom line and is an important cost-control measure.

Inventory control operations handle this task through ID association with every item removed. Item removal may occur only when an employee assigns his or her ID or pin to the product via a whole host of technologies. As with possible food spoilage, the human factor plays a crucial role here.

Benefits of Inventory and Menu Management

Some may view the use of technology in inventory management as disruptive. Taking the time to input user IDs and access codes can be perceived as a burden when a customer may be waiting. Aside from the aforementioned business intelligence aspects, the inventory and menu management component of an RMS help in other ways. Nutritional aspects may be improved. In an age where demographics prove that the number of elderly will increase dramatically, nutritional aspects must be considered. Additionally, most inventory and menu management systems also have the ability to monitor the actual nutritional aspects of a particular dish—from sodium to cholesterol. If you want to know, for example, how much you may need of a certain food item given the average age and number of expected covers, this software outputs the answer.

Reservations and Table Management

An RMS may also contain an electronic software module for reservations. This may be software that is part of, or separate from, the POS. It is simplistic in nature. The name, number in party, date, time, and so on are inputted here. With many restaurants still using a handwritten reservation book, many software companies see the restaurant sector as one full of opportunities as opposed to other saturated industries. Remember Oracle bought Micros and Priceline bought OpenTable.

Those who incorporate technology into their reservation operations and procedures may widen their potential business by moving online. Due to the increasing level of reservations that are being made online, restaurateurs are starting to purchase monthly services from Internet companies such as OpenTable for their solutions. They are the Expedia of the restaurant world, taking reservations for many restaurants in different locations (see Figure 4-2).

The Web site *www.OpenTable.com* is a great example of a portal specific to the hospitality industry. When its reservations are interfaced with the on-site system, which may or may not be made by OpenTable, significant volume increases may be seen. Data can also be captured from the RMS, as they can from the POS for future marketing or customer loyalty efforts.

With the advances in mobile technology, customers are also expecting more from restaurants. For reservations, aside from access from common travel apps, or less so, the restaurants app, customers want to reduce their waiting time. Access to the waiting list before arrival is a common mobile customer expectation.

After reservations comes table management. **Table management software (TMS)** is designed to allocate the reservation/wait/walk-in list with appropriate tables or locations and services within the establishment. TMS is the matchmaker between a dining party and a table with its assigned server and may take the form of an application on a computing device or even a kiosk. TMS is considered standard on large-scale RMS systems and as an add-on for smaller POS systems. TMS standard functionality includes the following:

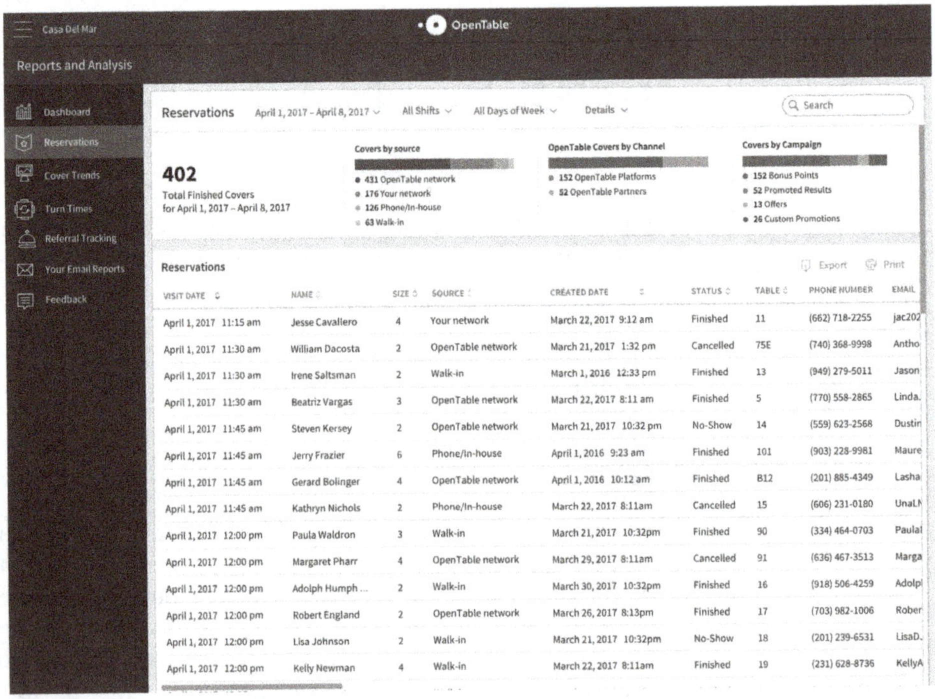

FIGURE 4-2

Restaurants with computerized reservation systems have access to data that helps them better understand their business and improve performance in the future.

(Source: OpenTable (Priceline), Inc.)

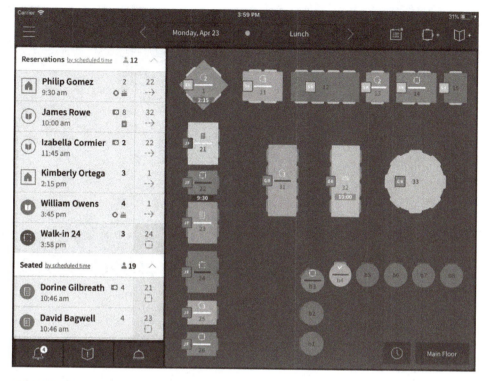

FIGURE 4-3

Table management systems such as GuestCenter from OpenTable provide a bird's eye view of a restaurant, as well as specific details of each table. Armed with this information, restaurant staff can better serve their guests and ensure efficiency during a shift.

(Source: OpenTable (Priceline), Inc.)

- A map view of the entire front-of-the-house seating
- Alerts on open, long-duration, and dirty tables
- Reservation/wait list assignment to tables
- Track covers for more efficient kitchen and server management
- Record and view shift notes for each day

Look at Figure 4-3, for a sample TMS screen from OpenTable.

With table management systems, operational staff can better control and manage the flow of customers within a restaurant and offer timely service to the benefit of both the client and the business.

Interfaces

An RMS, particularly its POS component, often needs to interface with other systems. If the restaurant is in a hotel environment, the system must be incorporated into the larger hotel system. Interfaces will be discussed in more detail in Chapter 5.

Since an RMS is geared toward day-to-day restaurant operations, any back office components such as human resource and accounting software may require an additional interface. Certain technology vendors are actually offering restaurant solutions that take into account all offices within a restaurant—thereby widening the definition of an RMS. You may see more of these offerings in the future.

3. Self-Ordering/Online Ordering

Although management has many options in taking and handling customer food and beverage orders, diners are seeing increased self-ordering options at their disposal. The success of online ordering has led to further advancements. With most consumers possessing

FIGURE 4-4
Menu boards are becoming more digital, allowing for easier changes and customer interactions. *(Source: Courtesy Micros/Oracle, Inc.)*

GPS-enabled smartphones, applications from multiple vendors such as Yelp or Postmates or delivery apps such as UberEats or Grubhub can find the nearest cuisine option(s) based upon location. Even restaurants are now creating their own applications that sense when a smartphone enters their premises and launch (with the customer's permission) their own software on the consumer's phone to proceed with any searches or orders among other features. Digital signage is also becoming more sophisticated and interactive (see Figure 4-4). In fact, some cell phones using near field communication (Chapter 2) can obtain everything from coupons to nutritional information from signage by merely pointing their phone toward it.

For certain food and beverage segments, kiosks are seeing increased usage. **Self-ordering kiosks** are stand-alone or networked devices that mainly allow for order-taking in food and beverage settings. In other settings, they may provide currency, tickets, or even room keys. In the hospitality industry, kiosks are seen as a labor-saving device. Like all technology, the delivery of customer service should be taken into account. While technology such as kiosks may replace or free up labor, sometimes our customers would rather be served by a person.

Table ordering systems take different forms. Some offerings include touchscreen battery-operated computing devices with wireless connections, while others rely on tablet PCs, even electronic readers (e-readers) or the location's mobile app. If table ordering systems are Internet enabled, customers have a world of information at their fingertips to aid them in such decisions as food and wine pairing. In conjunction with table ordering systems, server paging systems can be incorporated where your server wears an alert that is activated by a button at your table should you need his or her services. Newer technologies include facial recognition and even automobile recognition during drive-through, which would bring up the customers past orders for quicker service.

4. Proprietary versus Nonproprietary RMS

Proprietary is synonymous with *private*. Proprietary systems come from a single source. Mixing and matching software and hardware from other vendors with these components can be troublesome, if not impossible. Purchasing from a single source has both advantages and disadvantages. You may know whom to call if something breaks, but you only have that one company and its service providers as a resource. Further, imagine if a solution comes out tomorrow from a competing company. It may not be possible to integrate the new product with your system. Decisions such as these are common in technology. In the hospitality industry, they are most applicable to POS systems. There are some superior proprietary vendors. It is up to the restaurateur to weigh the good with the bad in making a purchase. Of particular note, IOS, Apple's mobile operating system, is increasing in usage in the restaurant industry, particularly in tablets. With many, often free apps, and mobile payment companies such as Square, technology adoption can be cheaper, however, often with less service.

5. Payment, Security, and Compliance

Currently, most restaurant customers prefer to pay mostly with credit and debit cards, followed by cash. The mobile payment method, where one pays via their mobile phone in a whole host of ways, while growing, still has not taken off as quickly as expected. ApplePay and Andriod Pay are two popular examples that require an NFC reader to communicate with the mobile device. With the many advances in both on- and off-premise technological offerings, security and compliance are gaining in importance. Recalling our discussion on encryption (Chapter 2), with the restaurant industry highly vulnerable to credit card breaches, the major card carriers (Visa, MasterCard, etc.) have mandated that certain steps be adhered to for outlets that wish to accept credit cards. These steps are contained in the **Payment Card Industry Data Security Standard (PCI DSS)**. They are summarized here:

1. Maintain a firewall
2. Change vendor-supplied passwords
3. Protect customer data
4. Use encryption
5. Use and update antivirus software
6. Develop and maintain secure systems and applications
7. Reduce access to data by a need-to-know basis
8. Assign a unique user ID to each computer user
9. Restrict physical access to cardholder data
10. Track and monitor access to all cardholder data
11. Regularly test security systems
12. Maintain a policy that addresses information security

These twelve steps are updated every couple of years or so. The same structure of twelve steps remains with newer technologies or obligations added within each. Of particular note is newer encryption such as **P2PE**, or point-to-point encryption (Chapter 2), where data such as credit card information is converted into an indecipherable code. Additionally, the new EMV (Europay, MasterCard, and Visa—the three companies that created the standards) is over half complete in the United States. EMV technology allows for more secure integrated circuits on the card in addition to the magnetic strip.

Another layer of security can be added if the credit card never leaves the customer's sight. The restaurant business is one of the few industries where the credit card is removed from the cardholder's sight to complete the transaction. Payment-at-the-table options are addressing this concern. Payment at the table can take many forms, from a networked device that sits at your table, to a portable payment solution worn by your server.

Finally, going back to the chapter interview, we see that many restaurateurs are using the advanced capabilities in digital video surveillance and exception-monitoring software to keep a closer eye on their business. If an exception is noticed, say a minimum number of free meals have been surpassed, management can now "go the tape" for that exact transaction and see visually what exactly happened.

6. Summary

Restaurant management systems (RMSs) are a critical tool used by management in restaurant sales and operations. If studied and used properly, RMSs will enable different locations and employees to join together in a more profitable business. Their importance, however, must be placed in a wider management setting. An RMS is a tool used by people. While this is true of technology in general, it is even more applicable here. A study of any restaurant will reveal numerous items that are not, and need not be, touched by technology. Sometimes in hospitality, more art than science is needed. In restaurants, this is particularly true. Nevertheless, an RMS, with its primary components, can give management more control over spending and sales.

With these controls, owners must also reevaluate customers' tastes and expectations regarding technology. If your clientele expects a certain amount of technology, it must be provided, such as server call buttons. This rings true for the future. Of particular note is the increase of payment-at-the-table and self-ordering options. Credit card security is not only important, but mandated. Additionally, the online medium is being used for restaurant research and bookings. Any restaurateur must incorporate this foresight into his or her operations. With proper knowledge and application of the various RMSs, along with a keen eye to the future, RMS technology can help grow the single-site or enterprise business.

---

7. CASE STUDY AND LEARNING ACTIVITY

Case Study by Kyle Emmett

It's a Friday night and you and some friends head out to a great new restaurant downtown. The place is packed upon arrival and you put in your name for a table. You immediately receive a text confirming your spot and a code to show the bartender for half off the price of your first round of drinks (1). You enjoy the round of drinks while scrolling through the menu on a tablet that the bartender handed to you and pre-order appetizers to arrive at the table once you are seated. After a while you receive a text letting you know that the table is ready and asking if you are ready to be seated. You reply "yes" and you promptly receive another message letting you know your tab has been transferred to your table and offering to duplicate your prior drink order to be waiting at your table (2). You reply "yes" once again and head to the front of the restaurant to meet the host and be seated. Your next round of drinks arrives at the same time you are being seated and shortly after your appetizers that you had pre-ordered arrive. Over the next hour, you receive prompt and professional personalized service; not to mention exceptional culinary displays of skill. Your server appears when needed, but not over-attentive and you are able to scroll through wine-pairing suggestions at your leisure via a tablet at the table. As you finish an incredible dessert, the bar and dinner tabs appear on one bill, which you and your guests can easily split and pay via that same tablet at the table (3). Throughout the entire dining experience, the table management system and host have been fed instant data points of how far along your table was so that the wait list could be consistently updated. As you leave the restaurant, you receive an additional text thanking you for dining that evening and letting you know that there is a wine pairing dinner in two weeks that they are currently accepting online reservations for (4).

1. Historical data shows that guests are more satisfied when waiting with a drink and it leads to higher check averages overall.

2. This decreases the amount of time a table sits empty while you would wait to pay the tab and increases the check average through an automated selling point.

3. This reduces the time servers spend splitting checks and improves accuracy. This also reduces the risk of any credit card fraud as the method of payment never leaves your sight.

4. Based on what you ordered, an automated message is sent (you opted in for texts that evening for the wait-list) to encourage you to come back as well as create a reservation in the future so that the restaurant can plan staffing levels. Also, by creating an online reservation, you are providing an email address and other data points that the restaurant can utilize in the future.

Learning Activity

What other opportunities can you identify in the dining experience to utilize technology to improve the customer experience as well as increase sales, retention, or efficiency for the restaurant?

8. Key Terms

Electronic cash register (ECR)
Payment Card Industry Data
    Security Standard (PCI DSS)
Point-of-sale (POS) system
P2PE

Restaurant management system
    (RMS)
Self-ordering kiosks
Snapshot by day
Table management software (TMS)

Table ordering systems

9. Chapter Questions

1. What are the five main components of an RMS?
2. Why is integration so important among the various RMSs?
3. Explain proprietary versus nonproprietary purchasing decisions.

4. Which self-ordering technology do you see as the most important and why?
5. What is P2PE?

CHAPTER 5

Hotel and Resort Technology

Courtesy of Jeanette Estrada

Chapter Objective

- At the end of this chapter students will gain an understanding of the technology used in hotels and resorts.

Two Questions Addressed in the Chapter:

- What are the core technologies used in hotels?
- How can technology satisfy repeat guests?

Learning Objectives

- Understand the main ways that technology can be used competitively in lodging
- Draw the guest life cycle circle and explain why it is a circle
- List the main components of the PMS
- Understand the importance of the three key interfaces
- Explain why a simple interface is important

Chapter Introduction

Interview

Jeanette Estrada is an IT professional whose introduction to the hospitality industry was serendipitous, considering in 2002 she began her hospitality career by accepting a position in human resources at the then Sofitel Miami. Unable to resist the lure and appeal of the hospitality industry, she spent subsequent years managing IT departments for several global chain hotels and resorts in her hometown of Miami, Florida.

Currently, she is senior project manager in the Global Hotel Technology Deployment department for Hilton, managing franchise hotel openings and conversions for the Hilton Family of Brands in the Caribbean and Latin American region.

Jeanette received a Bachelor's degree in Management Information Systems from Florida International University and is a member of the South Florida chapter of HFTP (Hospitality Financial & Technology Professionals).

1. Jeanette, please share a brief overview of your background in terms of your education, work experience, and current role and responsibilities in working with hotel technology.

After graduating from FIU with a Bachelor's degree in MIS, I held manager and director positions in IT Hotel Operations at several hotels and resorts in Miami. Currently, I work for Hilton as senior project manager for Hilton's Global Hotel Technology Deployment department. I am responsible for managing hotel opening and conversion projects for the franchise estate in the Caribbean and Latin American region.

2. With so many sectors of IT, what attracted you to the sector of hotel technology?

To be quite honest I did not set out to make a career in hotel technology! Nevertheless, what has kept me interested is the complex IT environment found in most hotels and resorts. Technology touches every aspect of hotel operations, and IT professionals must be knowledgeable, if not proficient, on a variety of technology.

3. What trends do you see emerging, particularly in the areas of (a) guest expectations and needs, (b) service delivery methods, and (c) technology developments and innovations?

Guests continue to expect high levels of service and rapid response times. Emerging trends like engaging with guests digitally via mobile apps, social media, and messaging is gaining momentum and can enhance the guest experience, help improve guest satisfaction, and assist in service recovery. One emerging trend that has created a buzz is robots and AI. There's much interest in how this technology will be adapted for hospitality use and how it might impact labor, guest service, and profits.

4. In this rapidly growing digital and mobile age, what impact(s) do you see bearing on hotel operations as we once knew them?

In this digital and mobile age guests have the freedom to control their individual experiences at their fingertips. This could mean fewer opportunities for hotel staff to engage and interact with guests. On the other hand, this technology has a potential to afford hotels efficiencies in labor and service delivery, which in turn could yield higher revenues. Finding a suitable balance and devising a strategy that gives guests the freedom to benefit from the available technology while seizing opportunities for meaningful and personalized customer engagement is key.

5. Hotel alternatives like Airbnb and HomeAway are on the rise. Although consumers book using digital platforms, the stay experience is generally very old-fashioned, in the sense that the host greets the customer, hands them a hard key, and wishes them an enjoyable stay. With how far hotel technology has come to make hotel experiences more comfortable and pleasant, do you think customers' usage of these hotel alternatives is indicative of a desire to be less technology focused while traveling?

No, I don't believe it's indicative of a desire to be less technology focused, just a desire for a different experience. In my opinion it's the appeal of self-service and a chance to experience a destination as a "local."

6. Shifting the focus back to a typical hotel operation, what are the most critical systems needed to run a hotel and the top technology priorities?

As far as critical systems go, PMS, POS, guest entertainment/Internet, accounting, and payroll/T&A are among the most critical. As for top technology priorities, a solid and scalable network infrastructure and design to support the planned hotel technology is critical, as well as information security and a solid digital/social marketing plan.

7. Who at the property level should be responsible for IT and, in your estimation, what does a hotel or resort general manager need to know about lodging technology? Where should his or her focus be to ensure a property is getting the best possible results and maximizing the benefits realized from technology?

There is certainly a need to have dedicated IT resources on property to manage and support the hotel information systems. A general manager would benefit from having basic knowledge and understanding of hotel information systems, but more importantly, should understand the key role technology plays in hotel operations so that IT is given the appropriate level of funding and support. The GM would also do well in engaging with IT and keeping the IT person informed of any key strategic initiatives in order to align efforts.

8. You are involved in the IT implementation in hotels in the process of opening. What challenges do hotel operators experience in the opening process?

One of the more significant challenges is the IT budgeting and procurement process, particularly when there are specific requirements and standards for hardware and software. Often hotel operators feel there are more cost-effective options and the challenge lies in demonstrating the value of choosing vendors and systems that are properly vetted. Procurement of hardware is often difficult in certain countries outside of the United States where because of either government policies on taxes and imports or geographic location it can be a costly and timely process.

9. What parting words of advice can you share with current and aspiring hospitality business professionals?

Whether you plan to be a hospitality technology professional, or explore some other aspect of the hospitality industry, it is inevitable that the technology surrounding our industry will impact your role in some way or another. Four key pieces of advice that I would like to share are the following: (1) Budget—get on the same page as your superiors and coworkers regarding the budget. (2) Be flexible—technology is continuously evolving; be amenable to adopting technology initiatives that may help your business run better or make your guests happier. (3) Be safe—always be cognizant of the security measures in place to protect private data and information. A data breach can cost a company millions of dollars, and even cause it to go out of business altogether. (4) Read the news—whether you read it on your tablet, smartphone, or in print, stay on top of breakthroughs and trends in the hospitality technology sector.

Interview with Jeanette Estrada

1. Overview

Hotels and resorts, especially large ones, are extremely complex businesses. In fact, they are made up of a collection of businesses (or **profit centers**). These profit centers include lodging operations, food and beverage outlets, retail stores, meeting rooms and banquets, spa, parking, and more. To run such complex businesses requires a strong reliance on IT applications and a sophisticated IT portfolio. Figure 5-1 provides an illustration of the breadth of the IT portfolio for a typical full-service hotel. The number of systems and their heterogeneity increase the complexity of a hotel/resort business. The average hotel may use up to 100 different technology applications to run its business! Systems integration (or the ability to exchange data between systems in real-time) is one of the greatest IT challenges facing hotels and resorts. In totality, the costs for IT are high, adding to the capital intensity of a hotel or resort property. Today, practically every department and business process relies on one or more technology applications. Some of this technology is guest-facing (i.e., **front-of-the-house**) and directly relates to guest services (e.g., PMS, Web site, and point-of-sale (POS)), whereas other technologies (e.g., accounting, human resources, and security systems) play supporting roles behind the scenes (i.e., **back-of-the-house** or **heart-of-the-house**). Finally, there are infrastructural technologies that are absolutely critical in empowering the property's IT portfolio and ensuring its integrity and reliability. These technologies provide the

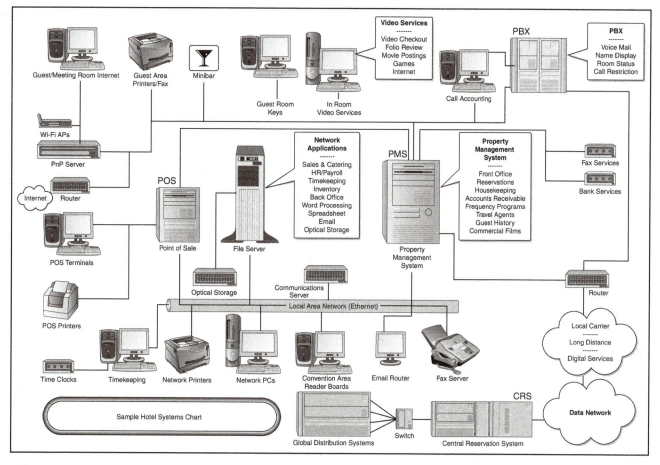

FIGURE 5-1
Hotel technology schematic for a typical full-service hotel.

foundation and backbone upon which all applications run. They include things like the operating systems, security applications, network monitoring, communications hardware, back-up software, and cabling.

The application of technology in business should be done purposefully, with the business priorities and strategic objectives driving technology choice and adoption. Technology should be serving, supporting, and enabling the business. The principal areas of focus include customers (revenue, service, and retention), employees (attracting, training, retaining, and equipping employees to perform their jobs), and owners (growing value). With these in mind, a simple formula used by companies like Marriott and Southwest Airlines is to take care of the employees. If they are happy, they will, in turn, take care of the customers, and if customers are happy, profits will come and satisfy the owners or shareholders. In the hospitality industry, major brands often suggest, if not dictate, what systems and technologies to use to ensure service consistency and enable consolidated reporting across properties. Regardless of brand affiliation or independent status, hotels and resorts turn to technology solutions for a variety of reasons. Some of these include the following:

- To improve profitability by driving revenues and/or reducing operating costs.
- To enhance and personalize service to wow guests and build loyalty.
- To extend marketing reach (especially globally) to new and existing guests in a cost-effective manner.
- To address labor shortages and labor-quality issues so that services can be delivered in a consistent manner.
- To collect, analyze, and communicate data.

- To provide managerial controls and reporting needed to maintain the health, strength, and integrity of the business.
- To provide a safe and secure environment.
- To differentiate and create strategic competitive advantage.
- To maintain competitive parity.
- To assist with legal and regulatory compliance.

2. The Guest Lifecycle

Hospitality is not about discrete transactions; it's about relationships. It's all about providing personalized guest services that meet or exceed guest expectations. In the end, it is about the experience and pleasantly surprising or wowing guests. Hotels and resorts that can create incredible and memorable guest experiences that impress their guests will have a definite advantage in the market place. Therefore, technology adoption should take a **guest-centric** approach in every facet of the organization's value chain (see Figure 5-2), looking at adding value in terms of services and amenities from the guest's perspective that ultimately contribute to the overall and lasting guest experience. Because every guest is different and has different needs, expectations, and situational factors, the notion of what constitutes great service or incredible experiences can vary widely. In essence, the quality (or perceived quality) of service delivery rests in the eyes of each guest. It is, therefore, incumbent upon hotels and resorts to offer various service delivery options so that guests can choose the appropriate delivery method or channel suited to their needs and situation at the time of the service interaction. Since hospitality managers are in the business of manufacturing outstanding, memorable, and personalized guest experiences, they must think strategically about guest needs and the architecture of the service delivery processes to appropriately take advantage of technology and ensure that the human touch and personalization as well as the appropriate internal or managerial controls are properly designed into the implemented solutions.

To help determine how and where to apply technology in a hotel or resort environment, it is helpful to understand the role and services of each department (e.g., front

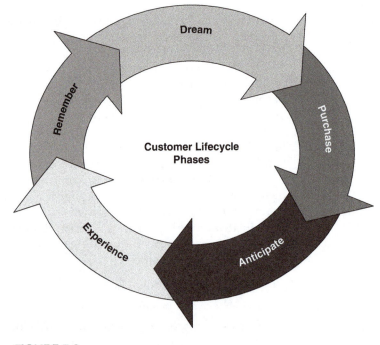

FIGURE 5-2
Guest lifecycle.
The customer lifecycle phases start with the "Dream" and end with the memory. A key to guest loyalty is that the guest remembers his or her experience fondly!

office, concierge, sales and marketing, accounting, housekeeping, and engineering) in the organization and the guest lifecycle (see Figure 5-2). It is important to realize that the guest experience begins long before a guest checks in, and it should continue long after bill settlement at check-out. The goals are to delight guests at every stage of their lifecycle so that they will be convinced to return again and again. Increasingly, hotels and resorts are turning to technology to enhance the guest experience. Every guest interaction (or service dyad)—whether it be in person, over the phone, or via technology (e.g., a Web site, kiosk, or mobile device)—is an impressionable moment or what is called a **moment of truth**. These service moments or interactions help to define a guest's overall level of satisfaction and influence one's intent to return.

The guest lifecycle starts with someone having an interest or need to travel overnight. This travel could be an exotic vacation, a trip to visit friends and relatives, a simple getaway, or a business trip. In the case of leisure travel, once the travel bug has hit, people typically research travel destinations, lodging providers, and activities in the area. This research helps to build excitement and establish guest expectations. Because of the many rich media tools on the Internet, the power of social networks, and the abundance of travel reviews, guests tend to be well informed and, as a result, pretty demanding. They know what they want and what they should expect and won't be satisfied unless their needs and expectations are met or exceeded. Business travelers will likely do some research as well, but their purchase decisions will be guided by company travel guidelines and policies.

Once a destination has been selected, it is time to book (purchase) lodging accommodations and begin preparing for the trip. The time between booking and the arrival date is called an anticipatory phase. In industry parlance, this is termed lead time to booking or **booking lead time**. This could be months in advance, or it could be last minute, say the day of or the day before arrival. Regardless of how long or short this lead time is, it is important to maintain the guest's level of excitement and address any questions or needs that might arise, such as questions about property location or amenities, activities and events, sights to see, driving directions, and weather. Eventually, the day of arrival (that is, the check-in date) comes. The guest stay starts with guest registration (or check-in), which marks the beginning of the on-site or stay experience. Please remember, however, that the actual experience really started at the very beginning of the cycle when the guest first began his or her search for lodging accommodations. The property is now faced with the ultimate test: delivering on all that was promised and has become expected by the guest up to this point.

Some innovative applications include Courtyard by Marriott's interactive digital signage (Go Boards) for information and way-finding, Starwood's deployment of Microsoft's surface computers for guest enjoyment, Rio's (Harrah's) use of Microsoft surface computing in its lounges to promote social interactions and guest amusement, W Hotels' deployment of interactive poolside ordering systems for added guest convenience and faster service, and Mandarin Oriental's and MGM's Aria in-room guest technologies like in-room controls, wake-up calls, digital TV, and music to enhance the in-room experience. Many major hotel chains are also focusing a lot of attention on mobile applications. Hilton's mobile application is a one-stop shop for Hilton Honors members to research and book their rooms, paying with cash or points, and prior to arrival complete their check-in digitally, selecting their room type and activating their room key with their phone's Bluetooth. Some hotels have even begun to implement text messaging with guests prior to arrival and during their stay. Prior to arrival, they text the guests to inform their room is ready, and during the stay guests are welcomed to text the hotel with anything they need. These are just a sampling of some of the many recent innovations that optimize guest and hotel interaction through technology.

The final stage in the guest cycle is the end of the guest's stay or the memories. This phase is established at the time of check-out but continues long after a guest's departure. Hotels and resorts want each guest to be able to relive and remember the experience long after the dates of stay have passed so that they will return often and tell others to do the same. Typically, hotel companies will use customer feedback solution technology such as Medallia to evaluate guest loyalty and satisfaction using hotel defined metrics in surveys. The surveys can be integrated with social network options as well, like TripAdvisor, where the guest is invited to write a TripAdvisor review on the hotel upon completing his or her survey. The survey results will be reviewed and analyzed internally by the hotel property and corporate offices, whereas the TripAdvisor review is available to the public to utilize in their research for a hotel to fit needs. In mobile apps like Hilton's, guests are also able to provide hotel feedback directly on the application, as well as track point accumulation and opportunities to advance from one tier status to another.

The lifecycle is drawn in a circular fashion to indicate that if every phase is executed well, the hotel or resort will have won over the guest and earned his or her loyalty for future (and hopefully frequent) stays. As one could surmise, there are numerous variables that must be managed within each phase. Careful attention to details is absolutely critical in winning guests over and earning their business as well as their loyalty. Therefore, perfect or near-flawless execution is a must. Otherwise, hotel or resort risks losing a guest for life—and, thanks to the Internet and social media, will likely lose countless more as word spreads quickly like wildfire.

To be effective, service processes must be carefully designed and planned from a guest's perspective. They need to account for the intended users' mind sets and technical abilities, the service work flow, company branding, aesthetics, and placement of the technology. Both form and function matter. As described previously, guests have specific needs and wants during each lifecycle phase. They select service providers that make it easy for them to do business and ones that provide great benefits at an appropriate price–value relationship. If a hospitality manager understands guests' needs and wants, he or she can then determine how best to meet them and determine ways in which technology can serve to support, enhance, or enable the service delivery process while also looking for ways to build in **switching costs** (i.e., barriers to change service providers) so that guests will remain loyal. By drilling down into each phase, we can develop a **guest interaction map**. This map looks at the various guest interactions, transactions, or moments of truth within each phase of the guest lifecycle and illustrates ways in which the interaction can be aided by technology. This tool helps to ensure that the right technologies are being matched with the right business processes at the right times and points of guest interaction. To be successful in delivering outstanding service, there must be a goodness of fit between people, business processes, and technology. An example of walking through the guest lifecycle to create a simple guest interaction map is presented in Figure 5-3.

Guest Phase	Dream (Research & Plan)	Purchase (Book)	Anticipate (Prepare)	Experience (Enjoy)	Remember (Relive & Share)
Property Goals	Inform & Entice	Convert & Monetize	Excite & Sell	Delight & Build Loyalty	Re-Engage & Win Back
Service Delivery Methods	• Virtual tours & rich media • Travel blogs • Guest reviews • Social media • Trip planning tools • Powerful search capabilities • Interactive maps • Collaborative shopping tools • Robust Web site • Language translation • Push-to-talk/live Web chat	• Online, real-time booking engine • Promotional pop-ups • Cross/up sell • CRM • Email confirmations • Currency conversion • Mobile booking applications • Reservation call centers • Travel agency • Corporate booking tools	• Personalized push messages with cross/up sell offers • Driving directions • Activity planner • Weather alerts and travel advisories • Destination guides & event calendars • Pre-blocking rooms • Advance/digital check-in • Mobile application pop-up notifications	• Mobile commerce • Check-in kiosks • POS • Concierge services • Itinerary management • In-room technology amenities • Guest safety & security • Guestroom climate controls • Rapid response system • Digital signage • Location-based services • Business center • Wake-up calls	• Guest satisfaction surveys • Photo galleries • Guest reviews & blogs • Guest profile updates • Loyalty points & statements • E-folios • E-newsletters • Social media

FIGURE 5-3

Sample guest interaction map.

3. The Property Management System

At the heart of any hotel or resort technology portfolio is the **property management system (PMS)**. This system is essentially the nervous system that runs the hotel or resort and the system with which most other property-based systems must connect or interface to exchange data (such as guest charges from the property's restaurant, bar, and retail outlets and other areas in which guests can make purchases). It was initially given this name because of its role in managing the property's room inventory and revenue; that is, keeping track of room availability and statuses, the guests who occupy each room, and the payments or revenues for rooms sold. Its original function was primarily administrative. Over the years as both the business and technology have changed, so has the role of the PMS. Its role expanded to revenue and sales lead generation as well as day-to-day operations and business reporting. Now, the PMS is integral to managing everything about a hotel's or resort's guests and their experiences, including their profiles and preferences, loyalty points, and CRM. It is hard to imagine running a hotel or resort today without the aid of a PMS. Many industry professionals suggest that the term PMS has become outdated, especially since these system functions are moving off of the central PMS and onto separate applications; instead, the term hospitality management system (HMS) seems more appropriate and rightly puts the primary emphasis on the guest experience (the reason for existence) rather than the administrative running of the property. For now, we will continue to use the term PMS in this chapter in order to remain consistent with standard industry terminology.

A PMS is a sophisticated management tool comprised of many modules. PMS vendors are continuously expanding their solutions to provide more robust application suites that can support more aspects of hotels and resorts and the guest lifecycle. The modules and specific functionality can vary by software vendor, but generally speaking, all PMSs will include (or have options to include) the categories depicted in Figure 5-4. Which options are purchased will depend upon the type or segment of hotel (e.g., full-service, mid-priced, economy, extended-stay) and services offered, what functions are performed at the property level versus at a regional or corporate level, corporate or brand requirements if affiliated with a lodging company, and one's preference toward an integrated solution and one-stop shopping versus purchasing best-of-breed applications (i.e., finding the best available application to perform each function). Cost may also be a factor.

While it is easy to underestimate the complexity and detailed functionality of today's PMS, it is just as easy to get bogged down in a detailed discussion of specific functionality and methodologies at the cost of "not seeing the forest through the trees." Simply stated,

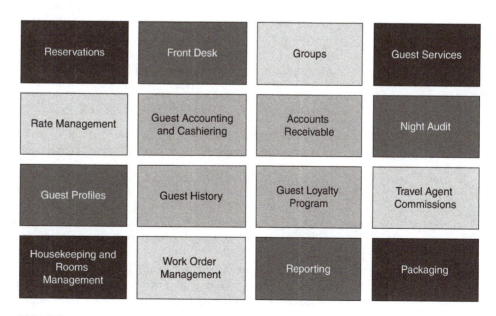

FIGURE 5-4
Property management system functionality.

a PMS is a room inventory management tool, a sales tool, and an accounting/billing tool. In its most basic form, a PMS must be able to perform seven basic functions:

1. Enable guests to make reservations.
2. Enable guests to check-in/register when they arrive and check-out/pay when they leave.
3. Enable staff to maintain guest facilities.
4. Account for guests' financial transactions.
5. Track guests' activities for use in future sales efforts
6. Track guests' complaints for user in customer service support
7. Interface with other systems.

Given the number of functions made possible by the PMS and the complexity of the system, access is usually limited to team members who have undergone the proper training for the modules of the system related to their role. For example, a housekeeping supervisor may only have access to the Housekeeping & Rooms Management module. Or, a front desk agent may have access to multiple modules, but his or her login ID may not have administrative access, meaning that he or she cannot unblock blocked rooms, or adjust past charges without manager approval. Each of these important functions will be discussed in the following sections. Where necessary, details will be included so that you can fully appreciate how PMSs perform certain functions.

Enable Guests to Make Reservations

The PMS works in tandem with the **central reservation system (CRS)** and the **revenue management system (RMS)** to manage, price, and sell guestroom inventory and ensure that the appropriate rates, availability, and selling rules and restrictions are made available as appropriate to all of the various distribution channels (i.e., sales outlets) used by the property. Additionally, the PMS must work with the guest loyalty program system to be able to access guest profiles, track guest history, and accrue loyalty points. While there are a myriad of ways in which a guest can book his or her lodging accommodations (e.g., online, on a mobile app, via travel agent, through a group block, over the phone with a central reservations agent, or directly with the property itself), the reservation record must find its way to the PMS to create the guest record or guest account.

Enable Guests to Check-In/Register When They Arrive and Check-Out/Pay When They Leave

Whether a guest has a reservation or not, this essential function of the PMS includes not only check-in upon arrival at the property but also the ability to interface with any self-service check-in kiosk and Internet or smartphone applications enabling check-in. Figure 5-5 provides an example of a guest-registration screen and illustrates the type of information captured in the Opera, a PMS from MICROS/Oracle Inc.

Enable Staff to Maintain Guest Facilities

The housekeeping functions of a PMS provide hotel or resort staff and management the ability to access some basic necessities when managing rooms:

1. Room type, room number—king, double, 101, 201, and so on.
2. Room status—clean, dirty, departing today, and so on.
3. Information about the occupant of each room—name, guest preferences (e.g., likes extra pillows), service recovery history (next page), and so on.
4. Internal operational information—inspections, maintenance issues, history, and so on.
5. Report generation, for example, the departures report listing guests due to check-out on a given date and the housekeeping breakout report detailing work assignments per housekeeper.

Managing discrepancies is a daily ritual in hotels. Discrepancies occur when the housekeeping department's definition of the status of a room differs with the front desk's

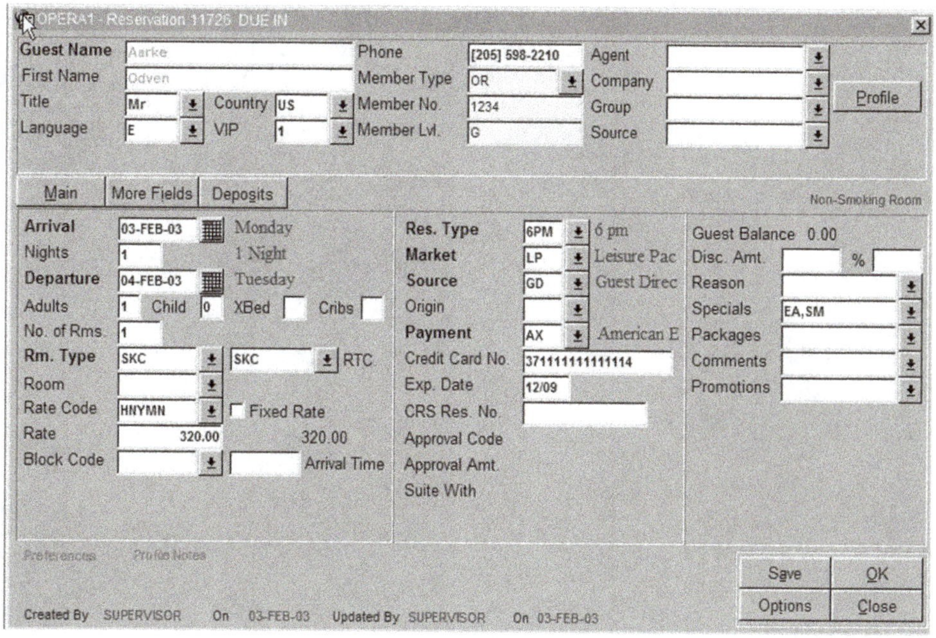

FIGURE 5-5

This reservation screen of the MICROS/Oracle Corporation Opera PMS contains many necessary pieces of guest information for various hotel departments.
(Source: MICROS/Oracle, Inc.)

status. This can result from many things. An example is when a guest checks out a day early without going to the front desk. A housekeeper will clean the room and report it as vacant and clean. However, since the room has not been checked out by the front desk, that department will display it as occupied. The PMS generates reports such as these to aid management in solving such problems. Figure 5-6 is a screen shot, again from the MICROS/Oracle Opera system, of a housekeeping screen and a field that displays the front office (FO) status. If the two differ, there is a discrepancy.

Account for Guests' Financial Transactions

Billing information such as credit card number, home and/or business address, and the specific type of room rate are accounted for here. Typically, a front office is divided into three eight-hour shifts with the overnight shift (generally 11 PM to 7 AM) left to complete the night audit. The night audit function involves generating a series of daily reports, monitoring internal controls, reconciling accounts and the day's business transactions, posting room and tax charges to each guest folio, processing point redemption stays for hotels with loyalty programs, balancing the books for the day, and rolling the computer date to the new business day.

Track Guests' Activities for Use in Future Sales Efforts

It is important that the PMS capture any and all information about a guest that is relevant and beneficial to future sales efforts. This information can also be accessed by the CRS and any CRM (Chapter 8) applications for sales and marketing initiatives. Figure 5-5 of the PMS is important. If staff members (or guest service associates) fail to capture all of the information requested on this screen, then the data needed for downstream services (i.e., service encounters or touch points such as the restaurant, concierge, or guest services that occur after check-in) will be incomplete. This could impede service or even cause service failures.

Track Guests' Complaints for Use in Customer Service Support

Inconveniences during a guest's stay are bound to happen from time-to-time. While some may be avoidable (i.e., the front desk agent forgot to check in the guest, and later a different

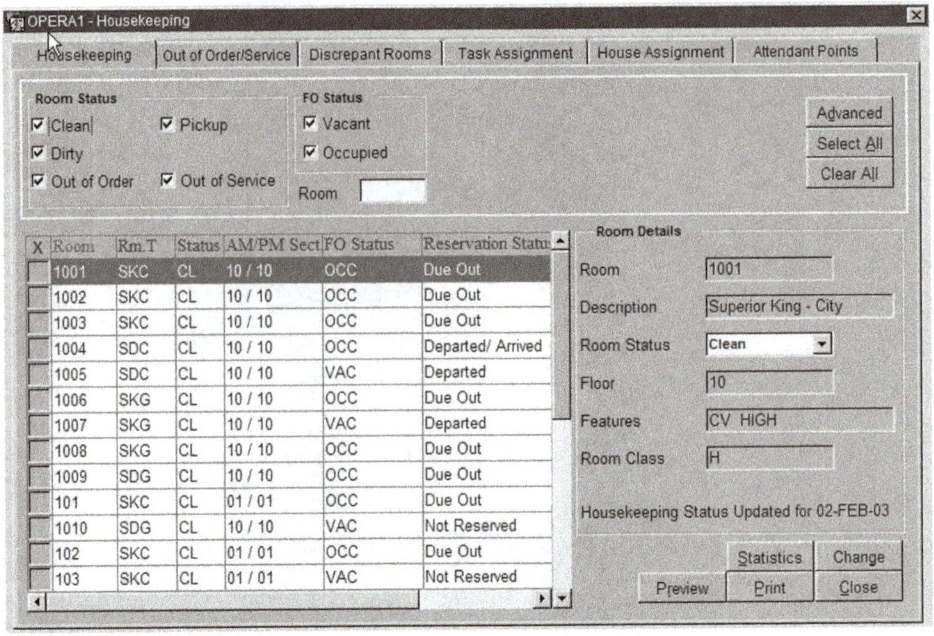

FIGURE 5-6

The management of hotel rooms can be a daunting task. With many different and constantly changing characteristics, organizations can benefit from department-specific modules of a PMS such as housekeeping from MICROS.
(Source: MICROS/Oracle, Inc.)

front desk agent checked a different guest into an already occupied room), others may be beyond the hotel team members' control (i.e., the external laundry service did not bring back any clean duvet covers, leaving housekeeping short of duvets and unable to prepare guestrooms in a timely manner). Whatever the case may be, it is crucial for hotels to utilize PMS and CRM applications to log any guest complaints, including follow-up (service recovery), to provide better customer service. For example, in a large hotel, it is very likely that a guest may express his complaint with one GSA (Guest Service Agent), but the following day, interact with someone totally different. If the GSA properly logs his complaint along with the service recovery offered, it will ensure that the guest does not have to repeat the entire story. It will allow the GSA to provide better service to the knowing that he had suffered a prior inconvenience in the hotel. Furthermore, when applied across an international hotel chain, this may help to identify more demanding guests so that both individual properties and corporate customer service support services may better recognize trends.

Interface with Other Systems

Effective systems implementation and seamless guest service around the property can only be achieved if the PMS is interfaced with other core systems and applications used throughout the property (refer back to Figure 5-1). Some examples of systems that must be interfaced with the PMS and why these interfaces are necessary are described in the following text.

Central Reservation System (CRS)

Real-time integration between the PMS and the CRS is necessary to ensure that all available rooms are listed as such so that they can be sold under the rules set and at the rates for which they are meant to be sold. Poor systems integration can result in undersold or oversold situations, both of which are undesirable situations, and hurt overall revenues. Consistent information regarding rates and availability in the CRS and PMS is important to guest service and to building trust with guests. If they receive different answers at different points of service, they begin to wonder what to believe, if they are receiving honest answers to their questions, and if they are being treated fairly.

Point-of-Sale System (Food and Beverage POS)

As the main system on the food and beverage side, the importance of this interface cannot be understated. In the past, the lack of an interface resulted in lost revenue and poor service due to the fact that these two systems did not communicate directly. Guest charges were sometimes processed *after* the guests checked out, which resulted in lost revenue, or guests were made to wait while a charge was manually added to a folio. Secondly, if a guest wished to dispute a restaurant charge and no data appeared on the front desk screen, the front office was at a loss and often deleted the charge at check-out to speed things along. Through a two-way interface, restaurant services and bartenders can verify that a guest is in-house (i.e., registered) prior to serving and posting charges. Both the total guest charge and the detailed guest check detail can be transferred from the restaurant/bar POS system to the PMS for guest billing. If questioned by the guest at the time of check-out, a front desk clerk can easily retrieve the check detail for the guest.

Hotel Retail POS Systems

If a hotel contains other retail shops such as gift shops, pro shops, spa, recreation rentals, and parking that allow room charges, these POS systems, just like the restaurant/bar POS system, must interface with the PMS to ensure that purchases appear on the room bill.

Back-Office Accounting

All of the financial data captured by the PMS must be transferred to the back-office accounting system to be appropriately reported in the accounting books so that the financial statements will all be up-to-date.

Sales and Catering System

Banquets and meetings are all part of a hotel or resort's operation and must be included in any revenue reporting of the night audit function of the PMS. In addition, the PMS and sales and catering system must share data required for the group business such as forecasting, room blocks, rooming lists, and room pick-ups (rooms that have been reserved within a group block).

Energy Management System

In some hotels, the PMS may interface with the **energy management system (EMS)** to control energy costs and maintain room climate controls at predefined temperature set points when guestrooms are not occupied. The PMS can send instructions to an in-room thermostat to change the temperature setting or speed of the blower or simply turn on or off the heating or air conditioning.

In-Room Amenities

Guestrooms have gone high tech offering guests a number of for-fee services. These may include high-speed Internet access, in-room movies, mini bars, and in-room safes. If there is a charge for usage, there needs to be an interface with the PMS to ensure proper and timely guest billing. These charges must be posted to the guest account prior to his or her check-out to ensure collection of payment. An interface to the guest television system can enhance guest services by enabling a customized guest welcome message upon entry into a guestroom. Hotels may also use technology such as a mobile app or in-room tablets that allow guests to request specific amenities upon arrival or during their stay.

Additionally, while not necessarily required to interface with the PMS, is the growing research related to TV streaming services in guestrooms. As of 2016 Year End, Netflix reported more than 90 million subscribers worldwide.[1] In an effort to provide a seamless, "like home" experience for business and leisure travelers alike is the opportunity to offer such streaming capabilities, free of charge and easy to connect for hotel guests.

---

[1] https://www.forbes.com/sites/greatspeculations/2017/01/19/netflix-subscriber-growth-continues-unabated-as-margins-improve/#1ced81d52dd7

Security

Most hotels and resorts use electronic guest locking systems. At the time of check-in, key is activated and authorized for the dates of the guest stay. On the date of departure, the key is deactivated. Hilton's Digital Key, for example, activates the guest's key directly on the mobile app, allowing the guest to unlock his or her guestroom through Bluetooth. Upon unlocking the guestroom for the first time, the guest is encouraged by the app to mask the room number for future uses so as to protect his or her privacy.

The Call Accounting System

Calls placed from in-room guest phones may result in local or long-distance charges. The costs of these calls are tracked by a property's telephone system (PBX or private branch exchange) and the **call accounting system**. Charges are then posted via the PMS to the guest folio.

Guest Call/Maintenance Tracking System

Particularly in large hotels, it is common for there to be some type of guest call/maintenance tracking system in addition to the PMS. A well-known system like this is Amadeus's HotSOS, where hotels can log guest requests (i.e., extra towels) as well as housekeeping and maintenance issues (i.e., lightbulb out in Ballroom A, carpet stained in Meeting Room D) in an effort to track the time tasks are completed, ensure duplicate calls are not placed for the same issue, and ideally reduce guest incidents and optimize customer service.

Telephone Service and Guest Messaging

The PMS must interface with the telephone system and voice messaging system to activate outbound phone and voicemail services upon check-in and to deactivate them and delete voicemail messages upon check-out. If a hotel does not have voice mail, the PMS must allow for messages to be taken and applied to individual rooms.

4. Three Key Interfaces

While all of the interfaces described in the earlier section are important, there are three interfaces that warrant more in-depth discussion. These include:

- Real-time interface with the global distribution system (GDS)/CRS
- The activities management systems
- Built-in revenue and yield management tools

Real-Time Interface with the GDS/CRS

While the integration between PMSs and GDSs/CRSs is rapidly evolving, this interface has traditionally been the single most important element in multiunit operators' and brands' decision about which PMS and/or CRS to implement. While brands, owners, and agents all have the same general goal—to generate as much revenue as possible from the sale of as many room nights as possible—historically, the integration of GDS/CRS and PMS data has been complicated in many ways due to the different business models and the varying relationships between these entities.

In short, most hotels want to sell as many of their own room nights as possible so they do not have to pay commissions or booking fees; however, the hotel does not want to leave any room empty that could have been otherwise filled by any booking source. Almost everyone else wants to sell as many of a hotel's room nights as possible in order to collect commissions or booking fees. Oftentimes, hoteliers must decide in advance how many rooms are to be allocated to various third-party booking agents, particularly if set prices are pre-negotiated under a merchant model-type agreement.

In a situation where there is no real-time integration between systems, rooms allocated to third-party booking agents, known as "blocks of rooms," are essentially removed from the hotel's inventory. As a result, the hotel cannot sell those rooms to potential guests, even if those guests would be willing to pay a higher rate per room than was given to the third-party booking agent for the block. This situation may or may not benefit the third party depending on the circumstances, but it always acts to limit the hotel's ability to manage or maximize its own revenue. In recent times, with the development of large, Internet-based third-party booking agents, there is even some concern that such situations may result in a single third party having the ability to negatively affect average room rates for an entire geographic area by controlling too large a percentage of the available inventory.

Real-time integration between the PMS and the GDS/CRS (and other booking engines) provides hoteliers and brands with much greater ability to manage their room inventory in real–time, in addition to providing a number of benefits relative to revenue management (discussed in a following section).

Because many GDSs and CRSs in use today rely on the collection of room inventory data aggregated from the local PMS at each participating property, a PMS must have sophisticated and reliable interfaces with the CRS and GDS used by the hotel brand. Many of the major hotel chains have invested significantly in these systems and interfaces in order to maximize sales opportunities and reduce the risk of unsold inventory. Chapter 7 will provide greater detail regarding global distribution.

Integration with Activities Management Systems

A number of lodging properties are comprised of fewer than 100 rooms and do not offer many additional activities or services beyond the basics that need to be managed within a PMS. However, larger hotels and resort properties generally feature a myriad of nonroom facilities and services such as restaurants, banquet rooms, meeting rooms, spa, golf courses, and tennis courts. Additionally, guests in these properties may desire to reserve specific services at predetermined times, many of which require preplanning such as spa treatments, golf tee times, and tennis lessons.

Many times, these properties will have entirely separate systems for managing nonroom services and resources. These systems often include golf tee time management, spa management, sales and catering, and other systems. It is not uncommon for some hotels and resorts with older or nonintegrated systems to require guests to schedule their various recreational activities and personal services in multiple reservation transactions with different staff members serving each area and with access to the appropriate booking system. When this happens, guests are often asked to resupply all of the same information provided at the time the room was reserved or at the time of registration. Having to repeatedly ask guests for their personal information is a sign of poor guest service, as is the inability to produce a comprehensive guest itinerary confirming all activities and services booked.

Guest service issues aside, using separate and nonintegrated systems for this purpose decreases revenues and increases expenses. Hotels and resorts can experience significant potential revenue loss when reservation agents fail to sell all available hotel services to guests when they call to book their rooms. Additionally, hotels lose even more potential revenue when guests cancel room reservations in a PMS that is not integrated with other property systems because the cancelled room reservation does not automatically result in cancellation of the spa treatment, restaurant reservation, or use of athletic facility. Staff may be scheduled or other guests denied reservations for various hotel amenities and resources based on false availability information in spa, tee time, and other systems because they are not integrated with the PMS.

Modern PMSs designed for use in large hotels and resort properties have integrated functionality that allows users, staff, or guests to reserve multiple hotel resources either in conjunction with or independent from an actual room reservation. Thus, each reservation provides an opportunity to easily and effortlessly (i.e., without a lot of data entry) upsell or cross-sell guests on additional services and amenities, helping to increase revenues per each guest. Also, when a guest cancels a room reservation, the staff member providing the cancellation is prompted to ask the guest if he or she would also like to cancel other activities at the hotel.

Integration of the PMS with other activities management systems, therefore, drives additional (nonroom) revenue and saves the hotel money by decreasing the incidents of "false no-shows" for various hotel resources.

Built-In Revenue Management Tools

In general, a hotel or resort's goal (relative to rooms) is to maximize revenue. To do this, one must carefully manage rates and occupancy levels. Contrary to what you might instinctively believe, maximizing room revenue does not necessarily mean selling as many rooms as possible. Since *Total Room Revenue = Average Dollars per Room-Night × Room-Nights Sold*, maximizing revenue requires hoteliers to consider both the number of rooms they sell and the price at which they sell those rooms. Some PMSs may provide hoteliers with some revenue management tools for managing room sales so as to maximize revenue and profits by helping to track key hotel performance measures such as **occupancy rate** (number of guestrooms sold or occupied as a percentage of the total number of rooms available or the hotel's capacity), **average daily rate** (ADR—total guestroom revenue divided by the number of guestrooms sold), and **revenue per available room** (REVPAR—total guestroom revenue divided by the number of rooms available for sale (that is, total hotel capacity) or hotel occupancy rate times the hotel's average daily rate). Many major international hotel chains utilize one or more revenue forecast and optimization systems that allow hotels to influence rate decisions based on forecasted demand/wash by market segment, group business on the books, and special events. These systems are integrated with the PMS to ensure consistency between rates and availability across all channels.

Just like airlines, retail stores, and financial firms, hoteliers must continually calculate and recalculate potential revenue models based on a number of variables affecting their businesses. Although a completely accurate projection of potential maximum revenue requires the development and processing of complicated equations with many variables, statistical data, historical business data, and assumptions about the future, basic calculations can be performed using historic sales and pricing data in conjunction with information that one can reasonably predict (such as major convention bookings, sports events, special groups, holidays). Most PMSs provide this basic functionality.

PMSs typically use a weighted historic average determined by the user along with the systems calendar (for holidays) and any additional information supplied by the user to set rates and predict availability for future room nights. While the functionality supplied by most vendors in this regard is currently not extremely complicated, it is fast and easy to use compared with stand-alone yield management systems that generally require a significant financial and labor investment that is often not realistic for a small property.

5. Graphical User Interface

You have probably never used anything but an intuitive graphical user interface (GUI). In addition, as college students, you probably have a higher level of literacy and cognitive capabilities than the general population. As a result, many of you probably take the concept of being able to "point and click" your way through any application for granted. The screen shots already presented in this chapter provide examples of the user interface for one commonly used PMS.

You probably never bothered to look at the user manual or instructions for the vast majority of computer applications you use on a daily basis. This is because almost all consumer-based technology applications from Google to iPhone apps have been developed with inherently user-friendly or intuitive GUIs. It is important to remember, though, that consumer-based information systems have been designed by large companies that derive billions of dollars in revenue from the widespread use of these systems. However, specific business-based applications, such as PMSs, have been developed by much smaller companies (with fewer resources) and are required in many cases to perform much more complicated tasks than their consumer-based cousins. So it should come as no surprise that the development and implementation of intuitive user interfaces for business-based applications such as PMSs have taken much longer than they did for consumer-based applications.

For hospitality professionals employing a PMS, however, there may be no single element of the system more important than the user interface. Not only must modern PMSs' user interfaces support the rapid training of a workforce that historically turns over almost two to three times per year, but going forward, the PMSs' interfaces will also have to support direct guest usage without the assistance of hotel staff. Whenever a choice is made regarding which PMS to use, study the interfaces. Are there other fields you wish to see? Can someone be trained on the system in a short period of time?

People (i.e., guests) have grown accustomed to self-service, and many guests will prefer to enter their own reservation information via a browser or self-register and make their own reservations, as opposed to relaying information through a hotel operator. Consumers have grown to expect business applications to have the same type of easy to use GUIs they are accustomed to in consumer products and Web sites. Direct guest interface also means much more than just accepting room reservations from computer literate people with sophisticated educational backgrounds. Educated consumers are not the only people in the world who have money and stay in hotels, so user interfaces must be intuitive even for guests who are not computer literate or lack high-end cognitive capabilities.

Direct guest interface in a rapidly shrinking world also means much more than just accepting room reservations from computer-literate people who all speak the same language. Thanks to many advances in translation technologies during the past several years, people have become accustomed to viewing Web pages in their native language. Both guests and staff now expect to be able to use a PMS in multiple languages.

As a result, newer PMSs must have robust user interfaces that are extremely intuitive and user friendly. Luckily, most do. However, many still do not, and telling the difference between the two is almost impossible for the average person sitting through a sales demonstration. There is an entire field of endeavor referred to as human factors engineering and a science associated with the development and testing of all those intuitive interfaces that people take for granted in their favorite consumer applications. In a sales demonstration of a system, a professional salesperson can make almost any GUI look easy to use. To actually determine the difference in levels of intuitiveness between two systems, however, requires somewhat extensive testing that generally is only affordable at the brand, chain, or multiproperty level.

You should understand, however, that the intuitive nature of a PMS's user interface is probably one of the most critical elements there is relative to the system's ability to enable a guest to make reservations. If potential guests, either via hotel staff or directly, cannot make reservations in the system quickly, efficiently, and easily, they will ultimately find a different hotel where they can. Hence, the intuitive nature of a PMS's user interface is a critical success factor relative to a hotel's obtainment of its gross revenue goals.

Security concerns around the world have called attention to security practices within hotels and resorts and various technologies that can help provide safer, more secure environments. Possible new interfaces may include biometrics such as retina scanning, fingerprint reading, and facial recognition software for individual identification.

6. Advantages and Disadvantages of External Technologies

Technology is changing the hotel industry at a rapid pace. In 2015, the first "robot-run" hotel called the Henn-na Hotel opened in Sasebo, Nagasaki, Japan. Throughout this chapter, we have also made reference to the impact of technology like mobile check-in, Hilton's Digital Key, and the rise of streaming services in television. Devices like Xbox Live, Google Chromecast, and Amazon Fire TV allow guests to keep up with their favorite shows, on demand and from hundreds of channel, regardless of time zone or hotel channel line-ups. Applications like Uber provide guests a simple way to get around town and charge to their personal or corporate credit card, and Uber Eats allow guests to have their cravings delivered right to the hotel lobby. In-room technology can enhance guests' ability to control their rooms' lighting, temperature, and curtains without ever having to get out of bed. Review sites like TripAdvisor, accessible on desktops, mobile applications, and even sometimes on the landing page of hotels' Wi-Fi registration, allow guests to find the best restaurants, excursions, and sights to see in the language of their preference.

Technology in hotels also presents opportunities toward improved environmental sustainability programs. According to a 2015 article in the *Green Hotelier*, Starwood plans to cut energy use by 30 percent and water use by 20 percent by 2020 worldwide

(O'Neill, 2015). One initiative that they have implemented in an effort to reach this goal is the use of "daylight harvesting" systems that adjust indoor lighting based on the amount of natural sunlight. The use of motion sensors in areas like bathrooms in hotel common areas, conference rooms, and fitness centers also enables hotels to minimize their environmental impact by saving energy (Soule, 2015).

It is without question that the constant evolution of such technologies presents endless, advantageous opportunities for guest experience and hotel management. As guest profiles and information are streamlined through interfaced systems, hotels can deliver guests what they want, when they want, and data analysis can track this activity and develop more accurate reporting on trends. The less obvious question to answer is what are the threats or disadvantages? Some of these have been identified below:

1. **Best Guest Recognition**—The use of mobile check-in apps makes it more challenging for hotel team members to properly recognize loyalty program members for their status and deliver them their benefits.

2. **Guest Service**—Guests are turning more to voicing their distaste with aspects of their hotel experiences on social media than to the hotel team members directly. Airlines like United, Delta, and Viva Colombia have come under attack recently for negative traveler experiences posted directly on social media, giving the public the opportunity to judge what the company should have done even if it goes against clearly outlined policies. How a company responds to these cases is now under scrutiny of millions of people rather than directly between the affected parties.

3. **Transportation Service**—Hotel private transportation services may become obsolete

4. **Concierge Services**—Hotel concierge services may become less necessary as guests turn to completely unbiased review sites like Yelp or TripAdvisor, available in their language, whereas often times, concierges are biased by commissions or courtesies for recommending certain activities or restaurants to guests and may be limited to just one or two languages.

5. **TV Service**—Many travelers, particularly in the millennial generation, claim to catch up on their favorite TV shows on demand, right from their tablet. The need for hoteliers to have technology available in the rooms so that guests can stream onto the larger television screen (vs. an 8–10 inch tablet screen) is quickly rising.

6. **Food and Beverage Revenues millennial generation**—While some hotels boast award-winning restaurants, other hotels clearly offer food just to meet a minimum requirement of their brand's standards. With other, potentially much better, food options just an Uber Eats order away, why would guests spend money in those hotels' restaurants?

7. **Cost per Key Investments for Owners**—Bluetooth capable door locks for digital key, smart toilets, and remote-controlled climate controls in rooms represent significant investment costs for hotel owners.

8. **Generational Gaps**—While millennials and Generation Z are known for being tech-savvy, some members of older generations find advanced technology overwhelming. It can be a challenge for hotels to integrate more advanced technology features without over-complicating the experience for guests who are less tech-savvy.

9. **Hotel Direct Bookings**—Although distribution will be discussed in a separate chapter (7), it is important to note that direct hotel bookings always represent the most profitable bookings for hotels. There are no commissions to pay to third parties. **Online Travel Agencies**, or OTAs, like Expedia and Booking, have lower operating costs and can focus an important portion of their funds on marketing and Web page enhancements. This can make it difficult for hotels to compete.

10. **Security of Customer Data**—The extent to which customer data is so widely available on digital platforms—in PMS systems, mobile apps, and online profiles—leaves customers' private information and the hospitality companies that possess such information highly vulnerable to attacks. Companies should be sure to invest not only in the guest experience enhancing technology but also in proper information systems security.

It is important for hospitality professionals to consider all aspects of how technology is shaping the industry.

7. Summary

Hotels and resorts are complex businesses requiring numerous systems to manage all facets of the business and guest details. Because of the competitive dynamics of the industry, hospitality managers must have a solid command of both the business and the technology used to support and enable the business. At the heart of all hotel and resort technology is the PMS, which could be located on property or above property through cloud computing. When looking to apply technology to guest services, it is helpful to understand the guest lifecycle and the specific guest needs within each phase of this lifecycle. It is also important to make sure that the things that guests value most are being provided and not lost in a property's quest to be high tech. It is all too easy to get caught up in trying to offer the latest technologies while losing sight of the basic elements of guest service. For example, several hotels and resorts have recently upgraded their in-room technology amenities with room controllers that can adjust the room's environment and ambiance, from climate control to lighting, music, and position of the window curtains. While guests find these technology advances to be impressive and contribute to novel guest experiences, they are left wondering why these hotels and resorts have gone to such an expense to wow them when what they are really seeking is reliable, fast, and free Internet access. Thus, the focus must be on value-adding technologies—those that enhance the guest experiences, garner guest loyalty, drive revenue, and reduce operating costs.

Another key consideration to keep in mind is the relationship between people, business processes, and technology. Service delivery must be carefully planned and designed. One cannot simply buy and install technology and then expect results. The technology is very adept at handling routine check-in and check-out transactions, but at many properties, guest usage rates have been disappointing and much lower than anticipated. In these situations, things were overlooked. One must consider a host of factors, especially since this technology serves as a face of the organization and is tasked with delivering a very important moment of truth. The corporate personality and culture must be embodied in the user interface. The device must be well integrated with the GDS/CRS systems as well (see Chapter 7) to provide on-screen personalization and relevant offers and room upgrade recommendations. Furthermore, just because technology is enabling the service interaction and facilitating the transaction does not mean that technology should completely replace people. One must find new ways to diffuse people into the overall guest experience to ensure that the human touch is not lost. Finally, the lobby design must be addressed to ensure that the kiosks fit in aesthetically and are placed appropriately for traffic flow patterns, visibility, power and network access, and security.

Because service quality (or perception of service quality) rests with the guest, hotels and resorts should offer multiple service delivery options to account for different situations and comfort levels. By doing so, guests can choose the methods best suited for their needs. In the end, technology coupled with people can contribute to superior guest service and memorable guest experiences, thereby driving differentiation and competitive advantage.

Finally, as technology continues to evolve, hotels and guests may start to enjoy more streamlined, efficient processes tailored to their needs. The rise of digital check-in, digital keys, and mobile-to-door services like Uber are radically changing more traditional hotel processes like checking in at the front desk and using hotel transportation services. While these advances can offer long-term savings for hotel operators, they also present threats to the guest service "human touch" that characterizes the hospitality industry. Furthermore, with more and more guest data being stored on virtual clouds, hotel leaders need to properly allocate resources in cyber security to prevent attacks. With the rapid pace at which hotel technology is evolving, all stakeholders involved in hospitality such as the investors, developers, hotel team members, and guests can expect to see important changes!

8. CASE STUDY AND LEARNING ACTIVITY

Case Study

A Day in the Life—Ana, New York City Hotel Manager

See How the Technology All Comes Together

Ana is the general manager at a large New York City hotel, boasting over 1,000 guest rooms and 60,000 square feet of meeting space. No two days are the same for her, given the large array of events, delegations, tourists, and corporate guests transiting through her hotel on a daily basis. To stay on top of it all, Ana and her team rely heavily on the variety of technology in place on property.

Front Desk—Her front desk team sees hundreds of arrivals and departures each day. The PMS used by her hotel allows them to see the arrival lists, identify their source (Travel Agent, OTA, Company, Loyalty Program, to name a few), and assign the rooms. Preferences of members of the loyalty program, along with any notes added on other guests' reservations, are used to pre-assign the best room for each arrival; for example, high

(Continued)

floor, non-smoking, or away from the elevator. Guests who use the digital check-in on the hotel's mobile application, which is integrated with the PMS and the e-checking dashboard system used by the property, will choose their own rooms and receive a notification on their smartphone when their room becomes available. Guests checking in at the hotel provide their phone number and receive a text message when their room becomes available. The PMS is integrated with the housekeeping department, so the front desk monitors the status of the rooms as they become available and are inspected directly through the PMS. Every morning, the front desk runs a CRM report to track the information about their loyalty program arrivals using the hotel chain's CRM database. From the PMS, they also run a service recovery report to track all complaints made the day before so as to provide managerial follow-up and ensure guest satisfaction. The PMS also provides reports like the credit report and trace report. The former tracks all rooms without sufficient credit card guarantee on file, while the latter tracks important reminders set by the front office team like "Mr. Rivera's birthday in room 603 on July 10th." Additionally, the front desk team relies on a key card system, which enables them to code guests' key cards unique to their room number and check out date. The PMS also has an integration with the credit card companies, like American Express and Visa, to preauthorize and charge guest credit cards.

PBX—In Ana's hotel, the operator or PBX team tracks all guest calls in a system called HotSos. Room 705 needs more towels? A request is logged in HotSos and assigned to a housekeeping runner. Room 1012's bedroom ceiling light bulb burned out? A request is logged in HotSos and assigned to maintenance. To guarantee that guest calls are resolved in an efficient manner, the PBX team tracks the request times on each ticket and ensures none surpass 30 minutes. Nowadays, many of Ana's guests prefer to send their requests electronically as opposed to calling the hotel operator, so Ana also invested in tablets for each guestroom. The information on the tablets is translated into five different languages, and guests can use the tablet to verify restaurant hours, order room service, and request amenity delivery to their rooms. Guests can also configure wake-up calls and seek information about activities and restaurants in New York right from the tablet.

Housekeeping—When Ana heads over to visit the housekeeping department, they are running their housekeeper room assignments for the day. The PMS has a report capability that automatically assigns the housekeepers rooms based on the amount of credits. For example, each housekeeper may be assigned 10 credits daily. A standard room may be worth 1 credit, whereas a two-bedroom suite may be worth 2.5. As the housekeepers complete each room assignment, they dial an extension configured into the guestroom phone indicating that the room is ready to be inspected. The housekeeping team also utilizes HotSos to log any deep-cleaning needs observed in guestrooms, common areas, and meeting space like curtain washes or carpet treatments to track and provide proper follow up.

Maintenance—Maintenance uses the PMS to block off rooms for their quarterly preventative maintenance schedule. They also stay on top of requests logged in HotSos in guestrooms, common areas, and meeting space in an effort to keep the hotel in top shape.

Revenue Management—Ana's Revenue team relies on several systems and external reporting agencies to optimize their management of the hotel's rates and inventory. Ana's budget allows for them to subscribe to STR, an external research company which provides a weekly analysis of her hotel's "piece of the pie" versus her competitive set. Her hotel also utilizes a forecasting system, which takes into account special events, forecasted productivity per market segment, and estimated wash (deleting unnecessary rooms from a room block) to properly price and sell her available inventory. Her team also uses a centralized revenue management database to lay the foundation of her hotel's rates and rate codes. This database is connected to external agencies like OTAs as well as to the hotel's PMS to provide real-time rates and inventory availability.

Sales—Ana's sales team utilizes a system separate from the PMS, called Delphi, which enables them to elaborate BEOs (Banquet Event Orders). These BEOs specify the catering booked, audio/visual setup of the meetings, and the meeting room setup. The banquets, stewarding, and A/V teams then take this information to order all products necessary for the event and set up properly on the actual day of the event. The sales team also runs reports from external systems like Cognos so as to obtain market intelligence data, as well as different lead response programs to manage requests for proposals from global companies and event planners. The sales team utilizes the PMS to generate their groups' house accounts, as well as the same inventory management system used by the revenue department to create the room blocks.

Food and Beverage—Along with relying on the sales team's BEOs, the food and beverage team also utilizes several different systems. For most purchasing needs, they use a purchasing system that holds all suppliers' electronic ordering forms, thus simplifying the ordering process drastically. In the hotel's restaurants, the food and beverage team also uses the Micros/Oracle POS (point-of-sale) system to log all customer orders and send them to the kitchen. The POS is integrated with the PMS, thus allowing the front desk to receive updated room charges on the guests' accounts.

Administrative Teams—The financial teams of the hotel utilize separate financial and accounting systems to process accounts receivable and accounts payable details. Employee time cards are processed through a system call PeopleSoft, and paychecks are delivered through an external company, ADP, system.

As you can see, this is just a mere glimpse of the array of technology integrated into a hotel's day-to-day operation and Ana's hotel is a prime example, given the size of her hotel and complexity of her operation.

Learning Activity

1. Approximately how many different systems, including external reporting companies, were identified across Ana's major departments?

2. If the PMS were to fail, what domino effect would it have on the hotel's various departments?

3. Pick any two teams in the hotel and describe how their communication is directly correlated by shared technology.

4. Based on the advantages and disadvantages of external technologies identified toward the end of this chapter, identify two opportunities this hotel faces as well as two threats or disadvantages to such a variety of systems.

5. This example described systems used by a large hotel property in New York City. Describe how this may differ if she ran a smaller property with just one restaurant and no banquet space. Also, identify how this may differ if she ran an all-inclusive golf resort and spa in the Caribbean.

9. Key Terms

Average daily rate (ADR)
Back-of-the-house
Booking lead time
Call accounting system
Central reservation system (CRS)
Energy management system (EMS)
Front-of-the-house

Guest-centric
Guest interaction map
Heart-of-the-house
Moment of truth
Occupancy rate
Online Travel Agency
  (OTA)

Profit center
Property management system (PMS)
Revenue management
Revenue per available room
  (REVPAR)
Security
Switching costs

10. Chapter Questions

1. What are the broad areas of functionality that a PMS must provide?

2. Since PMS is so critical to hotel and resort operations and guest services, what key considerations should one have when considering the selection and implementation of a PMS? Hint: Think about service delivery, operational issues, staffing and training, management needs, and so on.

3. What is an intuitive user interface, and why is it important to a PMS?

4. Why is it important to integrate a PMS to spa management, golf tee time, and other activity management systems?

5. What other hotel information systems rely on the PMS for information?

6. Why is business process integration so important?

7. When purchasing a PMS, what are some major considerations?

8. Aside from the chapter content, can you think of any other future PMS requirements?

9. Who on your staff should be trained on PMS usage?

CHAPTER 6

Technology in Meetings and Events

Courtesy of Corbin Ball

Chapter Objective

- Readers will gain an understanding of the technology tools available for meetings and events from planning through post-evaluation.

Learning Objectives

- Explain how technology makes meeting planning more efficient
- Understand the technologies used in the first phase
- Understand the technologies used in the second phase
- Understand the technologies used in the third phase

Chapter Introduction

Interview

Corbin Ball CSP, CMP, DES, MS, Owner, Corbin Ball Associates

1. **Please share about how your background as a meeting planner lead you to start your own meeting technology company.**

   I spent twenty years working as head of conference operations for SPIE—The International Society of Optical Engineering—running large international, citywide conventions and tradeshows. I then transitioned to twenty years as a meetings technology analyst, speaking, writing, and consulting on this topic.

2. **How have you kept yourself and your company ahead of the ever-changing technology of the last twenty years?**

   Hours of daily research. Attending about forty events/exhibitions yearly.

3. **What do you believe are the biggest barriers meetings and events face when integrating technology?**

   Lack of integration between tech tools (this is finally turning around). Human resistance to change.

4. **Technology is full of trends; which do you think is here to stay and will change the future of how we conduct meetings?**

   Mobile technology is changing the way we do business. The move toward fully cloud-based software is also a major change. Virtual reality/augmented reality (VR/AR) will eventually have a significant impact.

5. **The concern of technology replacing face-to-face meetings was once a major threat to the industry. With the evolution of hybrid events, do you think face to face is still threatened?**

   Despite the increased use of virtual meetings technology, face-to-face meetings and tradeshows will remain viable.

   Webinars and other virtual meetings are great for short information exchange. However, in today's multi-tasking and often distracting work environment, attention spans are short. Thirty to forty-five minutes is usually the maximum you can expect someone to pay attention to a Webinar while sitting in front of a monitor.

   Meetings, on the other hand, take people to a more focused environment with fewer distractions. As long as attendees are informed, entertained, and fed, event hosts can keep them engaged for days. At the minimum, we share a social contract to at least look like we are paying attention at an event. The opportunities for networking, brainstorming, and relationship building are usually far greater at face-to-face events than online. For an exhibitor, it is often the best way to meet so many qualified buyers in such a short time. For buyers, it is a great chance to meet vendors of interest—all together in one location, categorized and mapped for their choosing.

   Meetings provide a vastly richer, more targeted, and more focused learning experience than nearly any virtual meeting.

6. **Apps are a fast-growing event technology enhancement; what do you see in the future with apps for events? Will people continue to download native apps or has that convenience become an inconvenience?**

   Apps are currently standard operating procedure at most events. With the advent of 5G wireless technology and AI, apps will become much less important over the next few years. Rich information will be much more accessible anywhere/anytime. Intelligent agents will be at our voice command to provide the relevant information that we need immediately.

7. **VR and AR (Chapter 10) are now affordable technologies to integrate into meetings. Do you see this becoming an industry norm in future events?**

   Eventually. The major tech companies have invested billions in VR and AR—mixed reality. It will make its way into the consumer market first before we see widespread industry use (although it is quickly making its way into virtual site inspections). Apple's release of the iPhone X provides very significant advances in augmented reality. Android phones are following a similar path. Soon, AR will be commonplace with the phones we are all carrying around.

8. Artificial Intelligence (AI) is changing everyday life, from the way we manage our calendars to the way we shop for groceries. How do you think this will change the event experience?

This will have a big effect on our lives in general in the next few years. Finally, with Alexa and others, AI has gotten smart enough to understand most oral queries/requests. It will be a natural to use this interface to help attendees at events. Already, hotels such as Wynn Resorts, Las Vegas, is installing AI "butlers" in all guest rooms through Alexa Echo.

Interview with Corbin Ball

---

1. Overview

Improvements and advances in technology have brought about many of the changes in the meetings and events industry. In the 1960s and 1970s, the meeting/event manager's role was to ensure there were enough chairs in a meeting room, or enough white wine glasses on a table for a banquet. Today, the meeting/event manager is a very strategic position, utilizing forecasting tools, revenue management, return on investment (ROI), and expense management. Meeting/event managers have a wide range of technology available to them to increase revenue and minimize costs.

This chapter will walk through the life of an event from development to site selection, specifications, and technology enhancements and examine all the tools used along the way. It's important to note, few events currently use every technology named below. No two events are the same; they each have unique purposes, attendees, and desired outcomes. The role of the planner is to decide which technology tools are required and which would create a better environment.

Often the deciding factor of what to implement is a fiduciary decision. As technology develops, it generally reduces in cost and becomes more user-friendly. Comfort level of attendees and meeting planners also increases with further development. Many platforms may offer multiple technology solutions in one to bundle planners technology needs and decrease costs.

2. Planning Phase

The planning process of meetings/events has certainly become more efficient with the increased use of technology. Computers, both desktop applications and online tools, help to organize and analyze the vast amount of information needed to make the best decisions for a meeting/event. Meeting/event managers make use of desktop applications, SaaS (software as a service) (Chapter 2) and Web-based applications, the Internet, and portals as well as social networking sites to attract attendees to their next event and to customize the experience in order to maximize value.

Site Selection and RFPs

Meeting/event managers are now turning to the Internet and online search engines to aid in their planning efforts. Site selection search engines can help meeting/event managers find suitable locations for their events and even provide virtual property tours. Search engines can be convention and visitors bureau (CVB) based, National Sales Office (NSO) based, or third-party based. These search platforms are robust technology databases allowing planners to search for venues by specific attributes that are most important to their event. This helps narrow the selection process and allows venues to market their differentiating factors.

Meeting/event managers can post **request for proposals (RFPs)** to the Web, allowing vendors and suppliers to search, review, and reply to the requests. Industry listservs are also a popular source of information for meeting/event planning and preparation. Many meeting/event industry associations post information for insiders to use, or allow meeting/event managers to subscribe to RSS (Chapter 3) feeds for up-to-date information, pricing, and availability.

Event Documentation

The predominant planning software used in the meetings/events industry is still Microsoft Office. Meeting/event managers use word processing, spreadsheets, database management systems, presentation software, and project management tools to help plan, execute, and evaluate their events.

In 1949, four organizations formed the Convention Liaison Council, whose goal was to enhance the meetings, conventions, and exhibitions industry with the exchange of information, ideas, and best practices. In 2000, the Council changed its name to the Convention Industry Council and in May 2017 rebranded again to the Events Industry Council and now has thirty-three member organizations. The Council has launched many successful initiatives in the meetings/events industry such as the Certified Meeting Professional (CMP) designation and the **Accepted Practices Exchange (APEX)**.

The APEX initiative (www.eventscouncil.org) seeks to unite the meetings/events industry by creating and implementing voluntary practices and standards to create efficiencies throughout the industry. APEX focuses on seven core areas: industry terminology, event specifications guides (ESG), request for proposal (RFP) forms, housing and registration practices, contracts, post-event reports (PER), and meeting and site profiles. Interwoven into these core areas are suggested templates and software packages for planners to use. XML (Extensible Markup Language—Chapter 2) is a critical tool that helps APEX templates integrate with MS Office.

While MS Office still remains the main communication vehicle for event details, software development companies have seen this market as an area for growth and are developing robust event management software programs. The driving incentive to adopt these software programs is better financial management and increased data capture. Many site selection platforms have expanded their business models to include event management tools. Diagram, registration, and app software companies are also launching management software in an attempt to convert existing customers. Venues work in different programs than the planners and most major hotel or venues having different software as well. This communication gap is often seen as a handicap of the events business.

Registration, Housing, and Travel

As the drive for big data analytics grows, attendee registration software has become more robust than the traditional RSVP. Planners are expected to know demographics, dietary needs, education preferences, and many other details to plan the best experience possible. Large-scale meetings often use specific software programs for registration and sometimes will outsource this element to a third party. Those third parties usually can offer housing management as well, which is especially helpful to planners utilizing multiple hotels for a single event. Hotels may partner with a software platform that gives planners the access to link all their hotels into one Web site and manage them in one easy location. This is especially popular in hotels located near convention centers when all attendees will not fit in one hotel.

Travel management software is also available for events when air and ground transportation is organized by the planner for the group or for speakers, VIPs, etc. These management systems help streamline costs, organize details, and make changing travel plans easier. Programs are also able to manage expenses and allow guests to manage their own travel plans from parameters you as the planner set.

Marketing and Sponsorships

Event marketing has moved substantially to online vehicles. In addition to Web site and email communications, social media has greatly increased both the marketing and pre-event attendee engagement. Social media is widely used because it offers free resources to promote events. The challenge with social media is the maintenance of cross posting to current platforms and the time commitment needed to respond to inquires and comments. Social media does allow attendees a platform to communicate with each other before the event. This can foster networking, develop educational topics, and continue the conversation before, during, and after the event.

Sponsorship software is another popular platform for planners to utilize because it has a strong tangible ROI. Marketing of the event, booth selections, and branding opportunities allows sponsors to more easily purchase these items and therefore increases revenue to the event. Customer relationship management, tracking of payment, contract management, and real-time menu of options are some of the efficiencies that sponsorship software offers.

Internet Requirements

Bandwidth (Chapter 2) requirements are crucial for event planners to understand when planning for their event. Bandwidth needs vary by events based off the use of the Internet. Simple Web browsing and email checking requires less bandwidth than Web-based trainings, downloads, or streaming. Attendees carrying multiple devices (laptops, cell phones, tablets, wearable technology, etc.) means bandwidth accessibility on each device, so this could double or triple your usage. Planners should also consider the need for a dedicated network or shared network based off the bandwidth needed. While cloud-based computing and wireless connectivity are at the forefront, consider areas that may need a wired connection. Virtual Local Area Network (VLAN) is a technique to segment or isolate a network into functional areas that may require specific bandwidth or security attributes. These are commonly used for a network for general session, event staff, or presentation management systems.

The Events Industry Council created a calculator to aid planners in determining their need, http://www.eventscouncil.org/APEX/bwidthestimator.aspx. Planners should also ask the Network Service Provider (NSP) to provide bandwidth utilization reports after the program to record history of usage to aid in planning and contract negotiations for future events.

3. Event Phase

Technology helps to enhance the environment of meetings and events. Meetings are typically held to communicate a message and/or to increase learning. Every meeting or event requires its attendees to see and hear the presentation. Imagine a wedding without music, or a guest speaker without a microphone! Audio and visual equipment help to engage the audience while allowing the presenters or speakers to concentrate on their message.

Audio

A meeting/event manager should become familiar with some of the basic audio equipment needed to produce successful sound at the event. Audio systems help set the tone for the meeting/event and can evoke a variety of emotions. Depending on the needs of the attendees, an event can require the use of microphones, speaker systems, and recording equipment.

A meeting/event manager must determine the number and types of microphones needed for attendees to hear information at a meeting/event. Microphones can be placed in a fixed location, such as on a podium, or can be wireless, to allow a speaker to move around the site. Meeting managers must consider the number of speakers at a meeting/event, as well as the style of the speaker. Fixed microphones are best for a program with many speakers or for those that tend to speak strictly from the podium, while wireless microphones are good for energetic speakers that like to move around. The meeting/event manager must also consider microphones needed for audience response. Microphones have also advanced to soft-sided cubes, designed to be tossed around the audience to support interaction.

Additional microphones require additional equipment, such as mixers (mixing or sound boards), for the best audio quality. A meeting manager may want to consider loud speakers and sound systems (depending on audience and room size). Quality is an important component, not just for the audience at the meeting/event, but also for meetings that will be recorded. Digital recording devices can be used to record a meeting for future listeners for the purpose of transcriptions. Live streaming events should consider all audio in the event and the quality as the audio will be instantly viewed online and poor quality or uncaptured audio silences will deter the digital audience.

Music is a popular enhancement to more than just social events. General sessions, meal functions, and networking breaks all may contain music. Purchased online or played through a streaming service, music played publicly may be subject to licensing fees. BMI is an organization designed to represent songwriters and artists for licensing purchases.

Visual

Meeting/event visual equipment used to be limited to an overhead or slide projector. While some industries' events occasionally use those formats, video projectors and digital display equipment have become the industry norm. Video projectors interface with most computer systems (PC and Mac) and commonly use **LCD (liquid crystal display)** or **DLP (digital light processing)** technology. **LED (Light-emitting diode)** technology is being integrated into projectors in order to eliminate the need for bulbs, which are costly to replace in the traditional LCD projectors.

When selecting visual equipment, a meeting/event manager must consider several components based on the event location. It is important to make a note of the room size as well as how large the projection area (or screen) will be. The location of the projector and the amount of natural and room lighting will also assist the meeting/event manager in selecting the most appropriate equipment. As events and attendees become more experiential and dynamic, the traditional screen and tripod projector are no longer enough to engage audiences. **Image magnification** (I-MAG) allows guests in a general session to experience the speaker with a first-row seat, high-definition video detail. Second screen technology brings the presentation into the hands of the attendee via their own personal device and gives the chance to take notes, ask questions and chat with others in the room. **Projection mapping** eliminates the need for screens and turns any object, building, or surface into a projection area. Projection mapping can be used on a wall inside a meeting room or on the entire surface of a building. Projection mapping has expanded into the food scene being used on wedding cakes, transforming the traditional white surface into a storytelling experience. Theater is pushing the limits of projection mapping onto the faces of actors, enabling them to change characters instantly.

Intimate meetings technology choices allow attendees to share and communicate more effectively. Monitors replace traditional screens, eliminating the need for throw space that limits seating. Wireless presentation systems connect multiple laptops or tablets to the same screen with the press of a button. Boardroom tables have been replaced with smart tables that are touchscreen devices to view, share, and edit as a team. Smartboard devices that record written notes instantly to digital format have replaced the traditional whiteboard or flipchart.

A meeting/event planner must also familiarize himself or herself with different video standards for playback across the world. International standards vary and are not compatible with one another. The NTSC (National Television System Committee) format is used in the United States and Canada, the PAL (Phase Alternating Line) is used in Western Europe and Australia, while the SECAM (Sequential Color with Memory) is used in eastern Europe and France.

Virtual Meetings

Voice conferencing is connecting two or more sites via audio or a phone connection. In a voice conference, there is no need for visual communication. This type of virtual meeting is the most inexpensive alternative, with many service options available. Most beneficial is the short lead time in planning an audio conference.

Video conferencing involves connecting two or more sites via video transmission. Communication can be two-way or one-way. Advances in Web- and smartphone-based video conferencing have made this a more affordable option.

Rawpixel.com/Shutterstock

Social media has allowed attendees the chance to create their own virtual event experiences by live streaming event content from their smartphones. This can give great viral marketing for your event but also could pose legal issues. Speakers or other attendees may not consent to their image or content being broadcast without permission.

Real-Life Example: In 2015, the Floyd Mayweather and Manny Pacquiao fight on HBO and Showtime experienced the legal challenges of live streaming. According to CNN, 10,000 people had tuned into a single Periscope feed to watch the fight. The networks charged $100 on pay per view and brought in an estimated $400 million, but the amount lost to live streaming is unknown.

Like most technology, VR (Chapter 10) was initially very expensive, which made it difficult to integrate it with larger events. However cardboard VR goggles have made it affordable to create an experience that transports the attendees into another space without having to leave their chair. They can experience a customized product or location within a tradeshow booth before deciding to purchase. This also brings virtual events to the next level as attendees can, from anywhere in the world, feel like they're attending the actual event. Planners are also using VR to reimagine the site visit, graphics, and tradeshow designs. The traditional 2D floorplan is brought to life with VR. **Augmented reality (AR)** is the next step beyond VR, where digital overlays are implemented into your current reality.

Real-Life Example: Pokemon Go was launched in 2016 and took the world by storm. This AR game played on your smartphone encouraged players to explore their communities in search of Pokemon characters. AR technology turned your current environment into one where characters are waiting to be found. Users were exploring parks, businesses, and community locations in hopes of finding the rare characters. We will unpack Pokemon and AR/VR in another chapter.

Hybrid events, the combination of a digital audience via live streaming and the in-person audience of a face-to-face event make video capture extremely important. The purpose of a hybrid event is for the digital audience to feel as if they're in the room with the event. Factors to consider are video and audio quality, number of devices to record the audience and the speakers, Internet connectivity, and integration of the digital audience into the room. Social media is a natural platform for both audiences to participate together; however, the meeting organizer may have their own communication platform as well.

Real-Life Example: Digital event experiences are especially important in a global society and unpredictable political climate. In 2017, President Trump signed his first executive order that banned citizens from seven countries from entering America. Not only did this affect conference attendees from those countries, it impacted overall travel to the United States. This was predicted in a *New York Times* quote by Adam Sacks, president of Tourism Economics, an international firm that forecasts travel trends for several cities in the United States. He said the annual number of foreign visitors to the United States could fall by 6.3 million between 2016 and 2018 because of reactions to Mr. Trump's words and actions, such as pledges to pull out of international trade agreements. This could affect your conference attendance or prevent speakers from attending. Imagine if your event took place when the ban was instituted and airports were being picketed.

Presentation Management System

Speaker-ready rooms used to be a place where presenters could grab a beverage and work on their laptops in a quiet place away from the rest of a conference. Presentation or content management systems have transformed the room into a hub, where speakers access their previously uploaded content and can edit as needed. Such a presentation is held in a cloud-based system that any speaker can then access in any breakout room throughout the facility. This allows planners to adjust meeting rooms easily and reduces the need for speakers to bring their own computer or memory stick. AV techs can test presentations and update attendee facing documentation instantly.

Team Communication

The events industry used to operate by radio or push-to-talk devices to communicate between staff members and vendors. SMS and group messaging services have replaced most of these, yet still retain the same group communication channels. Screen sharing, shared online document, and storage platforms mean teams can view the same information together and execute onsite management digitally, instead of the thick binders that once never left a planner's side.

4. Attendee Experience

Successful meeting planners analyze their audience's consumer technology habits and integrate them into their event experience. If a large portion of your guests are using a step tracking device, do you set up a step challenge with QR codes—quick response two-dimensional codes—in strategic areas of the event? Event technology should play off what the guests are already doing while pushing their horizons to try new things.

Audience Response and Survey Systems

Increasing engagement, knowledge retention, and data collection are the three main advantages to audience response tools. Audience response can be a physical remote used for a customer to answer multiple-choice questions or type responses. SMS text or Web sites can also be used via a personal device to reply to surveys, give feedback, or ask questions. Speakers may use this to gain real-time insight to the demographics of those in the room and get a pulse on current knowledge of the audience. Anonymity is another advantage, so questions or feedback can be shared openly. These platforms can also serve as a survey tool, following the events.

Surveys about sessions used to be paper forms laid on tables and collected by hand following the event. Eventually they moved to scannable paper technology to reduce the manpower required to gather data. Today, surveys are mostly digital with live-time feedback, often integrating into audience response or event app tools. Push notifications can be sent via the app based on the breakout room you're sitting in to gather feedback.

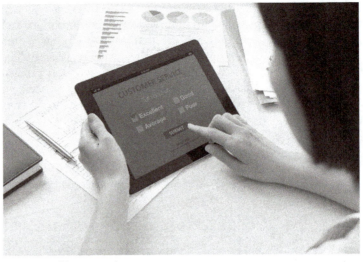

Bloomicon/Shutterstock

This is done using **geo-fencing technology,** a system that uses global positioning (GPS), beacons, or **radio frequency identification (RFID)** to create a virtual boundary that triggers texts, notifications, or emails. These location-based monitoring devices can also assist planners in tracking attendee data of how long they spend on the tradeshow floor, how many people attended sessions, and who skipped the lunch to eat on their own.

Mobile Application Software

"Apps" as they're nicknamed have become second nature to smartphone users, as they are software that perform a task or function of benefit to the user. Apple debuted apps in July 2008 and, in 2009, a study by Gartner noted 2.52 billion downloads. In 2016, that number rose 5,824.6 percent to 149.3 billion downloads. Event apps can be implemented as an app specific to that event for the organization and hosted within a hosting event app or live within an app that encompasses all events and other information between events.

In the event world, apps have been able to reduce the need for printed collateral including program books, session surveys, speaker profiles, venue maps, and sponsorship materials. One of the most important elements to a successful app is the integration into other apps. An event app will not replace other social media, email or navigation apps for users, because those apps are used on a regular basis and function independent of an event. When your event app integrates into them, the user will likely spend more screen time in your own app.

Wearable Devices

While some of our personal devices are getting larger screens, others are getting smaller and becoming wearable. Glasses, watches, and necklaces can track our steps, answer our calls, keep our calendars, and navigate us to that next meeting. In creating a mobile app it is now crucial to consider integration with these wearable devices. Most tech savvy guests will be carrying portable chargers for their multiple devices, but planners should consider the addition of charging stations to keep all devices running throughout the day. After all, with hotel room keys moving to smartphones, guests need enough charge to make it into their rooms at the end of the day.

Mobile Payments

Expanding on the restaurant chapter (4), wearable technology has also translated into payments. Cash bar or silent auction events can now offer technology of bracelets linked to your credit card to shorten lines commonly found at the end of events with guests waiting to settle payments. The consumer market has made purchases easy with your credit

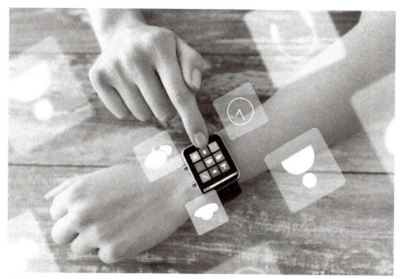

Syda Productions/Shutterstock

cards attached to multiple devices and apps that make money transfers and requests happen with a click. Event planners have to consider the ease of purchases during their events for merchandise, book stores, silent auctions, and donations. Onsite registrations may also require purchases, and depending on your registration software, can they facilitate charges onsite as well? Tax law can come into question when a company is based in one state or country and then sells products in another.

Signage

As seen again in the restaurant chapter (4) many venues and planners are moving to digital room signage for the ability to make quick changes and in an effort to go green. Touchscreen technology has increased the consumer's expectation of this signage leading to them wanting to see the other concurrent sessions, browse the restaurant menus, and see the navigation to the next meeting room. Signs are an area to integrate AI as well so that customers can verbally ask for what they need, and the sign is intelligent enough to customize the answer since it recognizes the attendees by the RFID in their name badge or Bluetooth in their phone.

Cheskyw/123RF

Event Capture

Social media and hashtags have aided planners in their ability to capture event photos, videos, and quotes. Photography companies, once a staple in event experience, have used social media to enhance their work with photo booths and tablet-based instant emailing. Technology companies have also used hashtag data to print photos linked with the hashtags for attendees to take with them. All photos are also created in a digital mosaic, giving attendees the chance to see their photo as a part of the larger picture. Drone cameras are used to capture events from angles no person could and offer time-lapse data of attendee movement to the event planners. Planners should consult with their venues on use of drones due to no fly zones and potential insurances needs regarding safety of devices.

5. Summary

Meeting/event managers have a wide variety of technology available to them to make planning and execution easier, more efficient, and more cost-effective. Managers can use audio/visual equipment to enhance the program content and set meeting/event tone. When planning technology into your event, the most important considerations are the goals and objectives of the event and how technology can support them and yield a favorable ROI to be discussed along with RFP in our final chapter. Before setting foot in a venue, the technology of site selection and RFPs is crucial for planner efficiency in terms of time and travel.

Once the venue has been selected, event documentation becomes the next challenge for the planner. Keeping numerous details and pieces of information organized can be streamlined with technology, but the process becomes manual again when your vendors receive that information due to their technology not speaking your language.

Understanding technology's impact on your bandwidth needs is a key takeaway from the discussion in this chapter. Most technology is void if there's not the system to support the devices. Some guests may rely on cellular data, but if your event is large enough (think a large sporting event), the cellular towers in the area may not be able to handle the volume, reducing the ability to text, upload, and post.

Virtual and Hybrid meetings are an inevitable shift in the meetings industry. Leveraging these to drive attendance, exposure, and sponsorship are the keys to success. In-person attendees not only want to connect with each other using technology but also want to interact with the virtual audience. AI, VR, and wearable technology are revolutionizing the way attendees navigate their daily routines and, therefore, how they participate in an event.

Meeting/event technology is always changing and improving. Continuous education is crucial to know the latest options and resources in technology. Planners should invest time in industry conferences, blogs, podcasts, and newsletters to ensure they're aware of the options and trends. Every event is expected to be better than the last one, so innovation is key.

6. CASE STUDY AND LEARNING ACTIVITY

PCMA's (Professional Convention Management Association) Convening Leaders 2017 in Austin attracted thousands of in-person attendees. Utilizing their Digital Experience Institute to live stream and record the event, PCMA was able to attract an additional 1,400 attendees from 24 countries. PCMA has leveraged a hybrid event strategy at their Convening Leaders event since 2011, gaining popularity each year with 2017 being no exception. Online attendance grew 6 percent over 2016. Of the 1,400 digital attendees, 46 percent spent more than six hours online.

Similar to face-to-face events, digital events, too, need contingency planning. In 2015, at a PCMA event, inclement weather caused a keynote speaker's flight to be canceled. In 2017, the keynote presentation was interrupted digitally due to buffering issues.

Learning Activity

1. How could an in-person or digital failure to deliver content affect the attendee experience? What resources could be used to troubleshoot the above scenarios?

2. PCMA's strategy with digital events is to drive revenue. After five years of launching their hybrid event, they recorded earning over $1 million in revenue. Name two ways that digital content could drive revenue. Name two ways that a digital attendee could produce revenue eventually.

3. During face-to-face meetings there's a strong demand for networking opportunities. Attendees want more chances to connect and discuss the content learned in the classroom. This poses a challenge for the digital audience with increased "white space." Name two ways a hybrid event can utilize these white spaces to enhance the online experience.

7. Key Terms

APEX (Accepted Practices Exchange)
AI (Artificial Intelligence)
AR (Augmented Reality)
Bandwidth
DLP (Digital Light Processing)

Geo-fencing technology
I-Mag (Image Magnification)
LCD (Liquid Crystal display)
LED (Light-emitting Diode)

Projection mapping
RFID (Radio Frequency Identification)
RFP (Request for Proposals)

8. Chapter Questions

1. Name three types of organizations that may host a database search engine for planners to easily find sites for events.
2. What are some factors that should be considered when choosing the right audio and visual technology for your event?
3. Name two consumer technology devices and explain how they impact attendance at an event. How can meeting planners capitalize on that existing technology?
4. When considering an app for an event, what is one of the most important features that should be available?

CHAPTER 7

Maximizing Revenues through Global Distribution

Courtesy of Melissa Maher

Chapter Objective

- At the end of this chapter students will have a deeper understanding of the complex world of reservation distribution.

Learning Objectives

- Define distribution and explain channels
- Understand the many roles of global distribution systems
- Explain the distribution core competencies
- Understand how quickly distribution changes

Chapter Introduction

Interview

Melissa Maher is senior vice president of the Global Partner Group for Expedia, Inc., where she manages all aspects of global business relationships with the company's top strategic hotel partners. Her team is charged with managing and enhancing relationships for the industry's ownership and management companies, key industry associations, and hotel groups. Based in Newport Beach, California, Maher also oversees the team responsible for driving the strategy, distribution and support of Expedia's gaming lodging supply division. Maher received an MBA in Hotel Administration from the University of Nevada, Las Vegas.

1. **Distribution is one of the most complex yet critical aspects of the hotel business. What are the key opportunities from the hotel perspective and the online travel agency perspective?**

   Distribution can be complex, but if opportunities are known, they can be managed. One opportunity is for hoteliers to understand their distribution costs, such as connectivity (e.g., global distribution system), meta search, and online travel agencies. These fees are important because hoteliers can utilize different distribution channels to support their revenue strategy. For example, a hotelier may want to target international customers and mobile same-day customers to fill their need periods, creating two different costs for consumer acquisition. It is important for hoteliers to research these fees and the overall return on investment of using these distribution partners. For Expedia, Inc., a big opportunity is to help educate our hotel partners about these fees and support them in researching the return on investment.

2. **With the previous question in mind, hotels have been differentiating themselves by using loyalty rates. What are the key opportunities?**

   From my perspective, the opportunity I see for hotels is to focus on what other factors drive guests to book direct. Research conducted by Deloitte on hotel industry loyalty programs found that a high-quality guest experience is expected by all guests including those not enrolled in a hotel guest loyalty program. As hotels roll out a strategy of loyalty book-direct rates, they may be overlooking a large opportunity to focus on basic guest satisfaction, which could impact the overall success of the hotel.

   I've observed another opportunity regarding guest acquisition for smaller hotel chains. These hotels have made the strategic decision to view their acquisition method across multiple distribution channels rather than focusing on one source of demand. Recently, Red Lion and Expedia, Inc., came together to provide *Expedia.com* and *Hotels.com* consumers with access to Red Lion's loyalty rates. This relationship proved successful when Red Lion saw four times the month-over-month increase in sign-ups for Hello Rewards. The collaboration between Red Lion and Expedia, Inc., is a great example of how a hotel company and a large distribution channel work together to support each other's strategy.

3. **What are the most important concepts and technologies to know about distribution to be successful hotel managers?**

   In my experience, there are several important concepts and technologies hotel managers should know. The advice I always give hoteliers is to utilize online travel agent (OTA) partners for their data. For example, our online portal, Expedia PartnerCentral, houses great analytics software such as Expedia, Inc.'s Rev+. Savvy hoteliers can utilize this data to help increase the business they receive from OTAs as well as use this data in their own revenue management strategies on property. Considering the future of online distribution and ecommerce, hoteliers need to think about embracing new technologies that are coming online. One of the most anticipated technologies that I have experienced is voice-search and voice-activation, which has grown in popularity through devices such as the Amazon Echo. This voice-activation software could potentially be used for guest services including making hotel reservations, ordering room service, and completing check-out. As the hospitality industry considers the next several years, they will need to embrace and invest in these resources to remain competitive.

4. **Today, there are so many different channels to distribute hotel products and accept reservations. How can a hotelier determine the channels to use and to pass over? What evaluation techniques and measures do you suggest?**

   Hoteliers must evaluate and decide which distribution partners bring them true incremental business that they may not be able to acquire through their direct booking strategy. The cost of distribution partners that bring incremental revenues are worthwhile. For example, one product Expedia, Inc., offers the "Package Path," a tool that enables consumers to bundle airfare, hotel and/or car rentals into one seamless booking. This is also a growing segment of the hospitality business. In addition, it is important for hotels to work with different distribution companies so that they can broaden their reach across the industry. From my experience, evaluation techniques are an important resource all hoteliers should use to understand the return on investment of each distribution partner. These evaluation techniques are especially important for the larger hotel chain companies. I recommend these hoteliers look at all variables of their distribution agreements. After all the different areas of the business are evaluated, hoteliers can then decide which distribution partners provide the business that is most valuable.

5. **Revenue management systems, specifically programs that use historical data to adjust the hotel's pricing strategy, continue to become the cutting edge product for hoteliers. What do you see as the future of these models? How will they impact current distribution strategies as we know them?**

   From my perspective, I anticipate that we will start to see the industry use more forward-looking and real-time data to evaluate shopping and search patterns. Forward-looking search information will enable hoteliers to anticipate demand and adjust their revenue strategies in real time to reflect the current demand of a market.

6. **There are different costs associated with various distribution channels both on the brand and OTA sides, which impact overhead and overall guest acquisition costs. How do you propose hoteliers manage them?**

   What I believe hoteliers need to understand is where these fees are coming from. I also believe a branded hotel should know what efforts the brand makes on their behalf. Specifically, they should know the costs of each part of a booking whether through their own Web site or through a distribution partner. The best way for a hotelier to learn about these costs is to reach out to their brands for clarification or to their third-party partners for more information.

7. **How does the influx of vacation rentals, apartment hotels, and alternative lodging impact the distribution of traditional hotel room inventory?**

   From my perspective, vacation rentals and alternative lodging are an important part of the travel industry. One reason consumers are drawn to this type of lodging is because many are in rural areas where there is minimal hotel supply. As these vacation rentals come online, they may impact supply depending on their location.

8. **Where do you look for emerging trends, new developments, and innovations in distribution? Who is leading the way?**

   I look at both small and large players in different ways. The small niche companies in the hospitality industry have a focus on rolling out unique ideas, and their size allows them to be more fixated on one product. I watch the larger companies for innovations on the technology front (e.g., Apple, Google).

9. **Going forward, what role(s) do you think travel intermediaries, especially online travel agents and wholesalers, will play? Do you see further disintermediation and/or consolidation?**

   From my viewpoint within Expedia, Inc., I see us evolving and transitioning from a pure distribution partner to more of platform company, helping hotel partners and the industry become more efficient. A recent example of this is the Vacations by Marriott announcement in September 2016. This relationship enabled Marriott's vacation Web site to be powered by Expedia, Inc.'s dynamic package path which allows consumers to add on air ticket, tour, attraction, or ground transportation to their accommodation. This exemplifies how Expedia, Inc., extended its technology, marketing, data, and analytics to support the travel industry in general to become more efficient for the consumer.

10. **What parting words of advice can you share with current and aspiring hospitality business professionals?**

    I would say work with companies that can give you a well-rounded, global experience. Additionally, it is important to find a focus in technology in your current role, because technology is the future.

    Interview with Melissa Maher

1. Overview

Since the early stages of commerce, merchants have wrestled with determining the *best* approach to delivering their products and services to the marketplace for purchase and consumption. All industries are tied together by technology; hospitality is unique in its reliance on technology as more consumers turn to multiple sources to find their best accommodations. The area of global distribution is one of the most complex aspects of the hospitality business and an area that has been greatly impacted by technology change with the rise of new channels or sales outlets. As technology evolves the way hotel inventory is distributed, so do the trends in the ways people find, research, and purchase travel. The term **global distribution** can be defined in this case as attaining the broadest possible reach to the largest available audience meeting a company's target market segments at the most affordable cost and with the highest potential for winning conversion (i.e., generating bookings). It is all about selling the right products and services to the right guests at the right times and prices under the right set of circumstances in ways that are convenient to guests (Stein and Sweat, 1998). When booking hotel and resort accommodations, consumers have many choices, both in terms of product selection and in terms of the tools they use to search for, research, and purchase their accommodations (see Figure 7-1). While clearly a marketing function, global distribution is completely reliant upon sophisticated information technology (IT) and is continuously being reshaped as new technologies, Internet developments, and mobile applications emerge. The marketing, revenue management, sales, and reservations teams need to work in tandem to deploy technologies that will aid the business in growing and capturing more market share. With new channels come new ways for customers to shop for and book their lodging accommodations and, hence, new ways for marketers to reach, interact with, and serve customers or guests. Because there are a series of tradeoffs among reach, richness, cost, and effectiveness or conversion (Evans and Wurster, 1999), it is challenging to determine the best distribution methods for each targeted customer segment. What a difference there is in today's distribution process and global economy from those our forefathers experienced when the concept of commerce first emerged! Thus, distribution is an area with some of the greatest opportunities to develop strategic advantages and drive revenues.

Until recently, hotel and resort distribution was characterized by adages such as "location, location, location" or "if you build it, they will come." Unfortunately, these tend to overshadow more rational approaches to selecting distribution channels and applying

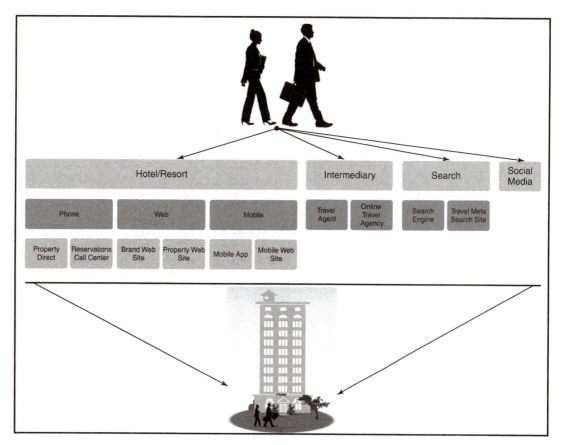

FIGURE 7-1

Common channels used when booking lodging accommodations.

IT to broaden visibility and win market share. Moreover, these traditional philosophies, by themselves, are no longer sufficient in attracting today's sophisticated and demanding consumers. Within the lodging industry, the area of distribution has become far too complex to be treated with such simplicity. It makes sense for organizations to pay attention, develop effective distribution strategies, and manage their channels carefully to maximize results. In some cases (often in larger chains), we see a position emerging called **channel manager**. This person, working closely with the revenue manager or revenue management team, oversees all of the different distribution channels used; makes sure content, rates, availability information, and selling rules and restrictions are up to date in each channel; and verifies whether each channel is properly representing his or her portfolio of properties.

The thrusts of distribution are market reach and penetration, branding, merchandising, and revenue generation. Supporting the global distribution function is a **global distribution system (GDS)** that in effect has become the circulatory system of the lodging organization (Estis Green, 2008). For the purposes of this chapter, we define GDS in the broadest possible sense. It is the entire network of people, systems, technology, and distribution channels that are used to help lodging providers sell their products and services. Given this scope, the GDS can be considered to be an ecosystem of sorts (see Figure 7-2). The primary focus has been on guestroom sales or reservations for individual and group travel, but attention is expanding into other areas such as meeting rooms, restaurant reservations, spa treatments, golf tee times, and more. A company's GDS must support two primary objectives. First, it must provide distribution channels that allow customers the ability to easily and quickly search for products and services they are willing to purchase with full (i.e., transparent) disclosure of rates and availability (what is often termed seamless, **single-image inventory**), and second, it must provide a means to conveniently conduct the transaction on the spot, with immediate confirmation that the transaction has been successfully completed.

To achieve these objectives, a GDS requires a clear strategy, dedicated resources, effective management, and a sound IT infrastructure. These are necessary in order to provide competitive advantage—and it can with access to new customers, better and faster service, sophisticated rate and inventory management, economies of scale, reduced overhead, lower transaction costs, enhanced buyer and supplier relationships, **cross-selling** (selling complementary products such as spa, golf tee times, restaurant reservations), and **up-selling** (room upgrades and packages), unique capabilities, and superior channel performance.

Generally, a GDS (or some part of a GDS) is the first point of all guest contact; it is also the initial and oftentimes primary source of data collection. Important guest data regarding one's stay (e.g., dates of stay, room preferences, payment information) are then used in downstream services and guest interactions (e.g., guest registration). Therefore, it is one of the most important technologies in a lodging company's IT portfolio. Remember, it is all about the guest experience and relationships with guests. One of the most famous customer relationship management (CRM) systems, Mystique, is used

FIGURE 7-2
The GDS ecosystem.

by The Ritz-Carlton Hotel Company, LLC. This system tracks and utilizes guest preference data to support the outstanding service offered to guests. Hotels and resorts must own these interaction points to collect the necessary data needed to create exemplary and memorable service experiences and build brand loyalty. A GDS is also one of the most complex components of a hotel or resort company's IT portfolio due to its technological sophistication, the complicated business logic and rules embedded in its applications, the numerous interfaces that must be supported to connect heterogeneous systems together to share data (both within the company and with the outside world), the volume of transactions and speed by which they must be processed, the uniqueness of room inventory and attributes across a lodging chain, individual guest needs, and the sophistication of the underlying database and search engine that powers it.

Within the lodging industry, distribution channels are being reshaped as the result of technological advancements; new and emerging players; and a shift in the balance of power among suppliers, buyers, and intermediaries. At the same time, the corresponding costs associated with technological investment and transaction processing are rising due to the complex networks and technological infrastructure (e.g., two-way interfaces) required and the sophisticated applications that must be in place to support seamless, single-image inventory across the spectrum of distribution channels that exist today and that will soon exist in the future. Complicating matters, executives have few tools and little guidance to help them determine when to invest, how much to invest, and how to assess or gauge the business value to be gained from the investment. Consequently, this is an important area of study requiring shrewd and decisive decision-making due to the strategic positioning implications and the high costs of doing business in today's competitive industry environment.

It is important for hoteliers to consider the strategic implications of using certain distribution channels while avoiding others. Consider, for example, how the discount airline company Southwest Airlines has intentionally chosen to limit the number of distribution channels used to sell its tickets to keep costs low and pass along savings to its customers. The company educates its customers on how and where to book its flights in order to get the best available fares. In doing so, it is actively seeking to drive consumers to its Web site, the least expensive distribution channel with the lowest overhead. Southwest Airlines' approach seems bold and is vastly different from the strategies employed by many hotel and resort companies, but it works well and contributes greatly to the success of the company. For hotels and resorts, a broad net is often cast in efforts to be everywhere the competition is and everywhere they are likely to find their target customers. Distribution channels are considered to be like retail store shelf space. Using this metaphor, the prevailing philosophy by many hoteliers is that more is better; more shelves carrying one's products will result in more purchases. While this seems logical on the surface, the corresponding costs that are associated with technological investment and transaction processing necessitate greater focus on better, proactive distribution channel selection, management, and assessment. Thus, it is important to use a disciplined approach to channel selection and have a strong measurement program in place to measure effectiveness of each channel used. Measurement should include traffic and conversion rates, volume of reservations booked, distribution and customer acquisition costs, revenue, profitability, and repeat usage. Marketing and distribution strategies and measurement programs will help determine how best to target one's distribution channel selection. The sections that follow will discuss the strategic significance of hotel/resort GDS. It will explore the many components of GDS, developments and trends in the distribution arena, and the importance of developing a **distribution strategy** to create competitive advantage.

2. Importance of GDS

As previously stated, the objective of a GDS is to distribute a company's products (in this case, hotel/property, guestroom, inventory, or meeting space) to as broad an audience as possible but in the most effective and cost-efficient means available so that they can be purchased. More specifically, the roles played by a GDS have evolved over time—from one of transaction-based emphasis to one of strategic value—but at any one point in time, a GDS fulfills five important roles, as illustrated in Figure 7-3 and described in the following.

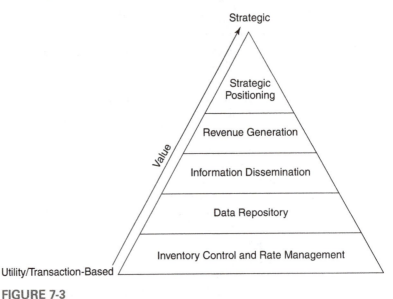

FIGURE 7-3
The many roles of a GDS.

The first role of a GDS is one of simple utility: transaction processing and maintaining, controlling, and reporting room inventory levels and hotel/resort rates. Initially, a GDS provided a simple accounting of rooms available versus rooms sold at predetermined rates, generally set by each hotel/property for some defined period of time (e.g., seasonal rates). Over time, this function has expanded in complexity and strategic importance as more emphasis has been placed on yield management to maximize a property's total revenue. Now, this function is responsible for the definition of room pools and rate categories, the allocation of rooms, and the rules and restrictions that govern the sale of these rooms. The system must support all decision-making regarding the setting of rates, the allocation of rooms, and the rules and restrictions. The system must then communicate this information to all points of distribution in real time, enforcing all the rules when a room is reserved or cancelled.

In its second role, a GDS plays an important function as a data repository and a learning system for guest history, preference, profiles, and buying patterns. This system is one of the primary collection points of valuable guest-related information and preferences. The value of the stored data increases with each subsequent guest encounter[1] and from data mining used to help a company in developing, positioning, and marketing its products and services. Because of the data collected, this system becomes an important feed to other core systems, including a company's property management system and data warehouse, which then enable a company to improve guest recognition, the customization of guest experiences, product positioning, and new service developments and product offerings.

Its third function is that of a communications vehicle. It disseminates vital information regarding inventory availability, rates (including rules and restrictions), and hotel property information as well as guest profile data to various points of distribution and service delivery in real time for access by all service associates to allow them to better perform their jobs, recognize their guests, and personalize the guest experience.

Fourth, a GDS represents a source of revenue, not just in terms of room nights or meeting sales generated and revenue maximization through yield management but also through fees charged for participation and for transactions processed. An effective GDS and skilled channel management will be key success factors, provide competitive advantage, and influence firm profitability. Since the cost of distribution can easily reach 35 percent of a room's daily rate (Estis Green, 2008), effective management is essential to containing overhead. Mismanagement of distribution channels will only accelerate the profit margin erosion that results from agent commissions and transaction fees.

Finally, a GDS is strategic. It plays an important role in a company's positioning, provides access to markets, allows a company to implement unique functionality and

---

[1] Kirsner (1999) terms this interactive, iterative learning process *progressive profiling*.

selling strategies, builds strategic alliances through **interorganizational systems** (connections with systems from other organizations such as airline GDSs, OTAs, Internet distribution systems, etc.), and provides a product which is used to sell to and attract franchisees and management contracts.

GDSs play a critical role in the sales process of any product or service. In the hospitality industry, significant advances in GDSs have raised the stakes of competition by providing access to more markets, creating new sources of revenue, and enhancing guest service (Connolly and Moore, 1995) while changing the overall economics of the booking process. More importantly, the methods of booking lodging accommodations and meeting space have shifted to alternative approaches that are cheaper to operate and require greater involvement from the customer, thereby freeing up traditional booking channels to process more complicated scenarios. As they continue to evolve, GDSs will reshape how travelers plan and arrange accommodations for personal vacations and business trips and how hotel/property companies interact with their customers. Without question, a GDS is a mission-critical application, and quite possibly, the lifeline of the organization. Any disruptions in service can severely inconvenience, if not cripple, a hotel or entire lodging company.

It can be said that a GDS is the cornerstone for the service delivery process in a hotel or property and for all property-based technology. Yet, one should not consider a GDS as a single system or entity. Rather, it is a collection of systems, technologies, telecommunications, people, and strategies, that, when coupled, provide an effective means of marketing and selling a hotel's guestrooms, meeting space, and other facilities. In most cases, it is the initial and principal data collection point that, in turn, feeds information to all other aspects of the organization and all subsequent processes in the guest lifecycle (namely, registration, in-house services, guest history, post-stay follow-up, and ongoing marketing efforts). Without a well-integrated GDS, functions like marketing, customer relationship building, data mining, revenue (yield) management, and labor forecasting, to name a few, would be severely handicapped—if not impossible to do.

A relatively recent focus of technology softwares are on the improvement of hotel revenue management strategies. These systems directly collect historical booking data from the hotel's GDS in which it is installed and support the hotel in making pricing decisions to optimize revenue and bring profit to the bottom line. One of the most popular software is IDeaS™.

The world of GDS is highly complex and requires that hospitality organizations master a number of competencies if they are to be successful in this area. Hamel and Prahalad (1994) stress the strategic importance of **core competencies** and competency building to achieve competitive advantage. The core competencies required of hotel and property companies with respect to distribution channels and GDS are included in Figure 7-4.

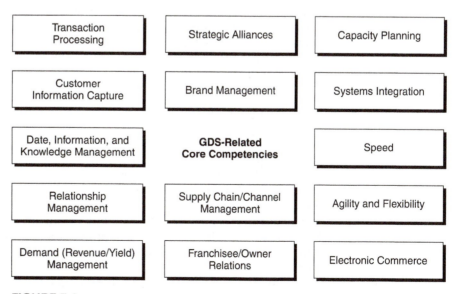

FIGURE 7-4

GDS-related core competencies essential for competitive advantage.

Essentially, GDS competitive advantage stems from excellence in and mastery of several key areas, including technology development and deployment, supply chain management, customer relationship building, knowledge management, electronic commerce. Finally, the GDS must also be fast, agile and flexible to change.

3. Developing a Distribution Channel Strategy

Being able to successfully manage something and invest in it requires complete understanding of precisely what it is one is trying to manage and how best to allocate firm resources to it. Alternatively stated, one must fully comprehend the concept of global distribution channels in today's context and have the ability to forecast where they are headed in order to select the appropriate channels and technologies to build competitive methods. Effective management of, investment in, and resource allocations to GDSs and their ensuing channels will result in improvements to a hotel's or property's profitability on two fronts: decreased costs and improved revenues. The fundamental principle at work here is that if a property or lodging company can effectively exploit its distribution channels, it can gain market share through increased sales while simultaneously reducing overhead. Both go directly to the bottom line, thereby improving profitability and competitive advantage.

One of the best illustrations in the travel industry of strategic choices and resource allocations related to GDS is Southwest Airlines, mentioned earlier. In the airline industry, it is not uncommon for airlines to list their flights and availability in competitor systems. Just as in the lodging industry, these airlines pay a booking fee for each reservation booked in addition to ongoing fees for participation and flight listings. To reduce overhead, Southwest Airlines has consciously decided not to participate in all airline GDSs and available travel distribution channels. Southwest is able to make these types of decisions because it understands its customer base and knows how best to reach its targeted audience. Perhaps this is why Southwest Airlines remains one of the most profitable airlines in the industry. These are precisely the same kinds of decisions hotels and lodging companies must make—but only after customer booking habits, market share, and other variables are better understood.

As transactional costs continue to rise, hotels and properties will need to determine which channels are most profitable for them and how they can yield the best results using these channels. This may mean discontinuing channels that are less productive or ones that cost more to maintain in favor of channels that yield greater room revenue and require less overhead to operate. The focus will be placed on distribution share per channel (i.e., the marketing mix or the amount of volume and revenue generated by each channel in the GDS network in comparison with the others to which an organization subscribes or in which it participates). With a growing number of hotel and property products and suitable alternatives, it becomes increasingly difficult to discern one property from the next. It also becomes harder to get the consumer's attention, since he or she is bombarded with an array of options, many of which may seemingly appear to be equally attractive. Therefore, it will be incumbent upon leading systems and GDS providers to find ways to rise above the noise and convert lookers into bookers.

Finding and Competing for Electronic Shelf Space

Gaining a presence in multiple points of distribution is analogous to finding shelf space in a grocery or retail store. More is generally considered better because it improves visibility, customer access, and convenience. Let's take leading Online Travel Agency, Expedia Inc.'s Market Place design, in this case more choices on the consumer side leads to better results. Referencing a viewpoint by the interviewee of this chapter, Melissa Maher; Expedia designed their marketplace with the consumer's preferences and search criteria in mind. Expedia finds the ideal way to present properties to their consumers is to allow the consumer to filter by price, locations, amenities, or other factors. This enables the consumer to find the best accommodation for their needs. To take this a step further, by the consumers aligning their needs to the right hotel at the right price, their expectations are also set at an appropriate standard. After twenty years of analyzing shopper behavior, Expedia found this strategy leads to the strongest conversion rate.

This is why lodging firms must make a strategic commitment to visibility to the consumer. This implies defining, developing, and implementing a strategy as well as investing in the corresponding technology to support this strategy. No longer can one afford to gratuitously spend money on marketing or distribution channels without knowing the appropriate target markets and anticipating the expected returns. To help hoteliers develop a global distribution strategy and evaluate various distribution channel options, a list of criteria has been provided in Figure 7-5.

Cost Implications

For lodging companies, connectivity to airline GDSs has been costly and problematic but necessary if they want to take advantage of the travel agent market, worldwide. The challenges of displaying detailed property information in an easy-to-use format and synchronizing databases in real time add to the administrative burdens of managing a GDS. In particular, the delays in transmission between airline GDSs and a hotel/property GDS, the batching of transactions, and the processing of error messages that result from incompatibilities between different systems create a cumbersome queuing process that must be closely monitored to avoid overbooking and to ensure that reservations are received at the property level before guests arrive. Manual and semi-automated processes also rely extensively on queues. Oftentimes, dedicated staffs are required to manage these queues. While improvements in airline GDS/lodging GDS interfaces help to alleviate the situation, they unfortunately do not completely eliminate the problems from occurring; and hence the queuing process still exists. Despite these shortcomings, hotels and properties are dependent upon the airline GDSs because of their extensive market reach, not only to travel agents but also to online travel agencies. To maximize travel agent bookings, airlines helped automate

---

Can the new distribution channel
- Gain access to new markets and new customers to drive top-line revenues?
- Strengthen customer relations and build lasting loyalty?
- Provide incremental bookings and revenue?
- Improve yield through rate lift or increases in average daily rate (ADR), occupancy rate, and revenue per available room (REVPAR)?
- Create switching costs?
- Build barriers to entry?
- Offer unique and sustainable advantages?
- Merchandise the property and adequately and appropriately convey its best features and value?
- Yield better information that can be used for competitive advantage or for creating or enhancing products and services?
- Provide easy and convenient access to single-image inventory and last-room availability?
- Be easily updated with rate changes, selling rules, restrictions, etc.?
- Be easily integrated into the company's global distribution network and managed on an ongoing basis?
- Streamline or simplify the technological complexity or management of existing distribution channels?
- Reduce the number distribution channels required?
- Eliminate potential points of failure and third-party intermediaries?
- Provide economies of scale?
- Reduce customer acquisition costs?
- Reduce operating costs or transaction fees and shift traffic to a channel of lower cost?
- Eliminate duplication?
- Change the balance of power in customer or supplier relationships?
- Alter the basis of competition or change the nature of intra-industry competitive rivalries?
- Enable new business opportunities?
- Track sources of origination for each reservation?
- Protect customer data and ensure privacy?
- Allow the hotel/resort to maintain the locus of control over room inventory and rates?
- Support multiple formats of content (i.e., text, graphics, sound, video, etc.)?

FIGURE 7-5

Distribution channel evaluation criteria.

travel agents by providing easy access to their mainframe-based reservation systems. These relationships proved fruitful for the airlines and quickly became a source of competitive advantage. For lodging companies to realize some of the same benefits as airlines in terms of access to the travel agency networks, they needed to list their properties in each of the major airline GDSs. Today, these GDSs help to further distribute lodging accommodations to various online channels. However, with advances in technology, new solutions have been coming to market, weakening the stronghold airline GDSs have enjoyed heretofore. These technology advances, while welcome, add to the complexity of the distribution landscape and make this a dynamic and exciting space.

To participate in this listing service is a costly endeavor. Hotels must pay listing fees and transaction costs for every reservation booked. Additionally, hotels are responsible for the information displayed about their facilities, rates, and availability. To maintain this information, the large lodging chains invested heavily in the development of interfaces between their GDSs and the airline GDSs. These interfaces are not only costly to develop but also costly to maintain. They require constant updating due to the dynamism of the airline GDS market and recent changes in the lodging industry. For example, the implementation of revenue management systems in many of the large chains resulted in thousands of price updates each day to the airline GDSs. Needless to say, the high costs and complexity of these interfaces put them out of reach of many smaller chains and independent hotels and resorts. This resulted in a definite disadvantage with respect to their representation in the marketplace by external sales agents (e.g., travel agents). The gap between the technology haves and the have-nots became evident. The Internet and the rise of alternative distribution systems (ADSs) have helped to give smaller entities and independents some of the same capabilities enjoyed by chains, thereby leveling the playing field.

Hoteliers should consider the role IT can play in building and supporting distribution channels and the subsequent economics of these channels, which include the total cost of ownership (TCO), operation, and maintenance for each point of distribution. Understanding and controlling this cost structure can be a valuable source of competitive advantage. Many of the interfaces between systems are costly to develop, maintain, and operate—especially for small properties and lodging companies, which cannot achieve the same economies of scale of their larger competitors. Because larger companies can share or leverage costs over more properties or rooms, they tend to achieve cost advantages more easily than smaller properties and independents. Initial interface development can cost as low as a few thousand dollars to as much as tens of thousands per interface, depending on the systems architecture, complexity of the interface, and the functionality. Although organizations like the OpenTravel Alliance (*www.opentravel.org*) and the Hotel Electronic Distribution Network Association (*www.hedna.org*) along with open systems and better standards have helped to improve connectivity between many of the technologies involved in distribution, the costs remain high. Therefore, hoteliers must estimate the value and strategic importance of each interface before embarking on its development. The ongoing support and maintenance costs must also be factored into the decision. Because the core technologies comprising the GDS environment are subject to frequent modification to keep up with market demands, these interfaces require constant monitoring and updating. Many properties and small lodging companies cannot afford the dedicated resources and lack the technical knowledge base to make these enhancements and modifications. Instead, they either choose not to participate in certain distribution channels, compromise the degree of integration, or outsource these services and become subject to the terms and service levels of their contractual arrangements with a chosen vendor. All of these decisions have strategic consequences.

The costs assigned to each channel vary and can be based on pre-negotiated volumes. Some channels (including brand channels) require fixed fees in addition to transaction fees. Transaction fees are generally based on net bookings (i.e., reservations booked minus cancellations), but in some cases, a transaction may be defined as any database query or inquiry (i.e., pay-per-click model). Approximate average costs (in U.S. dollars) that may impact a reservation are as follows:

- GDS fee: 10 percent
- Universal switch: 4 percent

- Hotel CRS (central reservation system): 3 percent
- Hotel Web site: $2 to $5

As stated previously, these costs should be evaluated based on ability to attract new consumers, revenue generation, and overall return on investment. One popular way to measure return on investment is the "look to book" ratio, also known as conversion. Ecommerce conversion is typically around 3 percent, if a distribution channel is bringing a hotel a larger conversion, this distribution source may be worthwhile to continue utilizing.

Understanding Share of Distribution

It is important for practitioners to consider which distribution channels will be most advantageous to them and subscribe or participate in only those channels. One of the common questions that is raised is "To which channels should a company subscribe?" A commonly held belief is that more channels lead to higher visibility, which, in turn, generates more demand. This may not always be the case. The quality of these channels and their links to the GDS must also be considered. The answer to this question is likely to vary from company to company and market to market. Each company must understand the sources of its business and the cost to acquire business through each of the distribution channels. Each channel has distinct costs; some are easily measurable such as transaction costs. Others are more intangible; for example, the cost to provide information to answer a guest inquiry that may or may not lead to a guest booking. To gain an advantage in this competitive marketplace, one must think intelligently about how resources are allocated so as to achieve an appropriate economic return. With respect to global distribution channels, this can be achieved only if a property or lodging company understands from where its business comes, how its distribution channels are used, how they contribute to the bottom line (this includes occupancy as well as profitability), and what the costs are to operate each channel.

When marketing professionals select media or places in which to advertise, they are advised to consider the medium and its targeted audience and compare them with the profiles of their customer base. The same must be done when considering investment in distribution channels. In addition, when selecting distribution channels, one should determine what reach the channel has, its visibility, the level of marketing provided by the channel operator, and the services that front-end this channel. This equates to broader distribution and visibility. For example, being part of an airline GDS has a profound reach. An airline GDS provides product representation to anyone or any service with access to that GDS, thus extending the potential audience for a given hotel or property. When determining which distribution channels to subscribe to and in which databases to market their product(s), hoteliers cannot ignore the reach of each channel and the popularity of its database. If the database is front-ended by a number of services, such as those found on the Internet, there is no need to join each service independently.

Hoteliers must also stay abreast of new trends impacting the way consumers shop and purchase hotel stays. By researching these trends, they can also ensure they remain relevant and a part of the most cutting-edge distribution channels. As mobile devices and Internet access become more accessible around the globe, more consumers are turning away from standard desktop booking and turning toward mobile.

The advantage of distribution channels versus traditional advertising is that more information can be captured regarding its impact and use via booking statistics, and other traffic or usage monitoring. These statistics are not always available for unidirectional forms of media. It is important to note that not all channels provide equal value and that some consumers use multiple channels when researching and purchasing lodging accommodations. In some cases, distribution channels may be redundant; in other cases, they may complement one another. As such, one cannot ignore the **look-to-book ratio** (i.e., the number of people who shop versus the number of people who actually make or book reservations). It is also important to consider the fact that channel usage can vary by market segment, accommodations needed, purpose of travel, or comfort level.

Inadequate GDS Technology Infrastructure

Even in today's high-level technology world, quite frankly, some hotels do not have the necessary technology and information systems in place to support the selling process from multiple locations via different channels and systems. Lacking last-room availability and seamless access to the property's rates create hardships and add to the overall level of frustration for the consumer. Those that are considered more advanced are still not state of the art. The industry's software and systems lack many of the functions required to support the industry's future directions. It is as if the software has put a stranglehold on the industry and given rise to a host of opportunities for outside players.

How Hotels Find Return on Investment in Third-Party Distribution

In order for hoteliers to be successful in their distribution strategy, they must branch out and make investments in technology beyond direct Web site. Although there are costs associated with these distributions, there are usually long-term benefits and a positive impact to net profits. The way these distributors work is simple; a hotel selects a channel to help represent its products and service offerings. That channel then subscribes to a wider network of its own, giving the products and services it represents broader distribution and visibility, thereby creating a much broader, virtual network for the hotel. When a reservation is booked in this broader network, a hotel receives the reservation directly into their connected system, third-party software, or by email/fax.

One should also remember the benefits of partnering with an online travel agency as well. There are two Cornell studies that make strong cases on the long-term benefits of being listed on these third-party distributors. The first is a 2012 Cornell study, that found just a one-percent improvement in a hotel reputation score online can impact a hotel's ADR to increase by .89 percent. This increase in hotel reputation score can also positively impact their occupancy up .54 percent, overall leading REVPAR to a 1.42 percent increase. This means that if a hotel improves their online reputation by 10 percent, they could see ADRs increase by 9 percent and occupancy by 5.4 percent. The second study, termed "The Billboard Effect," which was first released in 2011 and renewed in 2017, found that in an experiment of hotels listed on Expedia, Inc., Web sites saw an increase in overall reservations from 9 percent to 26 percent. This study also discovered that 65 percent of consumers that book direct with the hotel had visited an OTA prior to booking directly.

Typical models used in the distribution process include the following:

- *Agency model*—The agent or booking entity receives a compensation or flat fee for rooms booked.
- *Merchant or wholesale model*—A booking service negotiates room rates with a hotel in advance of sale. These are called **net rates**. It is then free to mark up the rates. The difference between what it charges and what it must pay the hotel or resort is its payment for service.
- *Opaque pricing model*—This approach is used by services like *Hotwire.com*. It allows hotels to discount rates while shielding their brand identities and maintain rate integrity. Guests make purchase decisions based primarily on price and location without knowing the service provider until after completing the booking transaction and committing to the purchase. This is a common way for hotels and resorts to sell distressed inventory at the last minute.
- *Expedia Traveler Preference model*—Pioneered by Expedia, Inc., consumers have the control to select to pay directly at time of booking or pay at the property upon check-in. Either way, the hotel pays the same compensation cost.
- *Pay per click*—A referral fee is commonly charged by travel meta search sites like *Trivago.com*, which generate leads and connects them with travel suppliers' Web sites to complete their booking transactions. Some prefer to use the term cost per click instead of pay per click.

The Rise in Meta Search Engines

As technology continues to evolve and grow, we see a rise in number of intermediaries in the selling process. While it is a commonly held belief that **disintermediation** will result as new electronic paths are built between the customer and supplier to create a more direct link, this thinking only applies to travel agents. The reality is that, in this digital age, the number of electronic intermediaries is increasing with greater seamlessness to both the customer and the supplier. Consider, for example, travel **meta search** engines like Trivago and Kayak. These search engine Web sites search and compare multiple travel sites to help consumers find the lowest rates and fares, they are especially popular among millennials and savvy online bookers, who are the future of travel. On the surface, they look or sound like an online travel agency, but they don't actually transact or fulfill the booking. They provide comparison-shopping services that then electronically link consumers with online providers who can transact the business. When a customer clicks on a link, he or she is redirected to a landing page within the booking process for the entity offering the product and price selected. These new electronic intermediaries match customer demand with products and services available for purchase. They are the information brokers operating on a pay-per-click compensation model; they earn revenue every time a consumer clicks on a listing. They can also earn revenue through sponsorship and advertising.

It is important to remember that each node in the distribution process, human or electronic, represents a potential point of service failure and a potential expense, typically a charge per transaction. Therefore, knowledge of and management of these players is critical. However, since intermediaries fall outside the traditional span of control of a lodging provider and since they are further removed from the primary source of information, it is difficult to motivate these resources to sell a particular brand or product and to educate them on how best to sell that brand or product. There is also greater potential for service delivery errors and misinforming guests due to incomplete information or general lack of knowledge. This is especially true when these intermediaries are less familiar with the products (i.e., lodging accommodations, facilities, and destinations) they are selling. The quality and timeliness of service delivered by these intermediaries can impact a guest's overall perception of the destination hotel, either positively or negatively.

Shift in Balance of Power from Supplier to Customer

As of late, we've also seen a shift in the balance of power between the consumer and the lodging supplier. The balance of power is moving away from the supplier in favor of the consumer. Consumers, armed with knowledge easily obtained from the Internet, develop greater expectations and now demand higher price–value relationships than ever before of any property in which they stay. These price conscious travelers also prefer a specific type of buying experience. A recent survey conducted by Adara Inc. found that 52 percent of U.S. travelers between the ages of 18 and 34 prefer booking hotels through online search engines as opposed to brand Web sites, compared with 37 percent age 35 and older. These Web sites and the tools that they offer allow consumers to quickly and effortlessly shop and compare products and services from one company to the next before making a buying decision. They can instantly tap into the many comments (good or bad) of prior visitors and factor this feedback into the selection and decision-making processes. Their efforts are expedited by push technology and smart agents, which help to filter out irrelevant or unwanted information, find the best travel bargains, and bring material of interest directly to the consumer's desktop in a manner that is easy to process and digest. This means consumers are now in charge; therefore, lodging properties must create, package, price, and deliver the perfect experience every time. In a digital world, there is no room or forgiveness for error.

New Models of Distribution and Pricing

Another important and related consideration resulting in the feeling of lost capacity control is that many of the newer forms of distribution are changing the model for how guestrooms are bought and sold. As a result, the sales, marketing, and distribution models are being turned on end, creating a new set of dynamics and a level playing field. For example, consider smartphone apps (e.g., iPhone and Google Android phones) and Google as two emerging booking sources as well as the influence of social media (e.g., consumer reviews) on the booking process. Consequently, hoteliers are uncomfortable because these new tools are ones in which they have little or no experience and ones in which they are slow to embrace. They have also come to realize that they cannot control all of the content or the brand image being communicated. Consumers, on the other hand, love and embrace the new model because it is consumer-centric and affords them control over their choices.

Accelerated Rates of Change

In the hospitality industry and almost all other industries impacted by technology, lately the only constant is change. Although for some, technology can be somewhat concerning, technology still remains the ultimate vehicle to further success and the future of travel. As a result of constant change, it is difficult to forecast the many changes on the horizon since industry leaders may not be looking in the right places or at the right indicators. By now, the business environment is characterized by the need to do more with less, faster and cheaper than ever before.

The cycle time for getting products to market and the number of competitors has heightened the complexity of competition. One area that has seen an influx of monetary and time investments is **A/B Tests**. These tests are defined as a controlled version (A) versus another version (B) to measure against a specific metric to find which version is most successful. A/B tests allow hospitality companies and online travel agencies to efficiently "test and learn" by introducing new advancements or changes to their Web site to a small group of users, measure the outcomes against the controlled version, and make a final decision. With trends changing so quickly, there often isn't time to test offline, rather instead hotels will run multiple and sometimes hundreds of A/B tests to measure which method is most profitable.

With technology in general and the Internet in particular growing at phenomenal rates, industry players cannot possibly keep abreast of the latest indicators or determinants of their business. The rules of the game are changing, introducing new opportunities for innovation and further revenues.

Relinquished Control of the Customer Relationship

In an age of digital distribution, lodging providers are increasingly concerned about losing control over the customer relationship. At a time where one-to-one marketing is paramount to success and winning customers over, lodging providers cannot afford to relinquish any control in the sales process or in customer relationship building. Because of the many distribution channels and intermediaries available and onward distribution, it is often difficult to track consumers, their identity and patterns, and the originating source of the booking. The problem is even more pronounced if the guest is part of a meeting or convention.

Control and management of the customer relationship are being involuntarily relinquished in favor of outside forces such as Google and alternative distribution systems that are now emerging. For example, Google recently introduced the Hotel Search Tool in 2011, software similar to the meta search format.

4. Trends in Hotel and Resort GDS

Disintermediation and Reintermediation

Until recently, travel agents had near-exclusive access to information, thus creating an appropriate niche in which to operate. However, the value they provide is diminishing as new, user-friendly tools become available to the general public that offer many of the same capabilities of travel agents. These new tools are providing the general public with full access to information and capabilities that, in years prior, only professional travel agents had enjoyed. At one time, travel booking systems were complex and difficult to use. Users required special training to operate them and interpret the screens and cryptic codes. Today, this is no longer the case. Graphical user interfaces and easy look-up tables have negated the need for specialized knowledge, making it possible for consumers to book their own reservations without relying on travel agents.

Automation of the GDS enterprise gives rise to the notion of disintermediation (i.e., the elimination of middlemen) and the thought that a flatter, less-complex network could exist. Do-it-yourself technologies are making the elimination of middlemen possible and are bringing consumers and service providers closer together. One recent example of this trend is the introduction of the "sharing economy" in which consumers can also be the providers of such services. Take Airbnb as an example, a company in which consumers can list their home, apartment, or other living space online for consumers to book seamlessly online.

For the hospitality and travel industries, more specifically, the focus has been on the elimination of travel agents and the role that they play as intermediaries. Instead, these services can be replaced by IT. Although it is true that automation can eliminate the role of middlemen, in many cases, these middlemen provide invaluable services and provide them cheaper than can be done internally. This is why outsourcing many functions has become so popular.

The Internet, as vast as it is, is creating just as many intermediaries as it displaces. For example, buyers need help in finding sellers and wading through the vast amount of information available. Search engines came to the rescue to provide this service. Through increased competition and greater consumer needs, these engines will be refined and become more focused and more powerful. As markets become more segmented and specialized, new players emerge to fill in and bridge gaps. Future intermediaries will add value and save time through their adeptness at transforming information into usable knowledge and subsequently providing services and convenience as a result of the knowledge gained. In an information world, it will be this new knowledge that will provide the currency of tomorrow. Mega portals formed through intra- and inter-industry alliances for one-stop shopping and aggregators will provide value through brand recognition, trust, convenience, and access to specially discounted rates that can only be provided through them.

Digital Divide

Because of the many facets of GDS and the complexities involved, hoteliers must consider GDS as more than just the reservations booking process or the company's CRS. It is much broader in scope with far-reaching implications. Competitive advantage will be derived less from the gap between the technology haves and the have-nots and more from the bipolarization that results between those who know how versus those who know not. This distinction is far less subtle than might appear. It is about who can effectively manage their distribution channels to yield the best results.

True, there will be gaps in what one company can afford versus another, with economies of scale favoring the larger chains. However, with many facets of the GDS technology readily available on the open market at affordable prices or accessible via outsourcing, the gap between the technology haves and the have-nots becomes very small. Therefore, the advantage will be in knowing how best to make use of this technology. This includes finding cost-effective uses as well as creating new ways to grow market share and build customer loyalty. The ultimate value will be in converting information into knowledge that then results in improved business performance, as demonstrated by the company's financials and market statistics. This can be realized only if the *right* GDS infrastructure is in place. What is right is subjective and variable by organization because each organization fills unique market needs and sets different goals. There is no one right answer, but there are some definite wrong ones. Furthermore, what is right today will likely change tomorrow, so hoteliers must be flexible and ready to adapt to meet the demands of tomorrow.

Transparency: A Hope for the Future

Many consumers love to shop and love to travel, and increasingly, they spend more time shopping for travel. In doing so, they are often quoted different rates for the same accommodations and dates being shopped. As one can suspect, this is frustrating to the consumer and needlessly consumes his or her time as well as resources for the hotel or resort with booking searches that don't result in converted sales. Therefore, it behooves hotels and resorts to provide seamless integration and single-image inventory with last-room availability and rate parity across distribution channels so the same availability and rate information will be quoted under the same set of travel circumstances. These are service issues and issues of trust. Therefore, hoteliers should strive to simplify things and make it easy and convenient for guests to book accommodations with a high degree of trust.

There may come a point in time when focus on the individual components of a GDS is less important. For example, when a person uses the telephone to place a call, he or she does not consider the many linkages and systems that are required in order for that call to be completed with an acceptable level of voice quality. The behind-the-scenes components are completely transparent during the course of the conversation. Within the lodging industry, the service levels and reliability are not to a point in which the various components can be treated as transparent as in the telephone example. Complicating the situation is the number of customer-interface options. Since each customer interface represents a critical incident, hotels and resorts must fully understand how to safeguard these opportunities and guarantee unblemished service delivery. Failure to do so will result in a tainted experience for the customer and a blemished image for the organization. The transactional economics of the GDS and its various components and linkages provide another reason that this level of attention and detail is warranted.

Packaging: The Bundling of Air Tickets, Lodging, and Car Rentals

One concept that has been in existence since travel agents began is a practice called packaging or bundling. We will refer to it as packaging. Packaging is the combination of air tickets, lodging, and car rentals together, benefiting the consumer that if they bundle these services together, they will pay an overall lower price. The way it works is that the airline, hotel, and car rental companies each offers a discounted price to the online travel agency, and the agency then bundles the items together under one total cost. This is a win–win proposition for the consumer and the hotel because they are able to capture a different customer segment while protecting their ADRs. This trend continues to grow over time as more consumers around the world begin to travel, especially by air.

Leveraging Technology to Reduce Overhead

The Internet provides hotels and resorts with many ways to service guests in a more cost-effective way than via the telephone or in person. As a result, hotels and resorts promote self-service and use of the Internet to help guests transact their business. There are also other technologies that can be used to help lower overhead. Outrigger Hotels and Resorts and JetBlue turned to the Internet and voice-over-IP (VOIP) technology to enable a home-based agency model rather than a centralized agency/office model. The result has been a lower overhead costs by not having to tie up money in real estate or office rental, power consumption, and so on. Employees also love the flexibility of working from home and their own savings of no commute costs.

United Airlines provides another example of a company deploying voice recognition systems that allow customers to make reservations by speaking in a normal conversational tone to computers. Using this technology, United Airlines is reducing transaction costs per reservation and boosting reservations productivity. The quality of voice recognition systems is improving and the prices of the hardware and software required to support them are declining, making them attractive and viable alternatives for the travel industry and others (e.g., financial services).

Smart Device Apps Applications

The proliferation of smartphones, smart watches, and tablets with Internet access makes mobile apps one of the most seamless ways to book travel. Almost all travel companies (including lodging providers, OTAs, and meta search engines) have entered this arena with several waves of applications. As the technology continues to improve and offer the option of personalizing to the consumer, so will these applications. Companies will continue to seek ways to provide convenience and value-adding services to guests to make it easier to do business with them and to win their loyalty. For example, recently Amazon introduced voice-activation booking through their Alexa voice products, Echo Dot and Amazon Tap. Consumers can now book their next vacation hands free and by their voice.

Shopping Bots

As technology becomes more advanced, smarter and more user-friendly shopping tools will become available. Many of these tools will function as shopping bots (that is, robotic, computerized agents that will carry out tasks for people), which will be powered by smart agent technology. Travel meta search engines provide the first wave of these tools. In the future, these tools will have the capability to read a traveler's profile and shop for available travel services and accommodations that match a person's needs and preferences with little to no involvement from a user—and all within a fraction of a second. They will then present a short list of options to the traveler or, if authorized, proceed directly with the booking process. Developments such as these will drastically reshape marketing and how hotels and resorts reach consumers. After all, how can one sell to a robot, a device with no emotion or human feeling? It cannot appreciate the unique attributes and sensual qualities that are presently sold by many hotels and resorts. As these robots catch on, Web site traffic will increase at a faster rate than conversions, creating less favorable look-to-book ratios. The challenge will be to attract these devices, appeal to the criteria they are seeking, create matches, and win the business.

5. Summary

A GDS is one of the most important strategic applications in a lodging firm's IT portfolio due to its revenue producing potential, role in building customer relationships and serving customers, and the need to focus on reducing costs. It is the cornerstone on which most other hotel/resort applications and services depend. Therefore, lodging executives must focus on this technology, monitor the emerging trends, and carefully chart an appropriate course of action. The rapid change of technology, the capital intensity of IT required to support a GDS, and the number of new distribution options being introduced to the marketplace makes managing in this environment difficult, confusing, and seemingly in a constant state of flux.

With tomorrow's leaders aggressively jockeying for position, the GDS arena is clearly in transition. The landscape is vastly changing as a result of consolidation, new technologies, distribution paths, and attempts to restructure the existing channels of distribution (e.g., bypass theories) to reduce the high fixed and variable costs associated with distribution. The future is likely to see major paradigm shifts for the lodging industry, such as revenue management programs that seek to implement dynamic or real-time pricing models (Davis and Meyer, 1998) and optimize by profit rather than by revenue, as is the case today. If hotels and resorts can channel reservations through services that allow them to yield greater contribution margins, they can improve their operating results and enjoy a competitive advantage over those unable to effectively manage their distribution channels.

With rising distribution costs, new channels entering the marketplace, and additional intermediaries gaining access to important customer information, hotel/resort companies must carefully evaluate distribution options, select appropriate partners and channels, and measure and monitor effectiveness (i.e., contributions in terms of *incremental* room-nights and revenues). Where possible, the number of channels should be simplified to ease the management and maintenance of them, to reduce the overlaps, and to reduce overhead costs associated with them.

Hospitality firms must begin to develop a comprehensive distribution strategy. The marketplace is getting too complex with its distribution channel offerings and too costly for companies to serendipitously choose which channels to subscribe. Likewise, it cannot leave these decisions to chance or defensive responses to competitors' moves. Gaining representation in as many channels as possible is a noble goal, but at what cost and at what value?

The dynamics of distribution have changed drastically over the years as a result of segmentation, greater competition, more demanding customers, and now, newer forms of technology. How a hotel/resort company uses a GDS to win sales and marketing advantages, to gain access to new markets, and to build and strengthen customer relationships and how a company ensures effective representation (i.e., presentation of rates, availability, product amenities, etc.) in each channel using the prevailing technologies should become top priorities. The ultimate goal of a GDS strategy should be to fully automate the entire booking process to create a cost-effective, streamlined, and hassle-free guest service that cannot be duplicated by anyone else.

6. CASE STUDY AND LEARNING ACTIVITY

Case Study

Understanding distribution—knowing the channels and technology in which to invest and how to effectively use and manage them—is critical to a hotel organization's competitive positioning. This is a complex undertaking that requires constant management and oversight. What follows in an example of how one company is using IT and its distribution channels to gain market advantages. The case is based on an actual company, but some of the names and facts have been changed to protect the identity of the company.

Company Overview

Hotel Eleganté is a global leader and technology innovator in the lodging industry. Its success and reputation are widely chronicled throughout the industry and in the trade literature. Hotel Eleganté has received numerous accolades for its programs, operations, and facilities, including high industry rankings for its use of and investment in IT. To many, its name is synonymous with quality, consistency, and attention to detail. Moreover, its employees' commitment to service has become a hallmark of the company's culture and core values, providing a distinct competitive advantage. These tributes notwithstanding, Hotel Eleganté's market position and distribution—in terms of globalization, location, breadth, and size—are esteemed by its competitors.

Hotel Eleganté's customers exhibit a high degree of brand loyalty, due in part to the company's highly successful, multi-brand guest loyalty program. Through an aggressive segmentation strategy, Hotel Eleganté's lodging portfolio spans the entire gamut of the lodging industry's segmentation (i.e., from luxury to limited service) and, with more than a dozen brands, is one of the broadest in the industry. The company likes to think it has the right product for any market location in the world, although some critics would accuse the company of over segmenting the market to the point where brands converge and confuse consumers. Hotel Eleganté's portfolio consists of over 2,500 hotels in more than 65 countries. The company's products typically rank top in their segments in industry surveys, and its growth in earnings per share surpass the industry. In almost all of the segments in which Hotel Eleganté competes, it outperforms the industry when it comes to sales, occupancy rates, and customer preference. The rate premiums the company commands allow its properties to earn higher REVPAR and ADR than industry averages and to outpace inflation rates.

Distribution Strategy

Hotel Eleganté was one of the early players in the industry to embark on electronic distribution. Today, Hotel Eleganté's hotels rank among the most booked properties in each of the major online travel agencies. Since the company introduced its first centralized reservation system in the early 1970s, it has witnessed many changes over the years in electronic distribution and in how hotel companies deliver their products and services to the marketplace. The industry is quite different in terms of distribution dynamics, competitive threats, and consumer behavior. Reminiscing about Hotel Eleganté's original strategy, one company executive remarked of its genuine simplicity and intuitiveness: "In the early days, the goal was obvious: to put inventory in front of as many people as possible to sell it." At the time, an open and close approach to inventory management worked well for managing room inventory in multiple distribution channels, with little need for sophisticated interfaces. Last-room availability and single-image inventories were not even imagined then, but over time, these concepts have evolved as the company grew and as the logistics became more complex for managing room inventory across multiple properties around the world. They are now critical in today's competitive marketplace and require complex, sophisticated, and costly interfaces.

As their strategy evolved, Hotel Eleganté developed interfaces to SABRE and Galileo, two of the largest GDSs. Through the years, these interfaces provided Hotel Eleganté with competitive advantage through first-mover advantages based on evidence collected by the company's marketing department. Over time, however, other hotel companies began copying Hotel Eleganté's moves. This required Hotel Eleganté to invest more to stay ahead of the competition and protect its lead. As the functionality of these interfaces become more complex and as airline GDSs and the company's CRS changed with time, maintaining these interfaces became more challenging and costly.

Hotel Eleganté's philosophy concerning distribution has always been to provide methods or channels that people want to use to book rooms and to provide a set of choices or options so that customers can select the channel best suited to their needs or convenience. In other words, Hotel

Elegante takes a consumer-centric approach. According to a marketing executive at Hotel Elegante: "Distribution is all about making it easy for our customers to do business with us." In her mind, channel selection must be driven by two key considerations:

1. How customers want to book with Hotel Elegante.
2. The revenue upside versus the costs of creating, maintaining, and using a distribution channel.

Thus, Hotel Elegante will enter any distribution channel that is indicative of how its customers want to buy its products rather than try to dictate how its consumers buy its products and services. To this end, Hotel Elegante will continue to fund distribution channels of higher cost so long as there is sufficient volume to justify their existence. For example, one executive at Hotel Elegante indicated he would like to eliminate the company's toll-free reservation call centers because they are so costly to operate. However, since a significant number of their customer base prefer this service and channel to others, Hotel Elegante will continue to offer reservation call centers as a distribution channel, but it will make them as operationally effective as possible.

Over the years, Hotel Elegante has successfully pursued a two-pronged distribution strategy that involved building relationships and developing loyalty with both consumers and distribution partners (or other influencers such as Convention Visitors Bureau and online travel agency sales managers). Hotel Elegante's competitive positioning today can largely be attributed to this strategy. Going forward, Hotel Elegante's overarching distribution strategy continues to be: "To make it as easy as possible to do business with the company by putting its products and services on as many shelves as possible." It accomplishes this objective by offering:

- A customer-centric sales and revenue management force capable of selling multiple brands.
- A fully functional Web site, visibility with online travel agencies and distribution partners, including meta search.
- A strong loyalty program and detailed customer profiles to recognize repeat guests and speed up the reservations process.
- State-of-the-art mobile applications for all smart devices and established social media presence, which attracts new customers.
- Long-term and mutual benefiting relationships with distribution partners such as online travel agencies.
- Easy access to a fast, reliable reservation system through the highest level of connectivity presently available.
- Real-time, two-way, seamless links to all its hotels, with single-image inventory and access to last-room availability.
- Hotel Elegante is currently researching opportunities to invest in a guest communication system, for their operations team to communicate with guests via a virtual interface while on property.

The company's reservation technology and distribution channels, support infrastructure, and revenue management to simplify the shopping process and add to the guest convenience. Through a competitive and real-time pricing strategy, Hotel Elegante maintains that there is "a logical and rational reason for every rate offered at every hotel." This approach improves rate integrity, and virtually guarantees that customers will be offered the best available rate given their qualifications, time of booking, dates of travel, and room requests.

Protecting Relationships with the OTA Community

Recognizing the important contributions of OTAs in influencing and stimulating travel, Hotel Elegante has spent years developing and fostering good relationships with the travel agent community. Programs to boost travel agent relations include access to last-room availability and all room categories, strategy meetings throughout the year with each online travel agency, special rates and amenity packages, competitive rates, up-to-date content, and maintaining communication.

OTAs presently deliver about 25 percent of all of Hotel Elegante's room-nights, chain wide. The company attributes this volume to its reservations and connectivity capabilities, its commitment and strong ties to the OTA community, the quality and breadth of its lodging portfolio, its strong customer service, and its access to last-room availability. Because of the significant contributions from the OTA community, Hotel Elegante continues to foster relations and develop programs that include, rather than preclude, travel agents. As one executive put it:

> Even if online travel agents influence only 5% of the company's business, this is still a significant chunk of business that cannot be overlooked.

Therefore, Hotel Elegante is extremely cautious about doing anything that might jeopardize relationships or be perceived as a threat or an attempt to undercut OTAs, out of fear of losing their business.

While Hotel Elegante could benefit financially from steering customers away from OTAs, it will not promote its Web site over online distribution channels or do anything that could be construed as an overt attempt to direct bookings away from the agents. Instead, it will assume the role of a cautious follower. Hotel Elegante will continue to monitor booking patterns, and as booking volumes shift over time with OTAs—or any other distribution channel, for that matter—Hotel Elegante will reinvest its resources accordingly to optimize customer access, booking volumes, and revenue and work to facilitate bookings through channels of lower cost.

Future Developments

Moving forward, Hotel Elegante will continue to explore innovative approaches that make it easier, faster, and cheaper for guests to book rooms at each of its brands. It will continue to look for ways to leverage its size and expertise to build unparalleled competitive advantages while maintaining an enduring commitment to its customers. It will also focus on exploiting Internet and mobile technologies to lower costs of distribution and increase booking volumes.

Future developments for hotel connectivity and IT will concentrate on functional enhancements, advances in revenue management real-time decision-making software, guest communication software, an operations platform to connect all departments more efficiently, and further centralization of meeting space reservations and group reservations. Additionally, capabilities will be expanded to incorporate electronic requests for proposal, better group handling, geo-coding, and cross-selling of properties and brands.

Learning Activity

1. Critically evaluate Hotel Eleganté's distribution strategy. Is it appropriate? Can you think of any other IT strategies which Hotel Eleganté might embrace or should be considering in light of emerging technologies?

2. How customer-centric is Hotel Eleganté's approach toward distribution?

3. How can Hotel Eleganté evaluate each distribution channel and measure its contribution to its bottom line? Create a measurement scorecard that can be used by company leaders to monitor the performance of each distribution channel.

4. Which distribution channel needs the most attention and why? Does Hotel Eleganté need to be concerned with channel conflict (i.e., one or more channels cannibalizing or taking business away from other channels)?

5. Are OTAs important to Hotel Eleganté? Going forward, what type of relationship should Hotel Eleganté have with OTAs? What role should they play? Should Hotel Eleganté continue to maintain these relationships? Why or why not?

7. Key Terms

Channel manager
Core competencies
Cross-selling
Disintermediation
Distribution strategy

Global distribution system (GDS)
Interorganizational system
Look-to-book ratio
Meta search
Merchant or wholesale model

Opaque pricing model
Single-image inventory
Up-selling

8. Chapter Questions

1. Discuss the many roles a GDS plays and why it is so important for a hotel company from strategic and marketing perspectives. How can it be used to achieve competitive advantage?

2. Why is a hotel/resort GDS considered to be a mission-critical application?

3. What core competencies must a hotel organization possess to excel in the distribution arena?

4. What are the key technologies and hospitality applications that comprise a hotel or resort's distribution system? Discuss the roles and importance of each.

5. How does distribution for hotel and resorts rooms differ from other types of products and services?

6. Should a lodging company strive for representation in any and all distribution channels? Describe and justify your response.

7. Why is the technology to support hotel and resort reservations so much more advanced than the technology used to support meeting space reservations?

8. How is the Internet reshaping lodging distribution and the ways in which hotels and resorts interact with their customers?

9. If a CEO of a major hotel or resort chain hired you as a consultant to help develop a distribution strategy for his or her company, how would you go about getting started? What sort of advice would you provide?

10. What do you consider to be the weak links of today's hotel/resort GDS? How would you prioritize these, and how can these limitations be reduced?

CHAPTER 8

Databases

Courtesy of Dan Bell

Chapter Objective

- At the end of this chapter students will understand how data is managed in the hospitality industry.

Learning Objectives

- List some ways databases can help in hospitality
- Explain how digital database are more efficient than other types

- Understand the new types of data being captured
- Explain how databases are used in both operations and sales

Chapter Introduction

Interview

Dan Bell is vice president of hotel sales in North America for Oracle.

1. Hi Dan, could you tell us about your background?

I've spent my career in the Information Technology Industry for three well-known industry leaders—NCR, MICROS Systems, and now Oracle (who acquired MICROS in 2015). I joined NCR following graduation from Penn State in 1983 as a sales executive, beginning my career in NCR's Rockville, Maryland, office with my initial territory in Washington, DC. Through career stops with NCR in Dayton, Ohio (where NCR was headquartered at the time), I assumed increasingly larger management roles leading sales, consulting, and support teams through stops in Richmond, Virginia; Atlanta, Georgia; Dallas, Texas; and again back through Atlanta where I was promoted to vice president of retail systems. I joined MICROS Systems in December 2002 in Columbia, Maryland. MICROS at the time was considered an "up and comer" in the industry and it was a fun and rewarding climb to be part of a growth company and ultimate industry leader, which attracted Oracle to acquire us. As part of Oracle Hospitality, I lead the North America Hotel Sales organization—over ninety employees serving the IT needs of hotels through the United States, Canada, and globally for large branded hotels like the Marriott, Hyatt, Hilton, and others.

2. What are Oracle's products and services for the hospitality industry?

Oracle has a "Cloud First" strategy for the hospitality industry. Everything we develop and release to the industry is cloud-centric—property management systems (PMS), point-of-service, distribution solutions, mobile solutions, hardware (POS and mobile), sales and catering, etc., are all cloud enabled. Our mission for the industry is to create exceptional guest experiences, reduce the cost and complexity of information technology, and deliver platforms that enable innovation. All of our solution offers are highly secure, offer integrated analytics, and are scalable globally. We're also incorporating our solutions into Oracle's cloud to include customer experience, customer relationship management and enterprise resource planning solutions as well.

3. How important is the cloud for hospitality organizations?

Cloud is now and the future for hospitality. Cloud provides a myriad of advantages to the hospitality industry including, but not limited to, increased agility to deploy new solutions/updates, data security, lower cost, and security. Our goal, in part, is to allow for hotels and restaurants to manage their business, while Oracle takes care of the IT elements to allow for them to serve their guests at high levels.

4. What are some other big changes you have seen in technology over your career?

I think the biggest thing has been the velocity of change, which is exciting to be part of. When I first started my career, the technology was considered leading edge, but now my mobile device has more storage than the processor that ran large grocery stores, which stood six feet tall or higher! The move to mobile, analytics, and anytime/ anywhere information has been fast changing as well. Cloud solutions will continue to mature and grow and I'm excited to see what's coming next!

5. How do you keep current with the latest technology trends?

To me, it's definitely important to be a student of the industry—not just the technology aspects, but the hospitality industry as well. Oracle does a great job with training programs related to the technology side of things and I serve on a number of technology boards, which keeps me fresh as well. On the industry side of things, I attend industry conferences like Hospitality Technology Next Generation (HTNG), HT Next, and HITEC and Oracle Hospitality hosts our annual user's conference called Oracle Industry Connect. I enjoy being a student of the industry and I attend the conferences to learn as much as I can in addition to presenting Oracle's solution offers for the hotel industry.

6. What non-technology skills are important for current and future managers?

I believe leadership skills such as the ability to lead from the front, empowering and challenging your employees, having a passion for serving others (internally and externally), and setting a clear vision while working together as a team will always stand the test of time. There's nothing more rewarding to me than building and leading teams of people from varying backgrounds, ages, ethnicities, and serving customers at high levels while achieving great results—the two go hand-in-hand.

7. What skills are needed to succeed in sales?

It may be surprising to some, but I would say persistence, a positive outlook, the ability to listen and understand a client's needs and how you can help them, knowing your solution offers, following-through on what you've sold the customer to ensure it met or exceeded their expectations, having an understanding of the industry you are serving, being aware of your competition and what makes you better without belittling them, and becoming a trusted advisor to your customer and the industry at large. Sales is definitely a career choice and the best sales executives I've met in my career exhibit the traits I've described and make listening and solving problems a priority versus talking about how great they are or their company is.

Interview with Dan Bell

1. Overview

Dan introduced us to some complex themes and Oracle is a company known for databases. Let's see if we can break them down. Databases are playing an ever-increasingly important role in the Information Age. In the hospitality industry, their effective usage can help every department better manage assets, expenses, and sales. This chapter will acquaint you with databases and their usage in the hospitality industry.

2. Structured Data and Database Basics

From check-in, to food purchasing, and to targeting customers, effective and efficient management of large quantities of data requires a database. You might keep a folder or notebook with different pages containing information. These papers have no apparent structure potentially linking them. When looking for specifics, you must go through each piece and extract it. In other words, they stand alone. Have you ever come across a written phone number and forgotten whose it was? You are almost forced to go through your cell phone name by name, or maybe recent calls. Companies that even to this day keep only paper records or noninterrelated computer systems face difficulties in data management. These are referred to as **flat files**. Flat files are usually text files that have no structured interrelationship. In the end, time and energy are wasted retrieving data with redundancies, while unseen relationships and potential couplings go undiscovered. What we need is to give that data structure. We begin there, with a conversation on **structured data**, or data that can be organized easily such as words and numbers.

Today, hospitality organizations take advantage of the benefits provided by databases. A **database** is an organized, centralized collection of data serving applications. Databases are a key element of most mission-critical applications and represent the most common type of back-end software systems. A property's databases store data on such things as its transactions, products, employees, guests, and assets and more. Such databases must be efficiently organized and easy to access. They must also provide data integrity and ensure the reliability of stored data.

Database Management Systems (DBMSs)

An important software component is needed to manage and edit the database. A **database management system (DBMS)** is that critical piece of software that provides users and database administrators with the ability to access and manipulate data. It is through this piece of software, with all the common software features such as menus and places to click, that most managers will interact with the database. Therefore, this section also discusses commercial databases, especially those used by contemporary applications.

DBMSs are available for prices comparable to word processing and spreadsheet packages. However, full-feature databases can cost half-a-million dollars just for enterprise software. DBMSs perform several key functions:

- Provide links between different files that are used together
- Allow the storage, updating, and retrieval of data in the database
- Apply data integrity, data security, and control constraints to the data
- Coordinate multiuser database access
- Support data reliability through backup and recovery features

The DBMS provides an intervening level of software between database users (and applications) and the data storage. Figure 8-1 shows where the DBMS works within a hospitality environment. The view of the database from the user's perspective is the **logical view**. There can be many logical views since different departments need to see data in different ways. The makeup and organization of the data on the storage device is the **physical view**. There is only one physical view. The DBMS takes the data from the physical view and presents it in the logical view.

The two views (logical and physical) of the data are used by the DBMS to provide data independence. This allows data models to be resistant to changes in the database's physical structure. This is convenient for system developers, who can easily change storage devices and data access methods.

Your knowledge of bits and bytes is expanded into more forms found in databases. Bytes form words and numbers that form fields. A **field** is a collection of bytes or data with specific meaning such as "Last Name." Next is a **record**, which is a collection of fields such as a customer's "Last Name," "First Name," "Address," and "Credit Card Number." A collection of records is a **file** such as "Customers," "Vendors," and "Employees," and a database is a collection of those files.

Just what provides that structured linkage lacking in flat files? It is how the rows of data are identified and related to the other rows in other files (sometimes referred to as *tables*). Since a database is made up of files, something connecting all of the files to one another is needed. The key here is linking files that have a field in common. Let's use an example of a simple database with only three files—reservations, front office, and housekeeping. At times, each department may be concerned only with its data. At other times, data from the other departments in relation to its department may be needed. In reality, each file would contain many more fields. Look at Figure 8-2. Each file has one or two fields that *uniquely* identify a record. In the reservation file, it is the reservation number. In the front office file it is the combination of the last name and street address. Two fields are used together here to uniquely identify a record in cases of guests with the same last name. Finally, in the housekeeping file, the room number is the field that uniquely identifies that record since there are no rooms with the same number. These fields that uniquely identify a record are called **primary keys**. If two primary keys are used together as in the

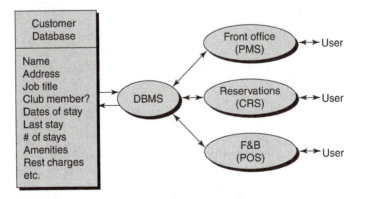

FIGURE 8-1

The DBMS serves as the link between departmental or user-specific requests and the database.

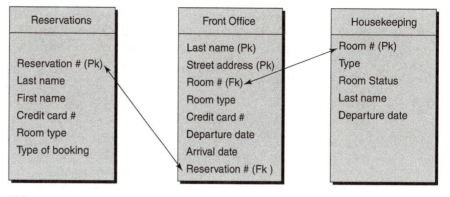

FIGURE 8-2

The valuable aspect of relational databases is the linkage of files. By connecting the files, you can make complex searches of the database as a whole rather than just the individual files. Here the three tables are joined by like fields—a primary key (pk) in one field and a foreign key (fk) in another. Primary keys uniquely identify a record. When two fields are used to uniquely identify a record, it is called a composite key. Foreign keys are primary keys in another relation.

front office file, they are called a **composite key**. The files are linked together where a primary key from one file is linked to a like field in another file. This like field is called a **foreign key**, which is just a primary key in another relation. In Figure 8-2, reservation number is seen as a primary key in the reservation file and as a foreign key in the front office file. When the reservation file is linked with the front office file, which in turn is related to the housekeeping file, all three files are linked, which allows the whole database to be utilized when needed giving us a **relational database** where the data is connected or related in an organized manner.

Through the DBMS, an important language is utilized. Using a data manipulation language or DML, users can manipulate the data in a relational database in various ways. For example, rows in a relation may be inserted, deleted, updated, displayed, or printed. For example, an airline cancels a contract with your organization. Without having to search name by name in your active corporate client list, you can search the database via a query for the airline's name and delete the related last names in a block. Other relational operations are used to extract answers to a user's queries. One example is the "Select" operation, which returns a new relation with a subset of the relation's rows. You'll look more closely at the "select" query in use in the most widely used DML in the next section.

Functions of a DBMS

Both large and small DBMSs provide the same general features, although they vary in sophistication. They include the ability to create and manipulate new files and records using DBMS commands. For example, a DBMS should allow the user to set up a (relational) reservation database with RESERVATION # and ROOM TYPE relations by defining the fields and field types, as in Figure 8-2. Subsequently, it should allow the user to populate the files by typing in new records, or by importing or reading the data from another application (e.g., a word-processed document or spreadsheet).

Another DBMS function minimizes redundancy among data elements to ensure database consistency. The fields shown in Figure 8-2 are stored just once. In a paper flat-file system, the reservation name may be found on many different documents. The ability of the DBMS to link and use files together eliminates this inefficiency and redundancy. DBMSs also support data independence, relieving the user of the need to know exactly how the data (e.g., supplier records) in the database is physically stored.

Data Extraction and Information Gathering

Once all the data is in place, you need to be able to extract it in a dynamic and structured way using a data language. While some DBMSs use their own proprietary DMLs, the data language of choice is *SQL*, the most widely used relational DML, originally developed by IBM. Queries allow a manager to extract specific data from a database. SQL, pronounced *sequel*, is used in products ranging from Access to Oracle. To find out which food items are at or below their reorder levels, for example, a food and beverage director might issue a SQL query:

SELECT ITEM_#, ITEM_NAME
FROM INVENTORY
WHERE ITEMS_IN_STOCK = REORDER_LEVEL

This query uses the INVENTORY relation and returns item numbers and names for inventory items that should be reordered.

DBMSs also provide security features to protect files and records from unauthorized access or modification. Unauthorized access is a high-level concern since hackers may be able to use what are known as SQL injectors to open up a database. In conjunction with network security measures, discussed in Chapter 2, through the DBMS, files can be protected by passwords to completely deny access to certain users, to provide read-only access, or to allow unlimited access. For example, the supplier file may have read-only access restrictions, protected by a password, to prevent possible fraud (e.g., rerouted payments).

Multiuser DBMSs are more sophisticated than the single-user variety and allow concurrent database access by tens or hundreds of users. If the inventory database described previously were implemented using a multiuser DBMS, two users on different terminals would be able to access multiple supplier records at the same time. However, problems occur in a multiuser context. The first is data integrity. For example, imagine a situation where two banquet managers retrieve an inventory record of fifty wine bottles, withdraw forty and thirty items each, and both end up with twenty bottles, potentially causing operational and security problems. Such problems are handled using file locks and record locks to restrict access to records in use. These locks are an important part of multiuser DBMSs.

Another problem multiuser DBMSs must handle is "deadly embrace," or deadlock, a situation that occurs when two processes require resources (e.g., records) held by the other. The result is that they would wait for each other, possibly indefinitely, if the ability to detect and break deadlock were not incorporated into multiuser DBMSs.

Distributed DBMSs and Cloud Computing

Distributed databases are becoming more and more common in this network age. The DBMS supports location transparency, relieving the user of the need to know where files are physically located. If, on the other hand, different properties use different databases, then problems can result. This is what is known as disparate databases. Ownership can be fragmented in the hospitality industry. Properties of the enterprise may be franchised and owned locally. Each property makes its own decisions regarding technology. A solution to this problem is **data-warehousing**, which is a collection of all the data from the entire enterprise centralized in one location. Its ultimate goal is "to integrate (this) enterprise-wide corporate data into a single repository from which users can easily run queries, produce reports, and perform analysis" (Connolly, Begg, and Strachan, 1999). A subsection of a data-warehouse is a **data mart**, which is a departmental-specific section of a data-warehouse created to simplify tasks and improve processing time. Data marts were created so each department could analyze and query only its data.

Recalling from the interview, Oracle, a company known for databases now has a "cloud (cloud computing, chapter 2) first" strategy for its hospitality offerings. The cloud, or off property computing and storage, is not only freeing up hospitality professionals to concentrate on service while someone else takes care of the technology, it has also led to new network database offerings. One such offering is blockchain. **Blockchain** is a large distributed permanent ledger that contains records of transactions that cannot be altered. Having a permanent record of a fixed asset in a hotel, for example, is advantageous in knowing its operating and accounting history. Blockchain in finance provides the backbone for the newer and debatable cryptocurrencies such as bitcoin. Cryptocurrency is a decentralized currency not backed by governments or precious metals, but rather through a decentralized computer network whose amount is in constant decline, creating value. Blockchain provides structure to decentralization, which brings us to our next topic of unstructured data.

3. Unstructured Data

Numbers and words found in structured data in our previous discussion on databases are easier to manage than unstructured data. **Unstructured data** is not organized like structured data and can be harder to manage. Think of it as a mix of things that need to be stored, such as emails, Web pages, and documents. Searching for meaning in a mix of things can be difficult. Now it gets even bigger, as in big data. **Big data** is so large that traditional databases are not capable of handling it. Examples include social media, wearable technology, camera footage, and the Internet of things. All of these are only getting larger. To attempt to organize all of these different inputs, one common new open source (public) software offering, Apache Hadoop, allows for more organization of all these data points using its own distributed file system. Recalling the conversation on SQL, in big data there is **NOSQL**, which is non-SQL for searches in these non-traditional data sets. Organizations are creating and receiving more information every day. Making use of it effectively is a challenge. Examples are discussed in the next section.

4. Database Usage

You have already seen some of the uses of a database through queries and commands. Much of what has been covered detailed database usage in daily operations such as inventory management or customer loyalty programs. With a good number of data captured on customers, databases can also provide the foundation for forward-looking events such as sales and marketing initiatives.

Analysis

Companies with a traditional database could find themselves with large amounts of data. At times it can be overwhelming. This stored data may have previously unseen relationships that could lead to future profit. For instance, after analyzing the data, it is uncovered that 80 percent of a hotel's weekend clientele comes from within a thirty-mile radius and has an annual income of over $75,000. Marketing initiatives could then be properly targeted to the records of a database with these same attributes and re-evaluated at a later date as to effectiveness. This creates a profile that can be used to help target data for a sales campaign. A **profile** is a set of attributes and relationships that classify an entity, in this case a customer. Using this profile, the organization may then spend precious dollars more accurately in targeting potential like customers. This is an example of data mining. **Data mining** is analysis of data for potential relationships. Most data mining is statistical and can involve model formation such as **profiling**, **clustering**, and **cluster mapping**. Clustering and cluster mapping involve the plotting and mapping of data with like attributes. Analytics also include, **predictive analytics**, which looks at your data to predict future events, and **social media analytics**, which looks at social media for behavioral analysis.

Setting up an analytical function beforehand can help a property take pre-emptive measures in preventing losses. Consider a frequent customer, Mr. Morrell, who has not stayed with a hotel in some time. In data mining, a trigger could be set to alert management of loyal customers who are not recent ones. A **trigger** in database terms is something that sets off another event. In this case, an email would be sent to the sales manager stating that Mr. Morrell is a loyal customer whose time between stays has lapsed and should be contacted. A sales representative may pick up the phone and gently state that much time has gone by since his last stay and offer a complementary amenity upon the next visit in order to retain Mr. Morrell as a customer. Customer retention is important in any industry, particularly hospitality. On the operations side, imagine a trigger set up to alert a restaurant vendor when a food or supply stock for one of the restaurants to which it sells dips below a certain level. A delivery could be initiated before the supply is depleted. Given the busy nature of the business, pre-emptive data management such as this can be a lifesaver. Aiding in this inventory management is a newer technology known as **radio-frequency identification (RFID)**. RFID is commonly used today in automobile toll passage (easy pass) and even in payment such as in gas stations. RFID is much more efficient than standard bar codes contained on packaging. RFID uses a tag that can be either passive or active that communicates through its embedded antennae with a reader that can then perform a number of actions such as raising a parking gate to unlocking a door. RFID technology is quickly finding many uses in our industry.

Customer Relationship Management (CRM)

Databases are also helping the industry to serve and target customers in personalized ways. One such initiative is **customer relationship management (CRM)**. The concept of CRM, sometimes referred to as *customer experience management* or other similar names, is defined by many different persons in many different ways. Dan Connolly, a professor of hospitality technology and e-commerce, defines CRM this way:

> CRM is a complex and multifaceted phenomenon that involves taking a customer-centric view to every process, guest touch point, and department across the entire property (or chain, if applicable) to create rich, unique, and personalized guest experiences. It is as much a way of doing business as it is a *mindset* or *philosophy* that must be embodied by everyone in the organization to become an essential part of the organization's culture. It is enabled by information technology and a series of software tools and technology applications that facilitate data collection, storage, filtering, pattern recognition, guest profiling, modeling, mapping, and more. The goals are to develop a holistic, 360-degree view of each guest, to create a segment of one, and to own each guest—for life!

CRM in Use

Databases are extremely important to CRM, incorporating all of the aforementioned functions. However, what these two definitions stress is the fact that CRM is not just a computer system tracking customer preferences. CRM is a *process*, *mindset*, and *philosophy*. Unless everyone and everything is on board with this initiative, it will not work. Applying knowledge from the chapter interview, we see that some CRM initiative "musts" include the following:

- All customer touch points (PMS, POS, CRS, mobile, etc.) must be engaged.
- All staff must be trained on its importance and gather data when *possible*.
- Access must be given to this data when and where appropriate.
- Staff must be empowered to react to data.
- The data must be centralized or warehoused.

More often than not CRM is accomplished through specific software that accesses the database. Many CRM offerings today are Web based, which means they are accessed through a browser. Data input accuracy is a must. While the name Thomas Nyheim or Tom Nyheim may be the same person, it could result in two different records. Consistency is a must. Let's take a look at CRM at work today (Figure 8-3).

Starting with the bottom tabs, you see that, via this software from GuestWare, you have a number of different views of a guest. This particular screen shot shows the customer preferences from *room type* to *wine*. As stated in the previous chapter, equipped with this kind of information, a hotel or restaurant is much better off anticipating a guest's needs. If the property is a chain, CRM can allow the organization to cater to the specific customer's needs all over the world. In an industry where the guest is king, CRM can provide the data to make sure that a guest is treated like one. Figure 8-4 shows another screen shot of GuestWare's software, this time showing the follow-up list. With just a tap on the phone, an employee or manager now has the potential to see what is and is not going on in the hotel and, more importantly, is able to react in real-time.

In sales, one of the most precious forms of data in a property's database is the *repeat customer list*. With the ability to purchase an item via the Internet, be it a room-night or an airline ticket, guests no longer are attached to a specific chain. Keeping them is a challenge. They are concerned with price and have less brand loyalty. If management is able to show them that they really know them and can cater to their every need, guests are less likely to choose another location. CRM is meeting this paradigm shift head on.

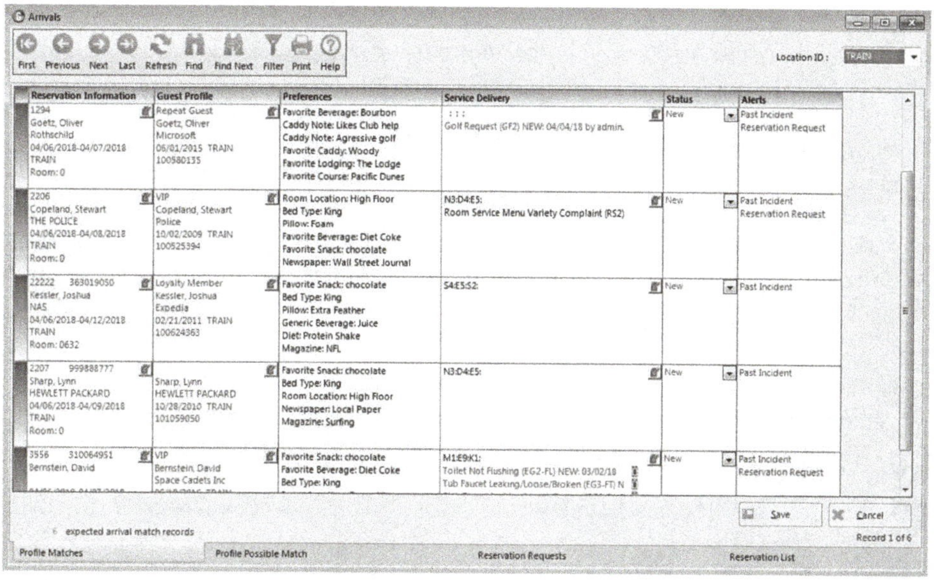

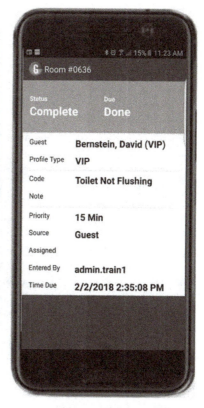

FIGURE 8-3

Software from companies such as Guestware provides a user-friendly way to store and access unique guest preferences data.

Screenshot of a software from Guestware

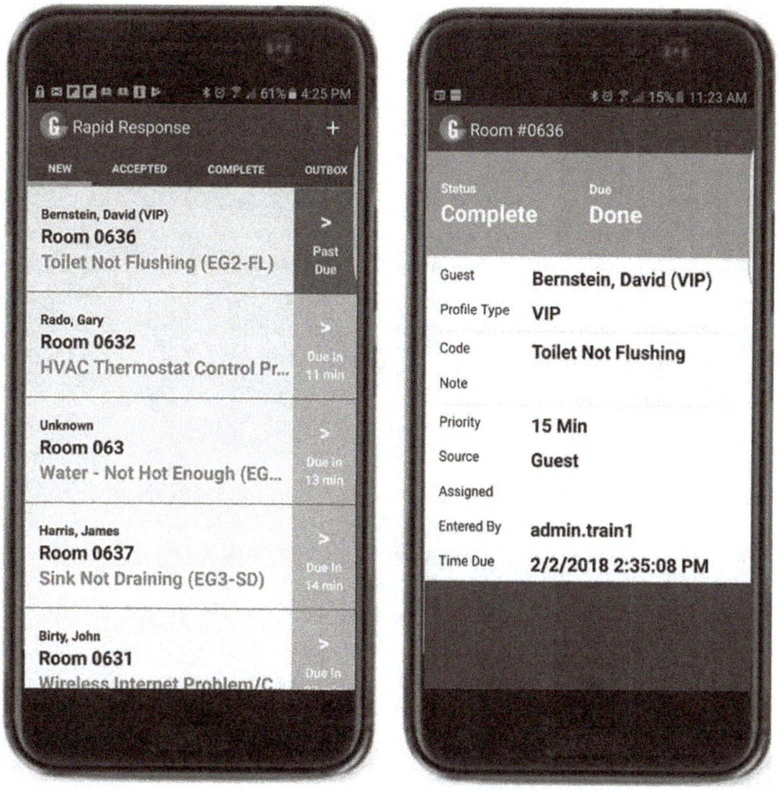

FIGURE 8-4

In the fast-moving hospitality industry, making sure that what was supposed to get done actually got done can be very time consuming. This Guestware follow-up screen aids in such efforts.

Screenshot of a software from Guestware

5. Summary

Without structured organization, companies doing business in the Information Age can find themselves left in the dark. Databases provide that structure. Their use at first was seen as a solution to the inefficiencies found in the flat file environment. It was quickly realized that real-time analysis could be done on data, and that initiatives such as CRM could actually help increase revenue and retention. However, moving to a database environment is not without difficulties. One of the largest impediments to organizations moving to a database is change. The old flat file environment allowed each department to control its own data. Political concerns are heightened at times when an organization is told to share its data. A database environment requires just that—data sharing. Another problem is that the tangible benefits of databases are often years away, as is the payback period, detailed in Chapter 11. The problems arising from different owners or management teams purchasing and using different technologies while serving the same customer are yet more obstacles to successful data management. Convincing management to purchase an expensive new system can be difficult. For that reason, newer agreements and management contracts often stipulate the technology to be used and how the data is to be shared. The reason is simple: Shared data used effectively can increase revenue. Finally, with advancements in big data and the sheer volume of new information, hospitality organizations now have more opportunity and challenges in managing all of the new data effectively.

---

6. CASE STUDY AND LEARNING ACTIVITY

Database Case Study—Loyalty

By Paul Manley, MS, PMP

Paul Manley, PMP, is a hospitality technology industry veteran who has worked for leading global hotel companies, systems vendors, and consultants. He is a project management consultant, educator, and an officer of the International Hospitality Information Technology Association—an association of educators and practitioners whose mission is to advance the use of IT in the hospitality industry through education and research.

The Situation

Hotel Company XYZ had multiple brands and was growing by acquisition, while organic growth was relatively stagnant. The challenge to achieve organic growth can be restated as three questions. How can XYZ maximize its marketing dollars to acquire and retain customers? How can it leverage its information-rich customer database containing tens of millions of unique customers across multiple brands while respecting individual hotel brand identities? What customer-facing initiative can it create to respond to competitors and to Wall Street analysts' questions? XYZ's current state of CRM was where most of their brands had their own unique points-based or service-based brand loyalty program. The XYZ future state and answer to all three questions was a unified, points-based loyalty program across all hotel brands.

While there were many business implementation and technological challenges, none was greater than that involving data. This includes the data-warehouse and transactional databases; the processes and technology rules that ensured data accuracy and integrity; and the business processes that captured and used the data. What follows is a brief description of the types of data XYZ kept, the various databases involved, and examples of the integration of business strategy and rules that impacted the databases.

The Creation of the Loyalty Database

Like many of its competitors, XYZ partnered with a loyalty system provider (LSP). They maintain the database of members, which includes the member profile information, member status, and transaction history that includes points earnings, redemptions, and, a few years later, their wish list. In addition to the database, XYZ had to transmit the checked-out guest (including members) folio information, centralize it, clean and validate it, and then integrate that data into the LSP system. The LSP system maintained the summary transactions for hotel earnings and free night redemptions along with points earned and redeemed with program partners such as rental cars, online flower shops, and merchandise. When a purchase was made with a program partner, the transaction details were received by LSP and points were posted. When a member redeemed their points, the partner was electronically notified to ship the reward.

The additional database challenge to create the new, unified loyalty program was to take the data from several brand databases and merge them into the LSP database. Among the data questions XYZ asked and answered were:

- ***How do we prevent duplicates from being created?***
  They added two of the existing program databases into a single database and then by doing a match using various rules that included credit card number, address, name, and phone number developed a fresh database. In an iterative fashion, they added one current database at a time to the fresh database until all current program members were in the new loyalty database. It should be noted that part of the effort included the omission of long-time inactive members and members whose name or identity could not be recognized.

- ***How do we respect brand identity?***
  The business requirement was to maintain existing hotel brand affinity when the old program was replaced with the new. To do this, the member's brand logo from their

previous loyalty program was printed on the new loyalty program card. From a database perspective, this meant adding a field to the LSP database schema to store brand affiliation. From a business rules perspective, it meant that any time a member enrolled, the channel through which he or she enrolled was captured so that the "brand affiliation" field could be populated.

- *How do we maintain an excellent customer experience during the transition?*
  There are several tactics involved including marketing communications and training for franchisees and call center agents. From a database perspective, XYZ needed to give call center customer service agents access to the old loyalty program data to investigate member queries around point balances, redemptions, and earnings. Since only the point balance was transferred from the old program to the new (and not the supporting transactions behind them), the customer-service agent needed access to the old data to answer questions.

Making the Loyalty Database Operational

There are actually several databases involved with supporting a loyalty program. In addition to the main member database, data marts are used to support the various marketing campaigns to acquire new members and activate existing members. These campaigns comprise seasonal promotions, email campaigns, and direct mail. Hotel companies access a variety of databases that identify market segments, campaign success, and filter opt-outs and do-not-contact attributes. Combining, for analysis purposes, the loyalty database with the enterprise customer data-warehouse can also provide additional insight into segmentation, behavior, trends, and other analytics.

Enhancing Database Capabilities

Once XYZ launched their new, unified loyalty program, many additional capabilities were added. These included:
- A credit card that earned points for any purchase and bonus points were given if the card was used to pay the hotel bill. The database challenge was to ensure that the loyalty program number was associated with the credit card. Due to banking regulations, the bank that issued the credit card had to allow anyone to apply for the card, so business processes were created to monitor new accounts and then update the credit card database with the member number.
- Real-time personalized offers through the customer service call center, mobile apps, and the Web were also added to the program. This entailed integrating the loyalty database, the call center system, and the offers database into a system that recognized the customer, scripted a relevant offer to the customer, and then stored the response back in the offers database so that it was either not offered again or offered at an appropriate time in a relevant context.

Learning Activity

1. What were XYZ's three questions that addressed growth?
2. In addition to a database, what are some other parts of a loyalty system?
3. What is brand identity?
4. How did XYZ prevent duplicate records from being formed?
5. What components of big data might be captured?

Case Study and Learning Activity Database Case Study—Loyalty
BY PAUL MANLEY, MS, PMP

7. Key Terms

Blockchain	Database Management System (DBMS)	Profile
Composite Key	Field	Radio-Frequency Identification (RFID)
Customer Relationship Management (CRM)	File	Record
Clustering	Flat File	Relational Database
Cluster Mapping	Foreign Key	Social Media Analytics
Data Mart	Logical View	Structured Data
Data Mining	Physical View	Trigger
Data-Warehousing	Predictive Analytics	Unstructured Data
Database	Primary Key	

8. Chapter Questions

1. What is the difference between the logical and physical views?
2. What is a flat file?
3. What functions does the DBMS provide?
4. What is CRM and how do you know if it is successful?
5. What is an enterprise search?
6. What is a profile?
7. How is CRM using the Web?
8. What is SQL and what does it do?
9. What is a trigger and how can it be used effectively?

CHAPTER 9

Information to Knowledge

Courtesy of Karen Sammon

Chapter Objective

- At the end of this chapter students will have a more thorough understanding on how data can be turned into knowledge

Learning Objectives

- How well do you understand your business metrics
- What are its parts and how can it be used effectively
- List some important characteristics of data and information

- Provide factors that get in the way of effective data interpretation
- Define the balanced scorecard and explain its main goal
- Understand the importance of hardware and software

Chapter Introduction

Interview

Karen Sammon is chief of staff and strategy at PAR Technology Corporation.

1. Hi Karen, Welcome back! Your background in restaurants, law, and technology make you a great fit for this interview. First off, can you refresh us on your experience and what you see as important right now in hospitality from an analytical standpoint?

I have worked in the hospitality industry for twenty years and with technology. Over this time, I have seen the positive impact technology has on restaurant and retail operations.

The pace of change today is accelerating as foodservice operators look for a digital connection with consumers. There are two macro trends that I think are interesting:

- Mobility, loyalty, omni-channel connections coupled with true cloud POS solutions enable operators access to real-time data and increase the ability to create a customized dining experience. Recognizing that the point of sale, marketing and service are wherever the consumer wants it to be, progressive operators are leveraging technology to create a frictionless experience.
- With increasing competition from grocery, C-Store, and emerging new concepts, there is increased need to drive digitization of all processes including the use of Internet of things to provide managers with visibility regarding operational effectiveness. Also, social media can instantly recommend or condemn and as a result, foodservice operator's need to protect their brand by ensuring quality, safe, and fresh food.

2. Aside from the basic ones, what are some newer metrics that hotel and restaurant operators should track?

Some of the newer metrics to watch would include loyalty participation rates, marketing campaign effectiveness and food safety program compliance. Restaurants may also want to understand which channels are fastest growing or represent the greatest proportion of their business so they can ensure they are optimizing (e.g., takeout orders from the mobile app vs. dine-in orders placed at a register).

3. How can one avoid getting lost in the new "Big Data" environment?

Restaurants have been generating transaction level detail for years. Improvement in this area won't be better tools per se, but the way in which machine learning at scale will lead us to ask better questions. We are already starting to see more data analysts working for restaurant operators collecting information from the POS, Internet of things, back office, and identifying ways to optimize operations and drive closer relationships with guests.

4. How can mangers turn data into business intelligence?

It is essential that managers ask a lot of questions about the data they are receiving. Data is only useful if it is the right tool for the right job. Operators need to make sure their data is accessible to the evolving toolchains they use for analytics.

5. What resources would you recommend for those interested in analytics for their operation?

The fundamental choice is whether the organization chooses to create its own analytics or to acquire them from a third party. In general, it is difficult for an organization to be able to model and create needed reports due to the cost of such development. There are a variety of purpose-built analytics options available in the market today. For example, PAR integrates our Brink platform with and supports many of partner solutions via our ecosystem.

6. Any advice for future hospitality professionals?

Choose your technology partners carefully and always check references. If it seems too good to be true, it probably is.

Interview used with permission of Karen Sammon

1. Overview

Karen brings up some great points on data usage within the present-day restaurant industry as one example. Let's expand on that and look at information usage. The present economy is often characterized as the information economy, digital economy, and now social networking economy. In such an economy, information is at the heart of all commerce, and knowledge is the basis of all competition. This is especially true in service industries like hospitality, where information becomes the essential ingredient to delivering unique, memorable, and unmatched service. Information also becomes a key competitive differentiator and can lead to competitive advantage. Differences in information, sometimes called **information asymmetry**, explain why firms respond differently and at different times to specific situations. They also explain how some firms can enter new markets or exit existing ones, launch new products and services, and respond more quickly to opportunities and threats than their chief competitors.

As seen in previous chapters, those who use information effectively can benefit. Thanks to information technology (IT), the good news is that managers now have better and timelier access to an abundance of data regarding business operations and how they are performing. Unfortunately, this also presents challenges, as there is an overabundance of data and insufficient time to wade through all of the reports to interpret them and apply what is useful. Understandably, it is easy for managers to be overcome by the volumes of data that bombard them each day. Therefore, today's managers must be extremely adept at gathering, analyzing, and using large quantities of data from a number of different sources about every facet of their businesses to see opportunities and patterns and to make smart business decisions in a timely and consistent manner. The business world is relatively unforgiving and intolerant of mistakes. As such, competitiveness and survivability depend upon one's ability to see and act upon opportunities that others don't see or before they see them.

This chapter's endeavor is to discuss how to effectively collect and use data to create information that can shape and guide managers' actions and decisions such as transactional data discussed in the interview. It focuses on using IT to work smart, not hard. It will discuss how to funnel important information to managers to enhance their decision-making, manage and control the business, guide the directions they set, and identify new opportunities for competitive posturing, positioning, and new product and service offerings. It will discuss the benefits of gathering usable information and applying it effectively and creatively to gain competitive advantage and to make it easier to manage the business.

To help frame this chapter and put things in context, consider the five questions presented in Figure 9-1. How readily you and others in your organization can provide consistent and agreed upon answers these questions will provide an initial and very rudimentary test to how intelligent your organization is and how in tune its management team is with the health of the organization and the business landscape—and this is just scratching the surface! As you will read, business intelligence and data analytics are quite complex and require a great deal of commitment from the organization and software resources. In essence, one wants to have the same type of detailed and sophisticated intelligence that the U.S. military and Central Intelligence Agency have, but focused on every facet of the business, its customers, competitors, suppliers, industry landscape, emerging trends, and so on.

What's Your Business IQ?

- Who are your top 10 customers, and what are they worth?
- Which of your products and services are the most (least) profitable?
- What are your guests' or employees' top 10 complaints?
- Who are the top 10 performing employees?
- What are your top competitors' major strengths and weaknesses?

FIGURE 9-1
A quick test of your firm's informational savviness.

2. Defining Business Intelligence

Over the past several decades, the hospitality business has steadily grown in complexity due to greater competition, more sophisticated customers, and more discriminating investors, not to mention rising costs and difficult economic conditions. While the craft elements of the business (i.e., personalized service) remain vital to the guest experience, a new sense of focus must be placed on the strategic use of resources and the hard numbers; that is, profitability and return on investment (ROI), topics which will be explored in greater detail in Chapter 11. Managing today's complex hospitality business requires effective use of information and a sophisticated **business intelligence** system that can gather, store, analyze, synthesize, share, and communicate information throughout the organization to those who need it, when and where they need it so that they may apply it in effective, value-creating ways (see Figure 9-2).

A business intelligence system operates much like the nervous system of the human body, providing important and timely information to management, the equivalent of the organization's brain, so that managers, their employees, and the organization as a whole can sense and respond to changing business conditions and know how to apply resources and where management must intervene to stay out in front of competition and customers. The key is to **informationalize** every aspect of the business (Davenport and Harris, 2007); that is, keep and analyze information about everything related to one's business and use it to inform business decisions. To achieve this, organizations must leverage information and IT and treat them as strategic weapons rather than just support tools. In doing so, decision makers will be armed with the *best* evidence and tools to perform their jobs in timely and effective ways.

The business literature uses a number of terms to describe various aspects of knowledge or business data gathered by companies (e.g., big data, business intelligence, knowledge management, customer analytics, data mining, decision support, and competitive intelligence). Sometimes, some of these terms are used interchangeably. Other times, they refer to different areas and different business processes and systems. For the purposes of this chapter, we will use the term *business intelligence* as the broad umbrella under which many different forms of intelligence gathering, knowledge management, information dissemination, and business technology fall.

Translating this view of business intelligence into a hotel or resort environment creates a much more complicated picture because a hotel or resort tends to be a fairly complex business entity run by a myriad of heterogeneous systems, many of which are

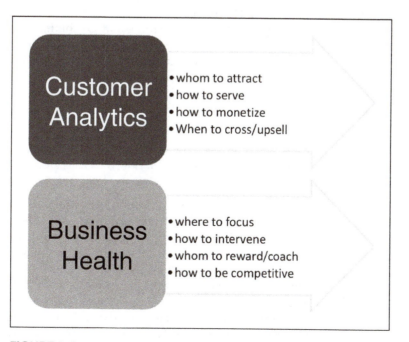

FIGURE 9-2

Key goals for business intelligence systems.

discussed throughout this book. Simply put, each key area of the business—from the front desk, restaurant operations, and retail outlets to spa services, meetings and banquets, and other hotel/resort services—is powered by a different system, often running on a different operating system (OS) and software environment with a different database system and data structure than other core systems used in the operation. These factors make it more difficult to collect, consolidate, and report data across an organization, causing challenges to answering simple operational questions such as "How much did the Jon Smith family spend at my resort during its most recent two-week ski vacation?" On the surface, this specific question seems to be straight-forward, but to find the answer, one must be able to identify every Smith family transaction involving an exchange of money across the resort operation—lodging, food and beverage, in-room services, spa services, ski rentals, and so on. This is difficult to do because of the many systems used to record these transactions (e.g., reservations system, Web site, app, third-party app, property management system (PMS), restaurant and retail point-of-sale (POS) systems), the differences in how data are stored in each system, the time between each transaction, and the fact that the Smith family name might not be captured or uniformly captured with each transaction. For example, if there was a cash transaction or transactions under J. Smith, John Smith, Jon Smith, and Jonathan Smith, it would be hard to associate these transactions the right Smith party to gain a full understanding of the Smith family spending during this one trip, never mind over the course of multiple trips and properties in the case of loyal customer.

Much of business success is determined by information and **knowledge management**—what is known, when, and by whom—and, then, how that information is put to use to outfox the competition. Good business decisions are a function of timely and accurate information in the hands of decision makers, knowledge of the context in which this information will be applied, appropriate and rigorous analysis, good common sense, experience, and speed (that is, the time to gather, interpret, and put the information to work and execute any resulting decisions). Moving forward, competition will continue to intensify in what appears to be a dog-eat-dog world. What will become important is how quickly companies can convert the reams of information they collect into knowledge that can be used for better decision-making, product development, and marketing/pricing promotions. Now with big data and the Internet of things, as discussed in the interview, it is even more important to ask the right questions given the increased volume of the data. In essence, we are talking about how fast companies can learn, and as you know, continuous learning is the lifeline of any organization. As managers, it is important to have access to the *right* information at the *right* time to assist us in making fact-based or informed decisions. This requires us to (1) constantly be in the know, (2) always have our fingers on the pulse of the organization, and (3) continually know what information is necessary to do our jobs and run our businesses. It also requires us to be inquisitive, to know how and when to ask provocative questions that will lead to new information and answers. Finally, we must also possess an uncanny ability to sense and respond to opportunities and threats before anyone else in our industry. These are some of the many traits of leaders in information economy. In looking at the future state of business competition, perhaps Bill Gates, chairman and co-founder of Microsoft sums it up best:

> The most meaningful way to differentiate your company from your competition ... is to do an outstanding job with information. How you gather, manage, and use information will determine whether you win or lose. (Gates, 1999, p. 3)

Leveraging information as a corporate-wide asset requires a strong, capable, and flexible **IT infrastructure** and supportive company culture. For these systems to be effective and generate value, hospitality companies must ensure that the infrastructure in place is capable of meeting a company's needs, both now and into the future with big data and the Internet of things. Critical components of an organization's information foundation include management's ability to monitor performance and enforce business rules (which should be programmed into all systems), query and reporting tools, proactive reporting, comparative reporting, and analytical tools that can help to find and identify hidden meanings in the data. The tools should be easy to use so that anyone can use them without first having to speak with the IT or marketing department.

To realize value requires alignment between people, technology, and business processes. The focus must clearly be enterprise-wide; that is on the entire organization. In many organizations, enterprise application integration (EAI) initiatives are well underway to connect and integrate all systems so that data can be shared and leveraged across the entire organization from loyalty programs to cloud-based food safety. The company's systems should be viewed as knowledge capture, creation, sharing, and policy enforcing devices. Collectively, they create a knowledge bank that can be shared by all employees throughout the company. In effect, these systems represent the brain trust of the organization.

3. Information as a Valued Asset

Information is one of a hospitality firm's most important, yet undervalued, assets due to its intangible value. It is highly coveted as its role is critical in every aspect of the hospitality industry, from guest services to marketing, decision-making, administration, and control of the operation or organization. With the hospitality industry increasingly approaching commoditization (i.e., no distinguishing differences in the products and services offered by the companies in the industry), companies must find new ways to differentiate their product and service offerings. Herein lies an important opportunity for the strategic use of information, particularly in the area of guest service. What information is known about guests and how that information is used to create personal, custom, and memorable (think wow) service experiences will be how hospitality companies set themselves apart and win guest loyalty.

The digital economy is powered by an infrastructure of highly sophisticated computer systems and communications networks that collect, analyze, and share information throughout the corporation and its value chain of social networks, suppliers, and allied partners to all those who need access to that information when and where their needs dictate. This economy is fueled by information and intellectual capital. To some, information might be viewed as a by-product of IT applications, but in reality, it is—or should be—the primary focus, for it is this information that gives IT its value and empowers managers and employees alike to do great things that provide them and their firms a competitive edge.

When we deal with data and information, we must remember four important characteristics. The first is the old adage, "Garbage in equals garbage out." It is imperative that the data collection processes (e.g., reservations, order entry, and lead development) are accurate, complete, consistent, and standardized. Accurate involves the ability to have processes in place to ensure *good* data via proper staff training and automated validation and error checking. Complete implies the ability to connect to various systems to gain all of the data needed, which is a major challenge with the systems in use today. Consistent and standardized suggest that processes, terminology, and data formats should be the same throughout the organization to allow for consolidation and interpretation. These data will be used downstream; for example, for subsequent processes such as check-in, guest profiles, function booking, **data mining** (recall our definition from Chapter 8: analysis and modeling, pattern/trend recognition, and identification of relationships), and social marketing, among others. Therefore, the accuracy of these later activities is only as good as the data collected during the initial guest contact points. Achieving this level of accuracy is a function not only of the systems in place but also the training front line employees receive and the culture of the organization. All guest contact associates must understand and appreciate the important roles data play and their own importance and the contributions they make in collecting and using data to benefit guest service and the overall success of the organization. This is essential to maintaining the integrity of the data.

To avoid service failures and bad (i.e., ineffective) management decisions, we must ensure we have the appropriate procedures and systems in place, and we must train our employees not only on how to collect data but also on the strategic importance of these data. In service businesses like those found in the hospitality industry, data are the raw ingredients used repeatedly in the guest lifecycle for the production of service and the resulting experiences. Thus, to produce flawless service, create positively memorable experiences, and wow guests, our employees require accurate and timely access to reliable data that can then be aggregated, ordered, and converted into usable information.

The second attribute we must remember is that data and information can be perishable. Most data are dynamic, not static. This means that their lives are generally short-lived in terms of their relevance or meaning. Think how quickly a tweet is pushed to the background. Consequently, the value of data can shift over time, given the context and how that data are being applied. Data that have surpassed their useful shelf lives may have limited value in a specific situation or guest encounter, but when they are put in a historical context and used to establish trends or patterns and predict future events, their value takes on different meaning and purpose. The opportunity costs, especially of missed opportunities, are where organizations are really vulnerable. In a time when speed wins, the opportunity costs can be rather high. Therefore, they must be carefully assessed and managed.

The third characteristic is that data and information are context-sensitive. Data without context have no meaning. In order to effectively use data, they must be treated in appropriate contexts for which they were collected and in which they will be applied. Finally, it is also important to remember that there is a humanistic element to data and information as well. Computers can help people organize and process data and information more quickly to find meaning in them, but humans must be able to recognize the value, see the meaning, and know how and when to apply this meaning (and when not to) in their jobs—from making managerial decisions to delivering outstanding guest services to developing successful digital marketing programs. This also implies their ethical and responsible use, which should never be overlooked.

4. Working Smart

Under the present economic environment, attention must be given to reducing or containing costs. This typically results in having to do more with less as financial resources are rationed and as people resources are eliminated. Under these circumstances, there are fewer staff and fewer managers to operate and manage the many diverse business activities associated with a hospitality enterprise. As managers' time is spread across a wider array of issues and business operations, managers are expected to oversee multiple aspects of the business without necessarily having all of the specific expertise—and certainly not all of the time—required to focus on the many important details to ensure smooth business operations, the consistent delivery of exceptional guest services, and the desired performance levels. Clearly, managers must figure out how to work smart if they are to be effective and productive and how to pay close attention to the numbers while maintaining high visibility across departments. They have little time to spend in their offices reviewing reams of reports, trying to decipher meaning in the numbers, and reflecting on what could have been. The conditions of today require hospitality organizations to apply IT to extend their managers' reach and knowledge across the entire enterprise without necessarily having to have a ubiquitous physical presence to know how the business is performing.

In the past and in many cases even today, a corporate office provides much of the reporting for key operating statistics, financial data, and online customer satisfaction surveys. This approach is neither efficient nor timely and can often lead to ineffective decisions. The resulting reports provide **lagging indicators** or historical operating information, making it difficult for managers to determine where and how to intervene to positively influence outcomes. By the time the reports are read, analyzed, and interpreted, the information contained within them is obsolete while the factors contributing to results are long forgotten. As properties become more automated, the local reporting capabilities increase, providing more timely information and alleviating many of the problems cited here. Yet, the number of disparate systems creates difficulties in gaining access to timely, meaningful, and consolidated data. At times, administrative staff re-key data from reports into spreadsheets to create customized and consolidated **flash reports**, a daily snapshot of key performance indicators and operating statistics (e.g., revenue, occupancy, average daily rate, and guest satisfaction scores), for management. Not only is this process inefficient, it is also prone to inaccuracies as a result of data entry errors. As previously mentioned, relevance is an issue due to the time involved in preparing the reports. Unfortunately, and perhaps surprisingly to some, these practices, as bad as they are, still exist today. With better systems and technology, these practices are changing, but the hospitality industry still has a long way to go, and the timing will be elongated due to the incompatibilities between many systems in use today and the lack of integrated solutions available for purchase.

Through advances in technology such as more open and integrated systems, greater organizational connectivity, and better reporting and analysis tools, the situation has greatly improved, giving managers access to more timely data as well as tools to help interpret the results quickly and effectively. With these tools, managers spend less time buried in reports and more time proactively managing the business.

5. The Balanced Scorecard

Over time, systems have evolved and now focus on providing a **balanced scorecard** (an organizational report card of key performance measures or dashboard of sorts) to top managers, a concept first popularized by Kaplan and Norton (1996). The balanced score-card may vary from organization to organization, but the underlying premise is the same: ascertaining the health of the business. In assessing performance, organizations should not rely on any single measure but rather on a composite set of measures that take into account the various stakeholders of the firm (i.e., guests, employees, owners and investors, suppliers, franchisees, allied partners, government, and community). The goal is to assemble a comprehensive and integrated measurement system that will allow managers to monitor performance, identify problem areas, develop intervening strategies, chart the performance of the organization against its overarching strategies, and aid in the development of future strategic directions. The system must not only report historical information but also predict future outcomes.

Traditionally, almost exclusive emphasis was given to financial measures. This approach, which overlooked other key measures, has proven problematic for several reasons. These include a historical and inward focus, a tendency to concentrate on short-term results, and an inappropriate assumption that everything can be quantified (Kaplan and Norton, 1996). In the words of Kaplan and Norton (1996, p. 24):

> Financial measures are inadequate for guiding and evaluating organizations' trajectories through competitive environments. They are lagging indicators that fail to capture much of the value that has been created or destroyed by managers' actions ... [They] tell some, but not all, of the story ... and they fail to provide adequate guidance for the actions to be taken today and the day after to create future financial value.

Certainly, financial measures are important and must be included, but they represent only one view of the firm. Instead of a single measure or single category of measures, what is proposed is a composite of integrated and telling measures or key indicators (sometimes referred to as **critical success factors**) across a variety of categories tied to each stakeholder group that will provide vital information regarding the health and performance of the organization. For each measurement category, management should define strategic objectives (or drivers), appropriate measures, targets to be achieved, and key initiatives that will be undertaken to achieve the established goals. Table 9-1 provides a worksheet that can be used in the scorecard development process to help identify and document key measures and goals and align them with the firm's strategy.

TABLE 9-1

Balanced Scorecard Development Worksheet

Measurement Category	Strategic Objectives (Drivers)	Measures	Targets (Goals)	Key Initiatives
Lodging Performance	Increase market share and improve profitability	ADR Occupancy percentage REVPAR Market share	↑ from $225 to $275 ↑ from 62% to 68% ↑ from $130 to $145 ↑ from 15% to 18%	Digital marketing campaign Weekend getaway promotion Corporate sales blitz
Guest Satisfaction	Improve guest satisfaction score	Guest satisfaction rating	↑ overall satisfaction score from 4.8 to 6.0 ↑ intent to return score from 4.2 to 6.0	Mobile check-in Digital signage In-room technology enhancements App redesign
Sustainability	Reduce energy and water consumption	Energy bills and consumption rates per room Water usage	↓ energy bills and per room consumption rates by 10%	In-room energy management system Energy saving lightbulbs Motion sensors Water saving devices Energy Star compliance

6. The Importance of Infrastructure

In order to achieve value from technology, a firm must have an appropriate, capable, reliable, and solid, yet flexible, technology infrastructure in place. Like a building's foundation, the technology infrastructure is the base upon which all technology applications are built. Simply put, the technology infrastructure is *everything* (i.e., people, technology, business processes, training programs, and organizational culture) necessary to support the flow and processing of data and information. It determines a firm's capabilities or limitations. A poor, ineffective, or inappropriate infrastructure will undoubtedly cause problems for the firm; namely, inhibited growth, unrealized potential, service delivery failures, and uninformed decisions. All of these are undesirable and could be catastrophic to the firm. While most of the infrastructure remains behind the scenes, its failure will quickly bring it into the fore. Therefore, one must not underestimate the importance of infrastructure, and one must not skimp in this area. Such shortsightedness almost always causes heartaches and growing pains at a later point in time. Instead, one should pay close attention to the selection, building, and ongoing maintenance and updating of the firm's IT infrastructure. This is not to say that the entire infrastructure has to be purchased at once; it should be scalable, adaptable, and purchased as needed.

Of particular note are the systems architecture (hardware and software design, operating systems, mobile apps, Social media integration, and programming languages), network topology and communications protocols, big data, the databases, data warehouses, data mining tools, intranet, security, systems procedures, organizational culture, and human elements. There is a broad range of systems in use within hospitality firms to run operations, link with suppliers and allied partners, and share data throughout the organization and across its value chain, the collection of all of the direct, indirect, and support functions, from supplier to customer, necessary to drive revenues and firm profitability. It is important for systems to be able to talk with one another; that is, share data back and forth with each other as business needs dictate. This sharing can be achieved only if the systems in use are able to talk the same language, which requires defining software, hardware, database, and communications standards at the onset. The data network then becomes the glue that connects various systems together. The databases are the underlying storage cabinets that house all data collected, and, in turn, allow users access to the data through queries, reports, and data sharing with other systems.

7. Summary

In the Information Age, competition is based on information, the time it takes to acquire this information, how the organization and its employees act on this information, and how soon they act. The possibilities and applications for business intelligence are virtually endless. Think about how business intelligence can help you to better manage and allocate resources, control operating costs, improve operational efficiencies and services offered, and drive revenue-enhancing opportunities. To manage the business by the numbers, IT and a good mobile technology infrastructure are required along with highly capable managers. A performance measurement and monitoring system is an ideal application to assist managers in carrying out their duties and should become standard parts of every organization's technology applications portfolio. While business intelligence tools are great assets for managers, they do not replace the need for good, strong, intelligent managers. Software applications can process the data, but someone still needs to interpret the results and make the decisions.

A more effective and productive manager, someone who is constantly in the know and armed with up-to-the-minute data, can spread himself or herself further across the organization and make better (i.e., fact-based versus gut-based) decisions. By being more informed, managers are in better control of their environment. They can, therefore, better coach their employees and raise the level of accountability for all departments, teams, and managers around the resort.

Leading business strategists suggest that the key to winning the future is to develop industry foresight and to stake one's territorial claim before anyone else. Following this advice, however, is not as easy as it may sound, especially when one takes into account how quickly things change in the high-tech era. Each day, the seeds of change are sewn. By using disciplined approaches and capable IT, these seeds can be spotted early on as they germinate, sprout, and grow into something big. IT applications are essential in helping us wade through that voluminous data to uncover trends, patterns, and meaning, but remember, technology is not enough. It is how we (and our staff) use the technology and the information it yields that will make a difference. As stated in the interview, learning to ask good, intelligent questions, having the systems in place to be able to answer these questions, and knowing how to interpret and apply the answers are important and required traits for hospitality managers. Knowledge, not location, is the key competitive determinant in the digital economy.

8. CASE STUDY AND LEARNING ACTIVITY

Case Study

Measurement before Management

Richard Sperry works for a major hotel management company. His corporate office has decided that his talents, honed as the head of strategy for the brand, need to be targeted toward the northeastern sector of the United States. This region has forty-five hotels and is presently the corporation's weakest performing region. Of particular concern to his boss is the ability of one of the competitors in the region to respond to market forces more readily, leaving the company at a major disadvantage. One competitor in particular always seems to have its finger on the pulse and adjusts its room rates perfectly to meet shifting demand seen in the region. Its package deals constantly meet with high approvals, and owners couldn't be happier.

Having been burned from the many "if you buy it, they will come," technology solutions offered by many vendors in the past, management is skeptical of purchasing new systems. Fortunately, Richard has a history of solving problems with little increased spending due to his ability to manage and use information effectively. Management is in clear agreement that the company is presently at a competitive disadvantage. Big data is little understood. Rather than react to every new offering a competing property may introduce to the marketplace, Richard and his boss concur that the best strategy to compete is to better use information to build a solid foundation of smart business practices blended with quality service offerings. The following five goals have been established and will be used as the basis of measuring Richard's performance over the next year:

1. Increase revenue by 5 percent
2. Increase occupancy percentage by 6 percent
3. Increase Guest Service Index (GSI) scores to 3.5 (on a scale of 1 to 5, with 5 being the most satisfied and 1 being the least satisfied)
4. Increase mobile reservations 10 percent
5. Reduce employee turnover by 15 percent

Current Systems

Luckily for Richard, each hotel recently upgraded its technology applications portfolio. Currently, each property shares a similar network infrastructure and common OS. High-speed Internet access is available at all properties on personal computers running Windows. Software, despite being upgraded, has not been standardized throughout the company. Among the forty-five hotels in Richard's region, there are three different PMSs, four different restaurant POS systems, and three different database architectures in use. Social media and digital marketing are mostly property specific. Additionally, word processing, spreadsheet, and other productivity software differ from property to property.

Current Procedures

Report compilation and dissemination requires each hotel's night auditor to scan weekly flash reports to the regional office where the numbers are entered manually into spreadsheet so that a consolidated report for the region can be prepared. Online guest surveys, the sole measurement for GSI scores, are emailed to the corporate office each week. The corporate office compiles the scores to create the GSI index and then emails a report to the regional office each month. The food and beverage director submits bi-weekly purchasing histories and nightly sales data to the on-site controller who compiles the data and emails a series of reports to the regional office. Each month, the regional office emails a series of summary financial and operating reports to the corporate office and each property in the region detailing actual performance versus budget and year-to-date statistics. These reports are then reviewed by the general manager and become the subject of discussion in executive committee meetings at each hotel.

Richard has some great ideas for a new strategy. He knows that he has to be able to measure what he is about to manage. Our learning activity is based on that theme.

Learning Activity

1. What are the key problems facing Richard Sperry and his organization as described in this scenario? If you were in Richard's shoes, how might you go about addressing these challenges? What would be your strategy and why? Be sure to provide appropriate justification and a specific (i.e., detailed and measurable) action plan.

2. Before any action is taken, what managerial measures must be implemented for the company's five goals, and how should these be implemented? What procedural changes are required at each property and at the regional and corporate offices? How should these changes be introduced, and who should lead the change effort?

3. Would any of data require access restriction? If so, who should have access, and to which data?

4. Evaluate the technology applications portfolio and infrastructure for Richard Sperry's company. What are its strengths and limitations? In what ways is technology being used effectively? Where is there room for improvement? What changes would you suggest and why?

5. If you were to design a balanced scorecard approach for measuring and monitoring performance and the overall health of the organization for Richard Sperry's company, how would you go about it? Where would you start? What issues might you face, and how can you overcome them? What would your proposed balanced scorecard look like?

9. Key Terms

Balanced scorecard
Business intelligence
Critical success factors
Data mining

Flash reports
Informationalize
Information asymmetry
IT infrastructure

Knowledge management
Lagging indicators

10. Chapter Questions

1. What are the characteristics of and differences between data and information? Why is it important to distinguish between the two, and how can one convert data into usable information?

2. Why should a business intelligence system be part of a hospitality organization's IT portfolio? Prepare a compelling business case to convince a skeptical hospitality industry executive why he or she should commit resources to secure and implement a business intelligence solution?

3. Why do hospitality managers feel a sense of information overload with big data? How can they cope? What strategies and techniques will you use as a manager to avoid succumbing to information overload?

4. As a hospitality manager in an information economy, what are the important traits for you to possess? What information would you consider essential to

be a successful manager? How would you use this information?

5. What are the core IT infrastructural components to a company's information systems and why are they so important? What roles can the Web and mobile technologies play?

6. Is information the basis of competition in today's marketplace? Can information provide competitive advantage? If so, how?

7. About what issues associated with data collection should a hospitality manager be aware? How can hospitality organizations improve the quality of their data?

8. Select a hospitality organization or department within a hospitality organization. For that organization or department, design an ideal balanced scorecard? What measurement categories and measures would you use and why?

CHAPTER 10

Virtual Reality and Augmented Reality Applications for the Tourism and Hospitality Industry

Courtesy of Neil M. Gupta

Chapter Objective

- At the end of this chapter students will have a deeper understanding of the complex world of virtual reality and augmented reality in hospitality

Learning Objectives

- Explain why virtual reality and augmented reality are such important technologies
- Understand the major technologies used in VR/AR
- Explain how VR/AR can be applied to hospitality

- Explain some new advances in VR/AR on the horizon
- See VR/AR in use in the hospitality and tourism industry

Chapter Introduction

Interview

Neil M. Gupta is an entrepreneur focused on virtual reality/augmented reality (VR/AR) and has been working on frontier technology for nearly a decade: developing technology as an engineer, designing products, and assessing the landscape and opportunities as a venture capitalist. Neil's goal is to help companies leverage technology into better products and user experiences. Neil is currently a Venture Partner with Indicator Ventures, runs his own consulting firm, and is the founder of the BostonAR meetup. Previously, Neil was co-founder and Venture Lead of the Sembler Innovation Office at Draper and also worked as senior technical staff on projects related to augmented reality and situational awareness. Neil has a certificate in entrepreneurship from the Stanford Graduate School of Business, and has his M.S. and B.S. in electrical engineering from Stanford and Northeastern University, respectively.

1. **It has been said that AR will be seen more in the hospitality industry than VR. Is there a place for VR in hospitality?**

   Absolutely. Hotel tours and vacation teasers in VR can help people decide where they want to go, and I believe this will be a big opportunity. In the room/suite you could have VR as a way to access front desk/concierge services, entertainment/TV, and relaxation/meditation to wind down. After the trip, you could re-experience it through 360° photos and videos you take along the way.

2. **What are some of the bigger roadblocks for AR adaptation?**

   For mobile AR, the roadblock will primarily be the limitations of the small FOV (field of view) and having to wave your arms around. This won't go away even as hardware/software gets better.

   For enterprise headsets like Google Glass 2.0, Vuzix m-series, and Epson moverios, the roadblocks depend on the industry, but this style of AR is becoming more widely adopted.

   Consumer headsets have the most roadblocks, as they are the most fickle customers. Almost every aspect of the headset has to get better, and some of that requires solving extremely difficult engineering problems in optics, manufacturing, computer vision, and more.

   In the future, bandwidth and connectivity issues will come into play and the need for 5G will become paramount.

3. **What sort of displays in AR are coming down the road?**

   In addition to headsets, we may see intelligent projectors that put information on the wall, floor, or ceiling.

4. **As one example, how do you see a hotel manager using AR?**

   Using facial identification and emotion recognition, the manager could ensure the smoothest experience possible for a guest.

5. **How about a customer in a restaurant?**

   Being able to visualize the actual portion sizes ahead of time.

6. **Are there other aspects of AR or VR, which someone in the hospitality industry should be aware of?**

   When it comes to technology, sometimes less is more.

7. **We are a very intimate industry, any privacy or security concerns?**

   Absolutely for both. Slowly, people will accept the technology, but these concerns will always exist and should be considered when crafting a customer experience.

8. **Finally, how can a manager in the hospitality industry use AR or VR as a competitive advantage?**

   Having 360° photos or videos of something can really make someone feel like they are there, and want to experience more. Given that we are in the early stages, even having the equipment available for people to experience might make a unique experience that gives a manager a competitive advantage.

Interview used with permission of Neil M. Gupta

1. Overview

Let's unpack the interview and take a real deep dive into the subject matter. This is our most in-depth chapter, due to what we see as its importance and future potential impact. **Virtual Reality (VR)** and **Augmented Reality (AR)** are regarded as the most world-changing technologies of the twenty-first century. VR and AR are considered to be very promising technologies for the hospitality and tourism industry, because the technology has the powerful effect of fooling the senses into believing one is present in a virtual world, by providing interactive 3D surroundings simulated by a computer. By stimulating our senses with computer-generated imagery, the mind becomes immersed in the experience and temporarily accepts VR/AR as reality (Blascovich and Bailenson, 2011; Burdea Grigore and Coiffet, 1994; Hale and Stanney, 2014; Jerald, 2016; Schmalstieg and Hollerer, 2016). VR and AR are used to create powerful 3D interactive visualization experiences for all kinds of purposes.

At the Internationale Tourismus-Börse, which takes place annually in Europe and Asia, and the World Travel Mart (WTM) in London, several tourism technology providers were demonstrating VR/AR content showcasing tourist destinations and attractions on location. These types of companies typically produce content in assignment from destination providers, attraction providers, and hospitality providers, and some offer a content management system (CMS) to travel agencies that they can use to develop their own immersive VR experiences for their clients. These terms and concepts will be further explained below.

These simulations can depict any tourist location or attraction reproduced as 3D imagery, controlled by powerful computers creating a complete **virtual environment (VE)**. VE, simply put, is a virtual digital environment generated so that the user with VR equipment feels present inside it. A complete VR system is regarded as the interface between the real-world user and the VE.

According to a report published in May 2017 by Grand View Research, Inc., the VR industry is expected to reach USD $692 billion by 2025, and the concept will expand from basic gaming to other applications like education, medicine and healthcare, architecture, sports, TV programs, movies and music, and many more (Virtual Reality Market Analysis, 2017). VR is gaining forefront attention in 2017 as various companies like Google, Microsoft, Facebook, HTC, and many others have come up with their own designs of VR head-mounted displays (HMDs). These devices will be further discussed in the sections below.

AR is an integration of the real world and the virtual world with the aim of providing additional information about something in the real world with information displayed in the virtual world. For instance, a person could look at a painting or a machine in the real world, hold up their smartphone or tablet in front of the painting or machine, and see on the screen the painting or machine with additional useful information, thus augmenting reality. In the case of the painting, the additional information could be about the painter, the painting technique, and the painter's life, for instance. In the case of the machine, the additional information could be about how to open the machine and replace a broken part.

AR technology is capable of revolutionizing the tourist experience by making possible the planning, previewing, and accessing of location-based information of the holiday journey and destinations, in an interactive and simple manner from a mobile device, during the holiday and in advance, from the comfort of one's home. Users can preview and book their hotel, access information while they are there, navigate around their destination, and translate written or spoken signs and conversations. Locating dining and entertainment options can all be done simply through an app on a mobile device.

In 2009, the first AR smartphone apps came out, using AR technology to add a layer of guidance, content, and entertainment to physical locations seen through the smartphone's camera view. Tuscany+ was the first app built specifically for tourism—an "interactive, real-time guide"—intended to enhance the visitor experience. The AR technology makes it possible to layer digital enhancements over an existing reality or real-life scenario.

As touched on in the meeting and events chapter (6), another world-famous example is Pokémon GO, an open-source, mobile multi-player AR-based game that since its release in July 2016 has taken the world by storm. It is an application with which players can collect points by walking around in the real world while holding their smartphone in a quest to find, catch, and collect virtual characters called "pocket monsters" through their phone camera viewfinder. These virtual characters are located near and linked to specific geographical locations. Pokémon GO already had more than 65 million players by April 2017 and is still rapidly increasing user numbers. With these numbers, it has become the most successful game of all-time. It is praised internationally by health experts because it gets people out of their houses and motivates them to walk around outside and connect with others.

Gastronomical providers have already started benefiting from the Pokémon GO craze, giving some ideas about more ways in which Pokémon GO type applications can benefit tourism. The game makes use of "PokéStops" that are strategically placed at sightseeing locations such as monuments and other public areas of interest; in the game, these locations are displayed with a photo and a brief description. Tour operators can design new tours according to the location of PokéStops or the known locations of rare collectable Pokémons. During the tour, players can expand their knowledge of the world around them in a playful and spontaneous manner, when they encounter PokéStops that have interesting historic, artistic, or cultural value.

Pokémon GO has made AR technology popular among consumers, and many variations on this theme can now be easily envisioned and introduced. This new technology can bring new opportunities to the hospitality and tourism industry. According to an article published by *Marketwatch.com* in July 2017, the AR market in 2016 was valued at USD $2.39 billion and is expected to reach USD $61.39 billion by 2023, growing at a CAGR (compound annual growth rate) of 55.71 percent during the forecasted period (Augmented Reality Market by Offering, 2017).

VR Definition

A useful definition of VR was created by Lavalle, professor in the Department of Computer Science at the University of Illinois at Urbana-Champaign, formerly principal scientist at Oculus, currently chief scientist of VR/AR/MR at Huawei Technologies Co. Ltd., and creator of a series of 71 VR lectures available on YouTube (Lavalle, 2016).

Lavalle's definition of VR: "Inducing targeted behavior in an organism by using artificial sensory stimulation, while the organism has little or no awareness of the interference" (Lavalle, 2015).

This allows us to break the functional elements down into four main components associated with VR (Milgram and Kishino, 1994):

1. *Targeted Behavior*: The organism has some "experience," which is designed by VR developers. Examples: walking, flying, space exploration, doing lab experiments, and interacting with other organisms.
2. *Organism*: Organism refers to the VR user and includes other life forms. Example: Human beings, animals, and chatbots.
3. *Artificial Sensory Stimulation*: With the integration of modern techniques of engineering, various sensory experiences of organisms can be replicated and the sensory inputs are replaced by artificial stimulation.
4. *Awareness*: With effective VR experiences, the organism experiences a smooth interaction and there is no friction between the user and the experience of the interface to the simulated world, thereby easily "misleading" the user into really feeling present in virtual world.

AR

Augmented Reality (AR) is regarded as a variation of VR. For this reason, AR is often listed in combination with VR, as "AR/VR" and sometimes "VR/AR." AR technology is beneficial to various industrial application areas, where there is a requirement for advanced user perception, and can help workers to have quick access to relevant information and instructions during the manufacturing processes (Azuma, 1997; Azuma et al., 2001).

AR Systems have the following characteristics (Van Krevelen and Poelman, 2010):

- Mix of real world and virtual objects in real environment
- Synchronize real and virtual objects with each other
- Highly interactive and runs in 3D in real time

2. Technologies for VR and AR

In this section, some of the technologies that enable the user to see and interact with the VR/AR application are reviewed. The technologies for VR/AR are still rapidly evolving. The software is becoming more sophisticated and faster, and the graphical imagery more detailed. The hardware is becoming less expensive and less bulky, but as pointed out in our interview, still not perfect. The user experience is getting better due to these advances in the technologies. AR requires more sophisticated technology compared to VR, but the key components for both, have remained the same since the 1960's, when Ivan Sutherland—who is widely regarded as the "father of computer graphics"—and his students invented several foundations of modern computer graphics. The race is on between the different VR hardware and software developers, and technology for VR is advancing so rapidly that reviewing the latest technology specifications is needed. The following sections give an overview of some of the relevant technologies for AR/VR. Check for updates before adaptation. Extensive footnotes are provided as a possible starting point for future purchasing research. We start with 3D scanning.

Overview of 3D Scanning Technology

Three-dimensional (3D) scanning is new technology that is potentially very impactful for the hospitality and tourism Industry, because it enables us to create realistic representations of tourist locations and attractions, by capturing a physical object's exact size and shape as a digital 3D representation (Retrieved on August 24, 2017, from https://en.wikipedia.org/wiki/3D_scanner; Retrieved on August 24, 2017, from https://www.ems-usa.com/tech-papers/3D%20Scanning%20Technologies%20.pdf; Guttentag, 2010). It scans and analyzes the real-world objects and the environment, in terms of shape and appearance, and constructs a digital 3D model. The environment at a place of interest can be captured and converted into this 3D model. It can then be explored by the public, either through a VR interface or via a traditional "2D" interface on a PC, tablet, or smartphone. These models can then be used in the production of movies, games, industrial design, prototyping, quality inspections, capturing of cultural artifacts, and incorporating realistic objects and environments into AR/VR applications. This allows the user to explore locations that are inconvenient for travel (Guttentag, 2010) and to pre-view locations of interest. Let's look at the main types of 3D scanning.

Types of 3D Scanning Technologies

Short-Range 3D Scanners (Retrieved on August 24, 2017, from https://www.ems-usa.com/tech-papers/3D%20Scanning%20Technologies%20.pdf). These scanners typically utilize a laser triangulation or structured light technology. Laser-based 3D scanners use a process called trigonometric triangulation to capture a 3D shape accurately as millions of points. Laser scanners work by projecting a laser line or multiple lines onto an object and then capturing its reflection with a single sensor or multiple sensors. The sensors are located at a known distance from the laser's source. Accurate point measurements are then made by calculating the reflection angle of the laser light. Laser scanners are very popular and come in many designs. The benefits of 3D laser scanners are that they are able to scan tough surfaces such as shiny or dark finishes. Additionally, they are less sensitive to changing light conditions and ambient light. Finally, they are often more simple and portable in design, easier to use, and lower in cost.

Projected or Structured Light 3D Scanners (Retrieved on August 24, 2017, from https://www.ems-usa.com/tech-papers/3D%20Scanning%20Technologies%20 .pdf). Also called "white light" 3D scanners, most structured light 3D scanners project a blue or white LED light pattern consisting of bars, blocks, or other shapes onto an object. The scanner has one or more sensors that look at the edge of a pattern or structure to determine the object's 3D shape. They are either tripod mounted or handheld. The benefits of structured light 3D scanners are numerous (Retrieved on August 24, 2017, from https://www.ems-usa.com/tech-papers/3D%20Scanning%20 Technologies%20.pdf):

- Very fast scan times: up to two seconds per scan
- Large scanning area: up to 48 inches in a single scan
- Versatile: multiple lenses to scan small to large parts in a single system
- Portable: handheld systems

Medium- and Long-Range 3D Scanners (Retrieved on August 24, 2017, from https:// www.ems-usa.com/tech-papers/3D%20Scanning%20Technologies%20.pdf).   These come in two formats: pulse-based and phase-shift. They capture millions of points by rotating 360 degrees, while a spinning mirror redirects the laser outward toward the object or areas to be scanned. They are well suited for scanning large objects such as buildings, structures, aircraft, and military vehicles (Retrieved on August 24, 2017, from https://www.ems-usa.com/tech-papers/3D%20Scanning%20Technologies%20. pdf). For medium-range scanning such as vehicles and large industrial equipment, phase-shift 3D scanners are the most suitable. Pulse-based 3D scanners can scan objects up to 1,000 meters away, while phase-shift scanners are better suited for scanning objects up to 300 meters or less. Benefits of long-range 3D scanners (Retrieved on August 24, 2017, from https://www.ems-usa.com/tech-papers/3D%20 Scanning%20Technologies%20.pdf):

- 3D scan of millions of points in a single scan—up to 1 million points per second
- Large scanning area up to 1,000 meters
- Good accuracy and resolution based on object size
- Non-contact to safely scan all types of objects
- Portable

360-Degree Video for Quick VR/AR Scene Generation

A very recent and increasingly popular VR imagery technology is 360° video, also known as spherical video, through which video recordings are made. This imagery is captured with an omnidirectional camera, or a collection of cameras set up in a circle or semi-circle. These videos can be combined into a larger connected set of panoramas and integrated into a VE. The user can interact with the video and view the panorama as if they were really standing in the scene at the point where the camera recorded the scene. The end user is in control of the 360° VR experience. when they see something of interest, they can control the flow of the experience, jump directly to the point of interest, and explore different aspects in more detail by moving in closer.

This technology has gained massive attention since the prices for the cameras dropped, and it was realized that this type of footage could deliver a virtual tour experience much faster than programming virtual scenes from scratch, as would be the case in normal VR productions. 360° video footage viewed in a VR/AR system is often referred to as VR. This can be confusing for people who are new to VR/AR technology and have not used VR that is based on real computer-generated graphics. However, 360° video is a useful way of quickly generating imagery for VR/AR applications and, especially for applications that depict real-world scenes; there is no need to create these scenes from scratch. One problem is that the cameras can be expensive and the imagery may need to be "stitched" together to create a larger VR experience, which can be time consuming. We now move on to what one would actually wear over the eyes, the HMD.

FIGURE 10-1
Picture of a generic VR headset.
zeljkodan/Shutterstock

VR/AR HMD Technologies

The AR/VR HMDs that are the most interesting to the hospitality and tourism industry are those that are "cordless" or "wireless," affordable, and easy to use. All HMD manufacturers are currently aiming to create wireless headsets because cables restrict the user's movements, and it is easy to get tangled up in them while the user is engaged in the AR/VR experience and unaware of the physical world around them. There is a whole range of HMDs (Figure 10-1), some wireless and some not yet, some only for VR, others only for AR, and prices range from high-end to low-end. This following sections describe various AR/VR HMDs through which the user can view the AR/VR application (Retrieved on August 24, 2017d, from https://en.wikipedia.org/wiki/Head-mounted_display).

Tethered VR Headsets

Tethered VR HMDs are smaller, lighter in weight, and more comfortable for the user, because the data is processed and sent via cable from the computer to the HMD. The current state-of-the-art models are reviewed below.

Sony PlayStation VR: PlayStation VR HMD was developed by Sony Interactive Entertainment and launched in October 2016. It is designed to be fully functional with the PlayStation 4 home video game console. The PlayStation VR system can send a view of the virtual game world to the PlayStation VR headset and a television simultaneously, with the television either mirroring the picture displayed on the headset, or displaying a separate image for competitive or cooperative gameplay. PlayStation VR works with two types of controlees, the standard DualShock 4 controller and the PlayStation Move controllers.

HTC Vive: The first version is not entirely wireless, but the next version (codename Oasis, release date rumored to be early of 2018) will be. The Vive headset uses "room scale" tracking of the HMD and the handheld controllers. It has a display resolution of 1080x1200, seventy infrared sensors: thirty-two on the headset and nineteen for each controller, a gyroscope, and an accelerometer. The front-facing camera in the HMD helps to identify any moving or static objects in a room; this functionality is known as the "Chaperone" safety system, because it will automatically display a grid to the user to show them the real-world boundaries of the physical space and any obstacles in it.

Oculus Rift: Developed and manufactured by Oculus VR, a division of Facebook Inc., it is not completely wireless. The positional tracking system (called "Constellation") is precise, has low-latency, and is sub-millimeter accurate. The tracking works via a USB-mounted stationary infrared (IR) sensor, which picks up light emitted by IR LEDs that are integrated into the HMD with the sensor located on the user's desk. This creates a 3D space in which the user can physically move around in the room. It uses "low persistence", that is, display an image for only 2 milliseconds of each frame. The combination of the high refresh rate, global refresh, and low persistence means that the user does not experience motion blurring or juddering of their view of the VE, as is typically experienced when viewing the VE via a PC on a regular monitor. It uses lenses that allow for a wide field of view. The separation of the lenses is adjustable by a dial on the bottom of the device, in order to accommodate a wide range of interpupillary distances. The same pair of lenses is used for all users; however, there are several facial foam-frames for the HMD with different thicknesses, so that the user's eyes can be positioned at the desired distance. This also allows for users wearing glasses to use the Rift, as well as users with widely varying facial shapes. Headphones are integrated, which provide real-time 3D audio effects.

Wireless VR Headsets

Google Cardboard 3D VR: A very simple, elegant, and cheap device to produce a VR platform was developed in 2014 by Google for use with a smartphone. It is a fold-out cardboard viewer. The platform is intended as a low-cost system to encourage interest and development in VR applications. Users can either build their own viewer from simple, low-cost components using specifications published by Google or purchase a pre-manufactured one. To use the platform, users download Cardboard-compatible 3D applications on their phone, place the phone into the back of the viewer, and view content in 3D through the lenses. It is wireless, and the user does not need a keyboard or mouse to interact with the applications. Interaction with the application such as selection and navigation is achieved with head movements and gaze duration. However, this can limit the number and types of interactions available to the user.

The Cardboard software development kit (SDK) is available for the Android and iOS operating systems. The SDK's VR View allows developers to embed VR content on the Web and in mobile apps. As of March 2017, over 10 million Cardboard viewers have been sold and over 160 million Cardboard app downloads have been made.

Google Daydream: Following the success of the Cardboard platform, Google announced an enhanced VR platform, Daydream, also for use with a smartphone and the Android mobile operating system. It is a true wireless HMD system. It works by inserting a smartphone into the HMD shaped "box". Compatible phones that are used in the Google Daydream View VR headset are Samsung, HTC, LG, Xiaomi, Huawei, ZTE, Asus, and Alcatel.

Samsung Gear VR: Developed by Samsung Electronics in collaboration with Oculus and manufactured by Samsung, it is used in conjunction with some smartphone models in Samsung's Galaxy line. The headset is wireless. The device offers Netflix, Vimeo, Hulu, and other content.

Wireless AR Headsets

In this section, we move on to the current state-of-the-art wireless "AR" as opposed to the previous VR headsets. Remember the difference?

Microsoft HoloLens: Developed and manufactured by Microsoft, it is a true wireless HMD. It is one of the first HMDs running on the Windows mixed reality platform under the Windows 10 operating system. It can run almost all Universal Windows Platform apps, which the user will see as almost transparent 2D Microsoft Windows that the user can move and interact with. The user can interact with 3D applications (called "holographic" applications), using the Windows holographic APIs. The HoloLens contains an internal rechargeable battery, with two to three hours of active use and two weeks of standby time.

Google Glass: Developed by "X" (previously known as "Google X") as a "ubiquitous computer" and released in 2013, it is an optical HMD that resembles standard eyeglasses with the lens replaced by a head-up display. The Google Glass 1.0 prototype flopped and was taken of the market because consumers had huge concerns about their privacy due to the unobtrusive recording features that were built into the device, capable of recording everything around it, unbeknown to the people in recording distance and so development ceased. After the release of Google Cardboard, consumer demand renewed and Google X is currently developing Google Glass 2.0. Google Glass consists of:

- *A touchpad:*   located on the side at the level of the user's right temple, providing a control to the device by swiping through a timeline-like interface displayed on the screen.
- *A camera:*   to take photos and record 720p HD video.
- *A display:*   a liquid crystal on silicon (LCoS).

3. VR/AR in Tourism and Hospitality: Rationales and Applications

Consumers and investors continue to be impressed with the advancements in VR/AR technologies and their implementation. As a result, these increasingly sophisticated technologies are also being envisioned and implemented for the tourism and hospitality industry. Let us look at a few areas.

Effective Policy Planning and Management

AR/VR technologies can really help your customer plan and organize. With VR technologies, travelers can experience bird's-eye views of their destination and have a detailed look and feel of the place before visiting. It can be an important and effective tool for tourist activity planning, as they can connect to each other via social media to get feedback regarding their previous experience.

Effective Entertainment Tool

VR technology has been implemented in various theme parks like Disneyland and other kids' entertainment parks to provide virtual experiences such as rollercoaster rides, flight simulators, and so on. Nowadays, the concept of 3D and 4D theaters are also on the rise in many places around the world.

Education Tool

VR has tremendous potential in terms of education, and effective research of many years has proved that VR devices and even the latest AR technology can serve as a great tool for entertainment. A VR model can be an efficient means of communication of large amounts of information because it leverages the user's natural spatial perception abilities. It allows tourists to learn about historic and cultural information before visiting the real site.

Virtual Attractions at Effective Cost

New AR and VR travel tourism experiences can be added to existing applications by modeling and animating them; digital content can be added or uploaded on demand, depending on the visitor's requirements, and can also be used for location marketing purposes.

Interactive Dining Experience

Dining and entertainment options are important to anyone planning a trip away from home. Recalling the interview, using VR/AR technology you can take virtual tours of restaurant locations, and even peruse virtual menus to help you make your dining decisions.

Easy Translation Capabilities

If your travels take you abroad, in a country where you have a limited understanding of the predominant languages spoken, AR can make translations. Using AR-equipped apps, the user can scan printed materials with their smartphone camera, such as signs or menus and have them translated into any language.

Real-Time and Reliable Navigation

Wayfinding in an unfamiliar place can be very challenging and frustrating. AR elevates typical navigation maps by adding digital elements such as arrows and other helpful direction and information to the map.

Booking Rooms

As seen in the interview, AR technology will allow potential guests to explore rooms before they make their booking. Travelers will be right there inside the room to see exactly what different sizes and floor plans are available. Potential guests may be persuaded to upgrade to a suite by seeing the additional amenities and incredible views, and how spacious it is.

Exploring the Property

Instead of relying on Web site images and ordinary paper brochures, potential visitors can learn what a hotel stay "feels" like. Through interactive experiences, travelers can virtually visit a hotel's restaurant, spa, or fitness center. An eco-friendly hotel might take users on a virtual tour of its rooftop herb garden or show off green building materials, helping to build customer loyalty. The Mansion at Casa Madrona uses an AR-printed brochure that can be scanned to immerse the user in the luxurious property.

Restaurant Experiences

Hoteliers can embed AR content on their restaurant menu, enabling non-native guests to read it in their own language. Taking this a step further, imagine a guest sitting in a hotel restaurant and being able to get suggested drink pairings, read customer reviews, and watch how the chef prepares the dish they are considering ordering. At the Inamo restaurant in London, AR images are projected onto the tables letting guests choose their own table theme.

Local Attractions

Guests often choose their hotel based on its proximity to area attractions. AR technology will not only allow users to view a hotel location but can also recreate significant historical events or cultural experiences of nearby destinations. Hoteliers could add an AR feature to their existing proprietary apps similar to "Paris, Then and Now," which shows users what different sites in Paris looked like in the past, based on where they are standing. Alternatively, guests can virtually try a local activity, such as a hang-gliding adventure, before choosing to go. In addition, opportunities for the hotel to advertise other services grows the longer a guest spends interacting with their app.

Marketing

Hotels can leverage AR tech on their Web site or billboards placed in airports and high-traffic areas. Scanning through a smartphone camera will trigger images and information about the hotel. A beachside resort may entice potential visitors by immersing them in a video from the viewpoint of a guest lounging in the sun while sipping a cocktail, a promotion for their happy hour drinks hovering in the foreground. AR may increase guest satisfaction as well, since the guest will know what to expect before they buy.

Hotel Management

AR will also impact business and back-of-house operations. The advanced AR technology can bring blueprints and artist renderings to life, letting potential investors clearly envision the result. In the realm of staff training, hotels can create real-life scenarios that teach skills and help employees more effectively interact with guests.

Although the AR trend for hotels is still in its early stages, it may not be long before cutting-edge virtual environments that include the feel of ocean breezes or the scent of cooking food become mainstream. The rapid adoption of Pokémon Go demonstrates how ready people are to embrace this innovative new tech trend, and hotels that ignore it will find themselves left behind. It is clear that AR has a profound role to play in the future of the hotel industry.

4. Emerging Role of Artificial Intelligence

The combination of VR/AR and artificial intelligence (AI) is made possible due to recently advanced technology parameters. AI, where computers perform tasks done by humans, and data-mining techniques have already been adopted by the hospitality and tourism industry for studying tourist behavior and forecasting their future demands (Goh, Mok, and Law, 2009). The recent advances in AI techniques and the increased availability and quantity of user data called "Big Data" (Chapter 8) have opened up more ways of using AI. AI can enhance the user experience through "customization." Rather than offering the same holiday or attraction to all users, big data can be analyzed with AI technologies and help match the desires, habits, and preferences of a tourist with the available offers. It can also become much more flexible and innovative in the offered holiday and attraction experiences, by using the data to create new combinations of offers based on user preferences.

Combinations of AI and VR/AR are expected to mature, with deeper integrations. These integrations provide an even wider range of opportunities, with product and service enhancements. AI technology is now also used to create cognitive systems that are capable of interacting with consumers in natural language, this is generally referred to as a "chatbot", a virtual robot animated by an AI, which means it can deduce and predict most likely events from previous events. As a result, the chatbot can answer all kinds of questions by itself.

Hospitality and tourism customers can talk to a chatbot in VR. This chatbot has a realistic looking virtual embodiment in the VE and customers can ask it for information about the tourist location or venue, rather than having to search for the answer themselves. For the tourism and hospitality sector, this could be envisioned as a virtual representative that can answer the most commonly asked consumer questions and pass on any complex issues on to a real representative, thus reducing the number of hours that a team member has to deal with answering the same questions repeatedly.

There are many opportunities for introducing AI within the tourism and hospitality services, especially for dealing with recurring tasks and customer service. Fitting these types of VR/AR-based chatbots successfully into the marketing funnel is a new challenge, although lessons can be learned from the AI-driven "virtual assistant."

Lets look at real-life examples.

5. VR/AR Adoption in the Tourism and Hospitality Industry

Now let's put it all together in real-life examples.

A. *VR travel production*: **The Hidden World of the National Parks**. This app was created by Google, a production company, a production team, and a creative content studio to coordinate the planning and oversee the post-production of the app, all directed by a cinematographer. The app commemorates the hundredth year of the US National Park system in an interactive 360° VR experience, combined with interactive storytelling and aerial images. The end user goes on a private tour with a park ranger, and can choose their own adventure within each park. Creating this app was an ambitious, complex project that took twenty-eight days on location, traveling with around forty cases of six different types of 360° recording equipment known as "rigs," thirty GoPro cameras, two Alexa packages, a prime lens set, and an Optimo 12:1 zoom.

B. *VR for the pre-purchase stage of hotel rooms*: There are several scenarios within this case, all allowing the end user to experience a room before booking, in addition to brand-building. **Best Western** created the "Best Western Virtual Reality Experience," allowing the end user to travel to all 2,200 Best Western locations. **Marriott Hotels** piloted a program at a location in London with the aim of brand marketing and sparking conversations about why people travel. In this program, end users could order a VR HMD with preloaded videos of distant holiday locations. **Hilton** has launched a 360° ad that allows the end user to experience the Hilton Barbados and tap "Book Now." **St. Giles Hotels** ran a contest to capture surrounding sights that could then be viewed on a VR HMD, Facebook, and YouTube. **Spring GCH Hotel Group** started promoting its 120 locations through VR, making VR apps for various HMDs of different quality and price range and for the Web. **Carlson Rezidor** is using VR to promote the design of their hotels before they are fully finished, aiming to increase the brand perception of their hotel group. Sri Lanka's **Cinnamon Hotels & Resorts** created immersive VR experiences to help potential customers make positive decisions.

C. *Behind-the-scene viewing of convention centers and event locations*: YouVisit, a company in New York, offers a production service for businesses and institutions to showcase their premises to their audiences, while inspiring them to visit in person. The end users stay on average for 10+ minutes in the 360° VR experiences that YouVisit created for their clients. Their clients include Swarovski, HP, Yale, PricewaterhouseCoopers, Cisco, various hotel chains, cruise companies and cities, over 400 educational institutes, and the U.S. Army. In August 2017, they reported that they had over 800 clients, with 24,500,000 visitors to the sites that they had created for them. Their clients have on average a 133 percent conversion rate from their virtual experiences. For a Mercedes Benz event, they created a 360° VR experience that placed the viewer in the middle of the event's fashion show, allowing the close-up views of the models and navigation to specific preferred perspectives of the fashion show. Additionally, they linked the actual fashion dresses to the different designers' Web sites. They also created 360° experiences of city attractions and the NASA Space center in Houston, the Carnival Breeze cruise ship, West Hollywood, and various convention centers.

Failures of VR/AR Adoption

Although the developments in this field are in the early stages, which limits the opportunity to point out real failures in the adoption of VR/AR technology specific to the tourism and hospitality sector, a number of serious potentially troublesome areas can be deduced from all three cases as a whole.

1. *Production problems:* Large or unexpected additional production costs, complex technology, inexperienced teams, and risky locations all contribute to potential failure in producing a good-quality end user experience, even before the product is launched.

2. *Exclusive market segment:* A common mistake is to only develop the app for high-end users of expensive HMDs and failing to include the casual visitors of Facebook, YouTube, and lower-end HMD users. Potential hotel guests will access VR through many different mediums, from expensive VR headsets to VR on a smartphone or simply a 360° ad on Facebook, so all of these mediums must be taken into account.

3. *Limited views and limited interactivity:* End users can view locations from only one 360° spot if the different 360° images have not been stitched together, thus creating a very limited view of the actual location and giving them a rather simplistic experience of 360° VR. In addition, the end user is unable to move around in the 360° space. These limitations could make the consumer exit the app much faster than desirable, thus massively reducing the time for client-conversion and brand-building opportunities.

6. Summary

This chapter covered a description of VR/AR enabling technologies, the current state-of-the-art VR/AR equipment and application areas, and cases of VR/AR applications for the tourism and hospitality sector. It reviewed the successes, failures, and challenges for the development and use of VR/AR applications to improve existing marketing funnel designs, thus improving client conversion rates. The cases are analyzed to illustrate how VR/AR apps can help customers with their pre-purchase decision-making, indicating that VR/AR technology is particularly suitable for supporting the customer decision-making process on intangible products such as the holiday or event experience. AI-driven chatbots are flagged as a new application area for the tourism and hospitality sector, particularly when it comes to answering the frequently asked questions from pre-purchase customers and helping those in the process of purchasing, thus helping reduce this type of repetitive, time-consuming workload of customer support personnel.

---

7. CASE STUDY AND LEARNING ACTIVITY

Case Study

Ms. Lyne is manager in a software company called VR/AR 4U. The company makes VR/AR/AI experiences for clients from the hospitality and tourism industry. This afternoon she has a meeting with Mr. Chang who is the customer experience manager for a large international hotel chain Coral Beaches. The 150 hotels are used for conferences, weddings, and anniversaries by holidaymakers from all over the world who want to enjoy the beach, the local attractions, and the luxury spa treatments that are available at the hotel and in the local area. The goal of the meeting is to define this VR/AR project.

The proposed VR/AR/AI application is called Coral Beaches VR/AR Tour Guide. It should provide potential hotel guests with a view of the hotel, the available rooms, the area around the hotels, the available activities, and wellness treatments. The hotel receives many phone calls and emails with frequently asked questions (FAQs) from potential clients that are looking at the hotel's booking Web site. The hotel management has decided to invest in the development of a VR/AR experience that can be downloaded for free, to give potential clients a memorable experience, showing them what it is like to be a guest at the hotel including showing the available activities and surroundings. The budget for this project is very generous, but the application must be finished as soon as possible, so it should not be too complex, and it should provide a very satisfactory experience for the user. You work for the Coral Beaches Hotel chain and you are the manager of this VR/AR development project.

Learning Activity

1. Create a short description of the proposed VR/AR application and user experiences you think are needed.
2. Create a list of any questions that need to be asked in the meeting
3. Create a list of success factors needed.
4. Create a list of challenges and pitfalls for the success of this project.

8. Key Terms

Virtual Reality (VR)   Augmented Reality (AR)   Three-dimensional (3D) scanning

9. Chapter Questions

1. Explain the difference between VR/AR and 360-degree video.
2. Describe how you see the influence of VR/AR being used in hospitality and tourism in the future?
3. Describe how you see the influence of AI in hospitality and tourism in the future?
4. In which sectors of the hospitality and tourism industry will VR/AR technology be the most beneficial?
5. In which sectors of the hospitality and tourism industry will AI technology be most beneficial?
6. What are the most important aspects to keep track of to make sure a VR/AR/AI development project will succeed?
7. How are you preparing for the future of VR/AR technology integration in the hospitality and tourism industry?

CHAPTER 11

Strategic Hospitality Technology Investment

Courtesy of Susan Patterson

Chapter Objective

- At the end of this chapter students will have a deeper understanding of the system selection process.

Learning Objectives

- Understand how purchasing differs when it is for a business
- Explain ROI and payback
- List some restaurant examples
- List some examples of what make up the total cost of a purchase
- Describe the purchasing process flow
- Explain how systems are successfully implemented

Chapter Introduction

Interview

We end the book, as we began, with an interview of a recent grad with a few years of experience. Let's talk with Susan Patterson who knows how to get help when she needs it from her coworker Spencer Rung.

1. **Can you tell us about your background?**

   I graduated from Penn State University in 2014 with a degree in hotel, restaurant, and institutional management (HRIM). Post graduation, I joined the Hospitality Leadership Institute as an extern where I sat alongside several Penn State hospitality professors and assisted in developing the first Big Data Management in Hospitality conference. I was assigned a segment to present during the conference that focused on Google Analytics and how the program can take mass data from online to develop a specific profile of the users demographic, interests, location, and activity on the specific site. Through this conference, I met my current CEO, Rob Grimes, who is a well-known entrepreneur in the hospitality tech industry. I interviewed for one of his start-up companies, Stratabare, which is a company that supports POS/PMS implementations for installations across the United States and Canada. I also spent a year with CrowdCompass by Cvent working as a project coordinator building mobile applications for events, conferences, and tradeshows.

2. **What are some common best practices in purchasing technology in hospitality today?**

   One of my coworkers, Spencer Rung, who is also a Penn State HRIM graduate, works more hands-on with our clients in purchasing technology from a consulting perspective. He explained that "when looking in purchasing new technology, whether it be an all-encompassing solution or a 'best-of-breed' approach, one of the best things to do is sit down with the departments that will be the end users to determine any concerns and to develop sort of a wish list of what the new technology needs to do in order to see a benefit to their business. More than likely you are going to have multiple options and this is when you really need to weigh what will be most valuable to your business and what the effect will be on the end user in both your business and the customer-facing end. Many vendors will be able to do a demo of their products for you and often will even be able to come on site to do a more personalized demo even with your own data if you choose."

3. **What are some common pain points in system selection and implementation?**

   Technology in hospitality is known to be well behind in the industry due to the mass effect it takes on selection, implementation, and training, especially with larger companies. By the time a company has integrated a new product into their business model, the next latest and greatest piece of technology is released. Spencer explained that "the first and often largest pain point for system selection/implementation is time. One of the things your business can consider is people who specialize in this process such as a consulting firm that will guide your company from start to finish allowing very little disruption to your operation. Another large pain point for selection is ease of transition over long-term viability. Many times, companies will opt for the less invasive and typically an older technology option to not disrupt their day-to-day operations when in the long run it is likely hurting those same operations. This really boils down to when the company decides to adopt a new technology.

4. **Since you graduated, what are some of the major things you have learned professionally?**

   From a management standpoint, over the last four years I have learned A LOT through my successes and failures as a professional in the start-up industry. Being a part of a brand new company has allowed me to have a more hands-on approach in building the structure and foundation of our processes, which has been a constant lesson in finding out what works and what doesn't work with our business model. Creating standardization and enforcing communication has taught me a lot about how to manage a business effectively. From a technical perspective, creating automation in your systems is extremely important when it comes to managing and organizing your data. To take it a step further, implementing systems that have the ability to integrate with each other is extremely important. It allows a company to follow a streamline process from start to finish as well as create summary reporting that allows the firm to save money and time while staying on top of critical issues due to the reporting features available within the systems.

5. How do you keep current?

- Conferences—HITEC, FSTEC, MURTEC, etc. (when able to attend)
- Hospitality Upgrade—Magazine
- HFTP—Published materials available on Web site
- CES—Also a conference, but a lot of new tech is announced here
- Many tech Web sites, The Verge, CNET News, CNN Tech, Forbes Tech News, etc.

6. What advice do you have for future managers?

Patience! Patience is so key in this high-paced, organized chaos, and "on your toes" industry. It is important to realize the reason why you implement technology in your businesses. Is it to define your structure? Is it to be able to track your numbers more efficiently? Is it to save time and manual error? These are important questions to ask yourself prior to moving forward in your choices. The next step is to understand that it will take time; the research, demos, and testing are only the beginning. Once you have decided on a program that fits your business goals, your team must be trained on the ins and outs of the system from the back-end setup to front-end user experience. The final and most time-consuming step is the actual implementation into your company. Even if every step is followed correctly, it still takes time for your end users to develop an intuitive approach to your new systems. Did you ever pick up a piece of new technology or open a new program and know how to work the entire system immediately? No, so patience is key!

Interview used with permission of Susan Patterson

1. Overview

Susan introduces us to some great themes on system selection in our industry. Notice how she also sought help when needed. Technology is vast. Colleagues and networks can really help. Making a purchasing decision relative to a strategic investment in corporate information systems is very different than a consumer technology purchase. When people buy consumer technology, they often tend to start any discussion about which alternative to purchase with a question along the lines of "Which smart phone is best?" The natural follow-up to this is "How much does the best one cost?" followed quickly by "How much do the other ones cost?" And so goes most of the selection process when it comes to buying anything from iPads to automobiles.

As technology consumers, people are programmed to think of quality and functionality as being somehow related, and, at the same time, they equate the most functionality with the best. Although there may be a great deal of validity to this type of thinking, when it comes to purchasing a tablet, it is often misplaced in the world of business-based information systems. This is because when it comes to acquiring technology for your hotel, restaurant, or any other business, it is not nearly as important to get lots of functionality as it is to get the right functionality for your business.

2. Reducing Expenses and Increasing Profits

The single most important thing to remember when you think about strategic investments in hospitality information technology (IT) is that these investments must generate a positive **return on investment (ROI)** just like any other strategic corporate purchase. In the past, many technology vendors and professionals have tried numerous arguments for why technology investments cannot be measured against a quantitative yardstick for ROI. These arguments are all weak at best and more often simply the result of laziness and ineptitude. This section will discuss ROI first in its most simplistic terms, and then in a more detailed manner.

One thing to always remember is that in order for an IT system to generate a positive ROI, it must either reduce costs or increase revenue in some quantifiable way. If a hospitality professional never remembers anything about detailed ROI calculations or information system minutia, he or she can always fall back on this most basic premise. If an IT system is worthy of the investment required to implement it, the proponent of that system must be able to quantify in a demonstrably objective manner the approximate value of specific savings (i.e., decreased expenses) and/or increased profits that the system will generate.

If you always think about strategic technology investments in terms of increased profits or decreased expenses, you will tend to make better purchase decisions. The problem is that quantifying cash flow based on a system's purported functionality takes time and effort for which many people do not have the skill or aptitude. It is not in the scope of this chapter to make you an expert in performing such calculations personally, but the following precepts should provide you with the knowledge necessary to make someone else (i.e., the system vendor's salesperson or your accountant) perform an accurate and objective analysis for you.

Decreased Expenses

Decreased expenses, or cost savings, are generally the first element of **payback** or when the purchase actually pays for itself either through new revenue or cost savings those systems try to achieve. Whenever the discussion of decreased expenses begins, business managers have a habit of thinking immediately of staff reductions. This is not completely unwarranted in the hospitality industry because staffing is usually one of the largest controllable costs. In restaurants, labor can be anywhere from 20 to 35 percent of total revenue. In hotels, when the **fixed costs** associated with property depreciation and other fixed asset depreciation and maintenance are excluded, staffing is usually the single largest cost element. Information systems are very often used to make manual processes more efficient or automate labor-intensive tasks, and labor cost is the one cost element that needs to be considered when assessing IT investments.

Implementing information systems that provide increased productivity can certainly lead to dramatic reductions in labor costs. However, decreased expenses associated with new IT can come in many shapes and sizes, and labor is not the only place operators can save money from new IT.

1. New technology can decrease the cost of maintaining systems. For instance, newer computer platforms that are more reliable perform better and have higher availability of cheap repair parts, and labor can significantly reduce the cost of hardware maintenance contracts. Other platforms include IOS with cheaper and sometimes even free apps available, usually for a fixed time period.
2. **Recipe management software** can help operators develop recipes that use even quantities of bulk ingredients and therefore reduce food costs by eliminating waste. However, this may not be a solution for higher-end establishments who need quality ingredients.
3. Periodic maintenance systems for kitchen equipment, HVAC, and other fixed assets can significantly reduce the operating costs of these systems.
4. Power control systems designed to monitor electrical usage and turn lights off when a room is vacant or cool buildings earlier in the day can significantly reduce electrical power consumption costs.

There are two important things to remember when looking at potential cost savings provided by an information system:

1. Fixed costs don't usually go down (that's why they are called fixed).
2. Each hotel, restaurant, and club has a unique cost structure.

Every corporate entity in the world has fixed and variable costs. Many times in hospitality, fixed costs are associated with guest service requirements that are not negotiable based on the organization's market position. As a result, a system may be capable of reducing the labor required to perform certain tasks, but may not generate any savings as a result.

For instance, imagine that a vendor can clearly demonstrate that a system reduces the time required to perform some task by 50 percent (from six labor hours to three labor hours). On the surface, this reduction would mean that the system saves $8 per hour multiplied by three hours multiplied by 365 days per year, or a total of about $8,750 per year (plus overhead and benefits). If the system only cost $10,000, this would appear to be a great deal, or would it? What if your hotel is a small, high-end property and you always have two people on duty at night because guests expect immediate attention twenty-four hours a day? Or maybe, it is a low-end hotel in a very bad neighborhood and you always have two people on duty at night for safety reasons. Now imagine that the task in question is performed by the night shift crew, which is otherwise unoccupied for the majority of its shift. In this scenario, even though the system can be clearly shown to reduce labor requirements, because the cost of maintaining the night shift is a fixed cost, and because those resources are not utilized 100 percent in the existing scenario, it is possible that implementing the new system could result in a $10,000 investment with no appreciable cost savings (and therefore a negative ROI).

Increased Gross Profits

There are two important concepts to remember when analyzing a system's potential to increase gross profits.

1. The assessment must include only increases in gross profit, not **gross revenue**. Gross revenue is total sales. Gross profit subtracts expenses or direct costs from gross revenue. Therefore, expenses from the new purchase must be considered.
2. The assessment must be limited to only those gross profits that are directly attributable to the new system and would not be achieved without the system.

Take particular note of the fact that this section is captioned "Increased Gross Profits" and not "Increased Revenue." All too often technology purchasing agents focus on revenue enhancement, probably at least in part because that is how vendors advertise. In fact, in a properly prepared ROI calculation, revenue exists only in the supporting detailed data. The actual top line ROI calculation is only concerned with increased gross profits.

When analyzing investments, remember that **gross profits** are equal to gross revenue less direct costs. If we use gross revenue in our ROI assessments, potential investments will look much more favorable than they actually are. This is an important point to remember because vendor advertisements for systems rarely include a complete ROI calculation, but very often highlight increased revenue. It is not uncommon to hear someone say, "I installed this new system and my sales went up X percent." The problem with this line of reasoning is that although it is appealing on the surface to say revenues are going up, without knowing the full cost of generating those revenues, it is impossible to determine if the system was a good deal or not.

For example, assume that the cost of implementing a new spa management system is $20,000. To objectively determine whether the new system would help book $50,000 per year in additional spa revenue, you would need to look at the details. If the spa is staffed internally and generates a 50 percent gross margin on every treatment sold, then the $25,000 first-year return makes the purchase decision very easy (assuming all of the projections are verifiable). However, if the spa is run on a contract basis with a 10 percent royalty on total sales, the annual payback of $5,000 may or may not justify a $20,000 investment (depending on the cost of capital and other factors). Although this example is obviously oversimplified, the concept holds true for all forms of potential increased revenue. You must convert incremental gross revenue projections to incremental gross profits before you can assess the potential value of a new information system.

3. System Examples

Different types of systems can generate various forms of revenue for an establishment. Depending on what the system is designed to do, IT can result in higher unit sales volumes or increased gross margins.

Revenue management systems can generate higher gross margins on room revenues while **restaurant menu management systems** can generate higher gross margins on food items by substituting less costly ingredients or by using historical sales data to accomplish the following:

- Develop more effective pricing strategies (e.g., menu mix)
- Create a more effective menu mix
- Schedule employees more efficiently within a shared app or online
- Improve functionality for offering and controlling promotions (e.g., buy one get one or happy hour pricing)
- Process credit, debit, gift cards, and mobile payments more efficiently
- Improve functionality for cross-marketing other services to existing customers (generate social networking coupon for other company-owned restaurants)
- Increase covers or average checks through the implementation of the new system (and by how much)

When analyzing the potential revenue increase, remember to attempt to identify an increase resulting only from the implementation of the new system. Any forecasted revenue increase due to other reasons, such as a change in the market, must be excluded. This is especially difficult if you plan to monitor the system benefits after conversion because additional revenue attributed only to the system is very difficult to quantify.

4. Cash Flow and Costs

There are many formulas for calculating specific cash flow relative to different types of investments, and a good technology investment can and should be reduced to a financial investment equation before a purchase decision is made.

$$ROI = (Increased\ Profits + Decreased\ Costs)/Investment$$
$$all\ cash\ flow\ must\ be\ adjusted\ for\ time\ and\ the\ cost\ of\ capital$$

There may be additional costs associated with operating the new system. These could include the following:

- Hardware/software maintenance due to automating a manual system or an increase over the old system
- Additional labor due to a short-term decrease in productivity after conversion (to be added to the up-front cost since it typically affects costs only during the first year)
- Costs of converting any exhibiting or historical data
- Costs of interfacing the system with other existing applications or mobile devices
- Communication costs
- Consulting services

There are a number of different things to consider when determining the total cost for a new system. The projections should include all costs associated with the project including purchase price, implementation, and training. Some examples might include the following:

Application software/mobile app	Operating systems/mobile OS
Network operating system workstations/mobility	Cabling and/or access points (cost of cable and cost of installation)
Servers/cloud storage	Printers
Uninterrupted power supply (UPS)	Backup system
Network training	Application training
Shipping	Hardware training
Consulting services	Furniture (new, replaced, modified, or constructed)
Additional payroll during training and conversion	System selection costs

Although hard cost savings are the numbers that most companies focus on when determining whether or not to move forward with a new IT project, there are other intangible or soft benefits that need to be considered as well. These might include benefits such as improved guest service, employee morale, or image in the marketplace. Although they cannot be included in the calculation, they are very important factors that need to be taken into account. Some examples include the following:

- Better morale from use of a more user-friendly system
- Overall improved productivity from a more efficient system
- Improved job retention rates due to higher overall job satisfaction

5. System Selection Process

Although the details of how to specify and select an information system are beyond the scope of this chapter, a discussion of the basic system selection process is necessary to fully understand how IT investments are made. The system selection process described here has nine steps. Although many of these steps can be performed in parallel, it is important that each is performed and that step 1 be completed before any other step in the process begins.

1. Verify/develop the conceptual design for the enterprise
2. Define functional and system requirements for the component application(s) and create organizational consensus on the requirements
3. Compile a request for proposal (RFP)
4. Develop a vendor short list
5. Solicit proposals
6. Assess proposals against criteria
7. Visit reference sites
8. Have vendors provide demonstrations
9. Final selection

Verify/Develop the Conceptual Design for the Enterprise

Selecting a particular system (POS, PMS, CRM, mobile app, or anything else) without first having reviewed the long-term IT strategy for the entire enterprise is like buying a pair of suit pants without knowing if you have a jacket, tie, or shirt that goes with them. They may be the best pants you've ever bought, but if you can't wear them with anything you own, you've effectively either forced yourself to spend money on items you hadn't planned to purchase or wasted whatever money you spent on the pants. So it is with information systems that each application should fit into an overall plan designed to effectively leverage your use of information to create additional shareholder value.

The world of information capture (collection), processing, storing, and reporting can be, and should be, divided along the same lines as functional operations within the enterprise. One example of how to do this is to divide all your business functions into a matrix, as shown in Figure 11-1.

A soon-to-reopen hotel might purchase many systems that require integration with existing hardware and infrastructure. The hotel wishes to integrate as much of the existing architecture as possible with the new purchases. What requirements of the system and captured data would integrate with what you already have? This is the endeavor of the matrix. Some of the fields have been filled in to serve as a guide in helping you tackle the remaining fields.

All too often, the critical first step is ignored. This is especially true when outside consultants are brought in to assist or when insiders from a single department or business unit perform the selection without interdepartmental involvement. It is absolutely critical to ensure that this first step is performed completely and with a solid look towards future operational and competitive requirements. Additionally, knowing

Functional Area	Specific Capability Requirements	Associated Data Capture Requirements	Involved Systems/Technologies
Unit Operations: Front Office F&B Housekeeping Reservations Engineering			Entire hotel network
Retail Operations (i.e., gift and pro shop)	Standard POS capabilities plus CRM	All relevant fields captured by credit card data with the addition of number of purchases to date and additional preference fields left blank to be named and utilized at a later date	None, however integration with the PMS is needed
Human Resource Management	Live updates on the Web—a must in addition to standard features	All relevant fields from I-9 IRS forms with the addition of property and department-specific fields	Payroll (electronic data interchange)
Financial Management and Control			
Communications			
Decision Support			Revenue, yield management, and CRM

FIGURE 11-1
Purchasing a new system requires proper planning. A matrix can help keep information organized.

your business today is unfortunately not enough. The successful purchaser will have an eye towards the future. Presentation on a mobile device must be the same as a workstation. Notice the "Retail Operations" section under "Associated Data Capture Requirements;" you do not know all the data fields to be captured that may be needed in the future, so you leave some room by requesting that certain fields be left blank on all devices and able to be named and used at a later date. Not all vendors will allow forward-looking requirements; however, it is vital to negotiate in what you can. As an operational efficiency and cost-saving measure, all systems and matrix-oriented decisions should follow this forward-looking thought process. You could thank yourself one day for the right decisions you made years ago and avoid having to purchase a whole new system.

The end-product(s) of this first step should, at a minimum, include a list of component applications that will be required to create the entire enterprise's information infrastructure, and a solid idea of the system architecture (including communications backbone) that will be used to host and integrate each of the component applications.

Define Functional and System Requirements for the Component Application(s) and Create Organizational Consensus on the Requirements

Once a long-term strategy and architecture for the entire enterprise have been developed and agreed upon, the task of selecting a particular component application can begin in earnest. Although the top-level or basic functional and system requirements for each component application should flow from the conceptual enterprise design, the detailed list of requirements necessary to properly evaluate alternative applications must be defined separately for each system. There are several key strategies that are worth employing during this step:

- Don't let management pick the new system. Create a system selection team and solicit both input and active involvement from the people who will actually have to use it. It is always best if you can select several informal leaders early in the process and win them over as champions of the new system by involving them in the selection process.

- It rarely makes good business sense to automate inefficient processes or move it into an app. More to the point, many of the system selection processes are often hampered by the identification of requirements whose only purpose is to preserve some non-value-added function within the organization. A key element of any system requirements definition process is the ability to objectively analyze the processes the system is designed to support and ensure that those processes are designed as efficiently as possible.

- Ensure involvement from multiple departments or business units within the organization (even if it appears as though only one unit is really affected or owns the system).

- Clearly define exactly what you need, or you will never be able to accurately or objectively compare which vendor's application is best suited to your business. You should not let your staff begin any serious conversation with any single vendor until you have developed a list of specific requirements.

- Most organizations purchase any type of application once in a long while and then use/ amortize it for several years. As a result, the level of knowledge of what is available is relatively low. It is worthwhile to attend a trade show or seminar or spend some time doing research (in-house or with a consultant) so you have an up-to-date perspective of what functional capabilities you should legitimately expect from your new system.

- As you speak with internal staff about requirements, remember to keep expectations in check. There are systems and vendors available that will do anything you want, but everything comes at a cost. When you start thinking about adding "customization" to a packaged system so that you can meet everyone's requirements, you add to the cost of the system.

One approach to defining and building consensus about requirements uses the following steps:

- Speak to colleagues and read articles about systems that have been recently installed in business units similar to your own. Use this research to identify common features expected to be in any system.

- Refer to your own enterprise system design documents in advance to identify minimal system and functional requirements (show stoppers) that any system you select will need to have.

- Speak informally with one or more vendors (preferably at a trade show or seminar where you can see many vendors' applications in a short period of time), and develop a list of features and functions that appear to be of value for your business.

- Combine all of the preceding to create a master requirements list. You can then use this master list as a group facilitation tool when you start to meet with members of your selection team.

- When meeting with members of your team, allow them to think out of the box and identify new functionality or features, but remind them constantly that everything comes with a price tag and the perfect system they want may not exist.

- Each requirement identified by the group should be prioritized, either relative to other requirements or against some absolute scale. Many people prefer using a scale of 1 to 5, where 5 is a show stopper, 3 is a legitimate need with the potential to add some value, and 1 is a desire with little or no chance of impacting system implementation.

The final output of these steps should be a complete and prioritized list of specific functional and system requirements for the component application.

Compile a Request for Proposal (RFP)

If a solid enterprise-level strategy and conceptual design have been complemented by a set of clearly defined component application functional and system requirements, compiling an RFP should be relatively simple. Please refer to the RFP appendix for a detailed model. There are several elements worth noting for inclusion:

- Never sign a contract that includes customization on a fee basis. If the system you are purchasing cannot meet all of your organization's requirements out of the box or downloaded, then your vendor should provide a firm fixed-price agreement to make the necessary modifications.

- Place all of your system and functional requirements in a numbered outline, matrix, or some other format that forces each vendor to address each requirement specifically and discretely.

- Always make the vendor include a clearly defined timetable for customization and implementation. Ensure the proposed contract documents include a process for remedy if the vendor does not meet the proposed delivery schedule.

- Make each vendor specifically address such support issues as training, help desk, mobility, and remote and local software maintenance.

- Make each vendor provide both a historic and a forward-looking build schedule. The historic build schedule should include a notation as to whether builds released during the previous twenty-four months were released on schedule or delayed. Make each vendor supply a specific statement as to whether future builds are included in maintenance costs. All mobile OS are to be included or at a minimum, dictate which one is the default.

- Make each vendor supply cost information using the same format (provided by your company in the RFP). This prohibits vendors from burying costs in different places and thereby making your selection process more difficult.

Develop a Vendor Short List

Developing a vendor short list can be both the easiest and the most short-sighted step in the system selection process. It can be the easiest because you can simply make a list of several systems that you have seen in advertisements and know about. It can be the most short-sighted because you may feel tempted to include any one of the many new and vastly improved products that enter the marketplace every day. Good places to start for lists and further information in this industry are the vendors listed with the AH&LA (American Hotel & Lodging Association) and the HFTP (Hospitality Financial and Technology Professionals) organization as well as the magazines *Hospitality Upgrade* and *Hospitality Technology*.

Developing a short list of vendors *before* sending out an RFP is an important element of the system selection process for any organization that purchases multiple systems. The reason is that if you constantly ask a long list of vendors to spend their time and resources responding to RFPs and proposing systems, they have little chance of being selected to provide; your organization will lose the credibility necessary to exact complete and earnest responses from multiple vendors.

There are several rules of thumb that people often refer to in the vendor selection process, but in the end, all of them are rules of thumb, none are cast in stone, and rules can never take the place of good old fashioned research.

One approach to narrowing the field of potential vendors that seems to work well uses the following steps:

- Refer to one or more well-maintained databases of systems like the one you are selecting. (A caution on databases and buyer's guides: the vendors listed in them often fund these guides. There may be several good vendors that do not appear in the guide you are using; therefore, it is important to use either multiple guides or a comprehensive database that does not rely on vendor advertisements for funding.)

- Use the databases to identify a list of vendor systems most likely to match your organization's system and functional requirements.

- Send a *request for information (RFI)* to those vendors that you think are the most suited to your needs. (The purpose of an **RFI** is to provide vendors a low-cost, low-effort means to supply just the information necessary for you to know if they should be on the short list.) Some basic questions that should be included in an RFI refer back to some of those rules of thumb such as the following.

- Can the vendor provide a list of reference installations similar in size and operation to yours, and is the vendor willing to provide a point of contact at each?

- How long has the vendor been in business and can the vendor demonstrate his or her company's financial stability? (Financial stability and time in market should not be sole determining factors for the nonselection of any vendor, but they are elements of risk that stakeholders should be aware of in advance of making a selection decision.)

- Use RFI responses and interviews with reference installations to narrow your list of vendors to five or fewer vendors who appear capable, responsive, and responsible.

Solicit Proposals

Soliciting proposals from good vendors is not as easy as you might expect. Vendors with good systems are in high demand and their ability to hire and train additional technical staff is limited by a global shortage of skilled IT personnel. As a result, writing detailed proposals and estimating the cost of significant customizations require the allocation of valuable people who could be working on other (profitable) projects.

You should therefore not expect good vendors to answer detailed RFPs in an unrealistic time frame. This often requires more advanced planning than most organizations are able to muster. It is not unrealistic to include an eight-week period for vendors to respond to your RFP. This is not because it takes eight weeks for a vendor to write a complete response. More often, it is because it takes four weeks for a vendor to determine that your project is worth dedicating the necessary resources to pursue and to ask all the additional questions and clarifications needed to answer your RFP accurately.

Assess Proposals against Criteria

Two critical elements of this phase are objectivity and sensitivity analysis.

One approach is to simply start by using the functionality matrix developed during the requirements stage, and ask each member of the selection team to grade each response on a scale of 1 to 5. It is important to make each individual grade each proposal independently. The purpose of independent evaluations instead of a group evaluation in a large meeting is twofold. The first problem with group evaluation is that some of the people will not read all of the proposals thoroughly. The second problem is that some people will allow their own perceptions to be changed without reason.

Eventually, however, the entire team should meet to discuss the results of the individual evaluations and attempt to reach a general consensus on the merits of each vendor's application relative to the specific criteria identified in your RFP. The important point during this meeting is to gain consensus on each specific functional requirement before allowing the conversation to veer towards whose proposal was best. In this respect, it is often of value if the manager responsible for the selection process has somebody to collect and compile all the individual evaluations from team members in advance.

Depending on the size and complexity of the project, the use of simple spreadsheets or complex decision support tools can be of great value. For smaller projects, it is easy to lay out individual evaluations, calculate average scores, and visually see how consistent various team member evaluations were. For larger more-complex projects, it may be appropriate to aggregate scores by category of requirement and then determine the average score and standard deviation for each category of requirements.

For smaller projects, placing the average scores in the same spreadsheet as priority for each requirement will quickly generate an objective score for each vendor's proposal. For larger projects, it may be helpful to use a decision support tool that allows you to build a requirements model and then perform sensitivity analysis on your results. The sensitivity analysis allows the selection team to see what the impacts of various requirement prioritization and/or scoring decisions are on the model's outcome. This is very helpful because it allows you to avoid lengthy discussions about decisions that do not change the model's outcome.

Visit Reference Sites

No matter how close or lopsided the results of your proposal evaluations are, you should always visit at least one vendor reference site for each of your top choices. Even if it is a mobile app, you still want to go to see how it works "in house." In addition, you should speak at length with several others via telephone if you don't have the time or resources to visit them.

It is important to bring your prioritized requirements matrix with you when you visit or call the vendor's reference installation sites and to have the same group of people make each visit or phone call.

In addition to seeing if the system truly does all the things you need it to do, some questions you should ask the people at the reference site are the following:

- Did the vendor install the system in accordance with the schedule laid out in the proposal, and if not, was the delay caused by the vendor or the customer?
- Has the vendor supplied the system in accordance with a reliable schedule?
- Have software and hardware maintenance fee increases been reasonable and predictable?
- Does the vendor provide reliable support in terms of help desk availability, on-site hardware service, and other factors? How often does the customer spend extended periods of time on hold, or wait a day and a half for a four-hour on-site service?

It is important to visit at least one installation site that is similar to yours. It is acceptable if one site is similar in size and another is a similar type of operation. If, however, the only reference installations the vendor can provide are for enterprises either significantly smaller or those that do completely different things than yours, you ought to consider the additional risk involved in migrating and/or scaling a system from one business to another.

Have Vendors Provide Demonstrations

The key to vendor demonstrations is to ensure that you do not buy a system based on the appearance or sales skills of the person presenting the demonstration. The reality in most instances is that the company purchasing a new system is replacing an old, much less functional system. As a result, a good salesperson could make almost any vendor's application look incredibly functional and robust to a room full of operators who have been working with dated technology for several years. It is important to remove this element of subjectivity from the equation.

The simplest way to make vendor demonstrations more useful and informative is to confine the vendor to a script. A favorite is the ice skating analogy:

- Each vendor has 40 (80 or 120 depending on the complexity of the system) minutes to walk you through a series of functions that you have scripted out (based on your RFP and functional requirements document).
- Following the 40-minute compulsory presentation, each vendor gets an additional 20 (40 or 60) minutes to provide a freestyle explanation of what makes his or her solution uniquely suited to your business.

By making the vendors stick to a tightly written and consistent script, you can be sure that each member of the team has the opportunity to personally verify that the vendor's system does in fact perform all of the functions identified in your requirements document. In addition to making sure you will receive what you think you are buying, this element of universal team verification and engagement is often critical to a successful rollout.

A note on vendor demonstrations: Don't ask a vendor to spend the time and money necessary to come to your site and perform a demonstration if you have not determined that this vendor has a viable and competitive alternative for your application. If you have narrowed the field to two vendors that you believe are head and shoulders above the competition in terms of being perfectly suited for your business, you should not ask other vendors to do demonstrations.

Companies will often have policies requiring the comparison of at least three systems to ensure competitive pricing. This is not a bad policy, but analyzing three alternative proposals does not mean making a vendor you have no intention of selecting spend thousands of dollars to do a demonstration.

Final Selection

Assuming that the vendor's demonstration verifies the information presented in his or her proposal, the final selection process is a foregone conclusion. In cases where the demonstration reveals weaknesses in a particular vendor's application that were not evident (or simply glossed over) in the proposal, final selection is less easy.

If you have more than three good candidates that came out of the proposal analyses (scoring) stage and only one was eliminated during the vendor demonstration, then you might choose to reconvene the selection team to discuss the other alternatives. In the end though, no matter how many selection committees are formed and how much input is received, the manager responsible for the system selection process has to be both willing and able to make a decision.

The final note on system selection is not much different than the final note on buying a car: You have to be willing to walk away. All too often in this business, you find yourself driven by the lure of being one step ahead of the competition, by the dull whine of Wall Street for any kind of news, or simply by employee complaints to jump into system acquisitions that do not make sense. During the past years, businesses within every vertical market segment have scrambled to increase capital spending on IT, particularly in digital marketing, often with very little real increase in shareholder value or corporate productivity. We now see software prices either stagnating or, in some cases, decreasing as rapidly as hardware prices. If the system you want is not available today at a reasonable price, wait twelve months and try again. Maybe concentrating on the free social networks for a year to the utmost and waiting for new software could be the way to go? It's better to have done the analyses twice and made a good investment, than to have done the analyses once and made a poor one.

6. Implementation

Now that you have purchased the correct system, a proper implementation procedure needs to be adopted whether it is hardware or software. There are ten steps.

1. Choose a project manager from your existing staff. This may or may not be the person who headed up the selection process. As hard as it may be, this must be a capable person who must be relieved of daily duties and given the lead to serve as your liaison with the vendor's project manager. This person is now the boss and your lifeline to the project's implementation. The project manager will take charge of the remaining steps in cooperation with your entire staff.

2. Set a schedule. This covers coordinating and confirming the specific delivery of the product and associated dates and any needed supplemental items. The contract and vendor schedule needs to be understood. What may be a good date for the vendor may not be for you. Implementation should be done at off hours

and off peaks so as not to affect business operations. Weekend nights are often a good time for business hotels, whereas restaurants might want to find a slow weekday. Resorts can adopt a new system during off seasons as can sports arenas and convention centers.

3. Establish a training system. Before tackling your own property, send a select group of staff from various departments to your vendor's site for initial training. From there, develop a training schedule for your property. When will it occur? For how long? What compensation will be given? How about perks? Training can be both a nice break from the daily grind and a chore. Try to make it as comfortable as possible. Training in the hospitality industry is often an afterthought due to high turnover. However, the greatest system in the world is useless if no one knows how to use it. Training needs to be taken very seriously or else all of the careful analysis up to this point can go up in smoke.

4. Meet with the vendor and exchange notes on steps 1 through 3. Resolve any issues to date and request specific information from the vendor on what to expect from the system and related elements during the upcoming time period. Communicate these facts to all involved to keep them in the loop.

5. Stop and analyze. This may seem like a good step to skip. However, you are approaching the point of no return—the implementation phase. Is everything and everyone ready? Has a contingency plan been put in place? An example may be paper records and systems/or cloud storage. Likewise, a good rule of thumb is to contact all the stakeholders in the company and remind them in the next few days you are adopting a new system and apologize in advance for any unwelcome occurrences.

6. Start implementation in *one* department. This entire department must adopt the new system. Old ways of doing things replaced by the new system must be discarded. The system must be totally embraced by all. Those in this first department will serve as additional trainers on the new system and importantly play the role of cheerleaders for future departments. These are the people who can spread the word that it wasn't so bad. Keep in mind that change is difficult and that people are creatures of habit. It is important to win allies early.

7. Stop and analyze. Has the new system affected the processing power of any in-place systems? For example, oftentimes new software may take up precious processing power of the CPUs involved to the detriment of other applications. Take care in monitoring all of the systems. It may surprise you that even the climate control systems may have to be fine-tuned to accommodate new additions. Your model for the new system's implementation is being set. Human comfort and settings deserve proper attention, particularly if the system is to be used for long hours.

8. Move on to the next department. With all the expertise and experience gained to date, the next department is usually easier. The important component here is to monitor the communication of the system between these first two departments. Is your network being adversely affected? For example, complex database queries of your entire customer database or large mobile video viewing, can tie up a network. Additionally, the connection to your outside network needs to be tested.

9. Stop and analyze again. Again? Yes, the third time is the charm and is critical since enterprise or companywide implementation is next. You are about to turn your whole location over to a new system (if your whole property is involved) and want to make sure that everything is okay.

10. Rollout the system propertywide.

Following these steps is safe and efficient. Oftentimes business requirements and the fast-moving nature of this industry can truncate some of these processes. Stay with these steps as best you can to avoid problems.

7. Summary

Judging by the amount and different types of technology used in the hospitality industry and presented in Chapters 1 through 10, it seems that every current and future manager must have a solid technological knowledge base. However, just as important, a manager must understand business. During the past in hospitality, many purchasing decisions were based on neat features and functionality of a proposed system under the assumption that future profits would appear one day. During this period, owners were often scared that if they did not have the current technology, their customers would go elsewhere. Many purchases refused to bear fruit. Today, with big data, the Internet of things, and digital marketing, new fears are arising. However, those in charge of making purchases have hopefully gone back to basics. Advancements in technology are still respected, such as mobility; however, business considerations come first. Simply put, any new system needs to either increase revenue or reduce costs. Understanding and utilizing financial metrics and definitions such as ROI and differing cost and profit structures are again the norm for management.

Hospitality is a fast-paced industry where wants and needs of any new purchase often boil down to something that works. Given the capabilities and price tags of solutions available in the marketplace today, more understanding is necessary. In reaching a determination on the potential purchase, a detailed system selection process is needed. From the beginning of the process where exact needs are established, to site visits of the system in use at the end of the process, all steps along the way are crucial and related. This is equally important in the implementation stage where analysis and testing are done along the many steps before it is committed companywide.

With understanding, proper usage, and analysis of the particulars presented in this chapter, the next technology purchase can be a successful one.

8. CASE STUDY AND LEARNING ACTIVITY

Case Study

The "411" on ROI

Let's take another look at ROI in this write-up on specific hospitality IT purchases from a leading IT consultant.

By Michael DiLeva

When proposing or developing an Information Technology project, there are plenty of acronyms that will be the center of the conversation, such as SaS, AI, PMS, POS, CRM, IP, and HDMI. The one acronym that we discussed in this chapter may be overlooked early in the process is ROI—Return on Investment.

Source: Case Study The "411" On ROI by Michael DiLeva

Unfortunately, the actual implementation and ongoing support of a hospitality IT project is a piece of cake compared to the challenge of estimating ROI. Of course, it's always difficult to model and project the future success of any effort or investment. But projecting IT ROI in hospitality, however, is further complicated by the fact that, when compared to other industries or businesses, hospitality often adds at least one additional layer to the decision-making process in the form of an owner, management group, asset manager, or even the franchisor. So not only are there often more constituents that need to be considered, but also all of those involved or impacted by the project may have differing—and sometimes even conflicting—goals and may be measured (and even compensated) differently.

So where to begin? The best place to start is to either conduct a self-analysis on your true motivations for the project

or document the goals of the sponsoring party if the technology request is coming from an external department. While it sounds overly simplistic, this initial step should help to flush out one of the most common pitfalls of an IT project—that the overall goals were not properly defined. Often, this step will also highlight if the project is merely "technology for technology's sake," or "we have to get a mobile app," or is designed to solve a real need, or to advance a core objective of the organization. While not as prevalent in today's era of tight budgets and reduced capital expenditures, recent history is dotted with examples of hotel companies and hotel executives pushing a technology project because of trade publication "buzz," because a competitor was doing it or because the nuances of the technology or product appealed to a particular constituent's personal interests—all of which are recipes for failure.

As an example of how differing constituents often have different objectives or areas of focus, some owners, asset managers, or controllers may be focused entirely on financial returns and have little interest in a project that does not offer a very high likelihood of crossing a particular hurdle rate (a minimum accepted rate of return). Other owners may take a more strategic and less financially focused approach towards IT investments and be willing to approve them if they improve the guest experience or increase the prestige of the property. Operations staff may be advocating a project for its impact on their particular area, such as its ability to assist them in meeting their operational goals (such as average speed to answer via an app) and not necessarily on how those goals translate to financial benefit.

Generally, project goals can be characterized as either quantitative (i.e., measurable) or qualitative (i.e., more related to "quality" and as such more indistinct and subject to broad interpretation). Examples of common IT investments and their goals include:

Investment	Goal(S)
Energy Management Systems	Reducing energy expenditures
Check-In/Out Kiosks and Mobile Apps	Reducing guest wait times or front desk and speedier service
Online Booking Software	Reducing booking costs or improving the ease of guest bookings
Maintenance Software Systems	Reducing parts or materials inventory or reducing maintenance cycles
Interactive Television	Eliminating printed materials or automating/digitizing services
Revenue Management Systems	Increasing ADR
Cloud Storage	Reducing maintenance and energy costs
Wi-Fi Upgrade	Maintaining viable systems architecture or enabling other IT options

For investments with Quantitative goals, identifying the precise goal for the project is relatively easy. Tracked metrics like ADR, speed-to-answer, and others easily lend themselves to specific numerical goals (increase 10%, decrease 20%, etc.). For investments with Qualitative goals, like "improving guest service," projecting returns is challenging, but not insurmountable. In these scenarios, it's best to attempt to identify any areas where such objectives are measured and guest surveys are the perfect place to start. Usually there are overall categories that summarize guest satisfaction and often such categories include specific queries on the very area that you're attempting to influence. For example, if implementing new check-n/check-out kiosks, an appropriate goal would be to increase the guest survey score on the question of "How was your check-in process" from an average of 3.9 to 4.25.

After all of this talk about the "Return" component of ROI, however, there are some points to keep in mind regarding the "Investment" component. "Investment" goes far beyond the price quote provided by your technology vendor or the bottom line figure on your purchase order. As was stated in this chapter, often, projects involve a myriad of "hidden" costs that, while not immediately evident when contemplating the initiative, nonetheless have a substantial impact.

Some other examples and re-emphasis include:

- **Training:** Is training on the proper use of the new system included in the bid and have you adequately accounted for the costs for associates to participate in training sessions (either in actual "hard" costs in wages paid during training sessions or the "opportunity" cost associated with the tasks that will need to be covered by others while staff is in training)? These include training on both using the technology and communicating the technology to the end user (i.e., the guest).
- **Maintenance:** Have all of the future maintenance requirements been fully identified?
- **Infrastructure:** Are there any infrastructure upgrades (e.g., HVAC, wiring, network) that are required for the new technology to operate properly?
- **Marketing:** Are there materials that need to be produced (social media, digital marketing) to advise the guest about the new technology, the benefits, or how to use it (to borrow a phrase from the great baseball movie "Field of Dreams," don't assume that "if you build it, they will come!")?
- **Processes:** Do new policies and procedures need to be developed around the technology (e.g., documenting how housekeepers should properly clean flat-panel televisions or auxiliary media connectivity apparatus)?
- **Legal Fees:** Does your contract require review by outside counsel or does the technology require development of proper legal terms of usage?

With so much to keep in mind, calculating ROI can seem intimidating and may even hinder some projects from ever getting off the drawing board. But as former British prime minister Tony Blair said, "Don't let the perfect be the enemy of the good." No projects ever go exactly as planned and few ROI projections are ever 100 percent accurate. Regardless of up-front projections, for some projects, ultimately breaking even may be viewed as a win.

The key, however, is to conduct proper due diligence up-front, define the project, goals, and expected returns as specifically as possible and ensure that everyone in the team is on the same page. As long as you do that, your project will start with a high likelihood of success—and may even help to make the deployment phase a lot less problematic.

Learning Activity

1. Name three examples of hidden costs.
2. What is the difference between qualitative and quantitative projects?
3. Provide an example of how differing constituents often have different objectives or areas of focus.

9. Key Terms

Fixed costs
Gross profits
Gross revenue
Payback

Recipe management software
Restaurant menu management
  system

Return on investment (ROI)
Request for information (RFI)

10. Chapter Questions

1. What is the difference between an RFI and an RFP?
2. What are the nine steps of system selection?
3. What are the ten steps of implementation?
4. How would you further the ten steps of implementation to multiple sites?
5. How do you calculate ROI?

6. What is the difference between a fixed and a variable cost?
7. Name three factors to be cautious of in system selection.

APPENDIX

XYZ Property Point-of-Sale RFP

Proposals in response to this request for proposal (RFP) are due by close of business on...

CONFIDENTIALITY STATEMENT

This document, its enclosures, attachments, and all other information, spoken or written, made available in regard to any information herein, are confidential and proprietary property of XYZ property. Any disclosure or reproduction of the above-referenced information in a verbal, written, photographed, photocopied, electronic, or other manner, without prior written consent of an officer of XYZ property, is prohibited. Even then, those so authorized may only use the information consistent with the consent and only for purposes of addressing the goals, objectives, and requirements contained within this document. All copies of any portion of this document must include this Confidentiality Statement.

Extreme care should be taken in the methods and locations used to review, discuss, and store this document. By receiving this document you assume full responsibility as outlined in this Confidentiality Statement and agree to be bound by all interpretations thereof. Unauthorized disclosure of the information contained herein as described in the previous paragraph, or as a result of eavesdropping of any type, will be your sole responsibility and punishable by the fullest extent allowable by law.

Table of Contents

Section H: Physical and Environmental Requirements
Section I: Implementation and Training
Section J: Documentation
Section K: System Upgrades
Section L: Contracts
Section M: System Costs

I. INTRODUCTION

A. Scope

Property XYZ is seeking a feature-rich point-of-sale (POS) system that will support the operational requirements for the food and beverage (F&B) outlets as defined in this request for proposal (RFP). This RFP provides the necessary information for you to prepare a proposal and also provides background information about XYZ. The purpose of the RFP is to effect the successful negotiation, execution, and consummation of a definitive agreement between property XYZ and appropriate bidder(s) to provide XYZ with a POS system.

B. Objectives

To select a full-featured POS system that will address not only the standard POS requirements but also the many unique operational needs of a full-service resort like XYZ, at a minimum, the final solution must:

- Provide a quick, simple, and straightforward solution for entering and tendering guest checks using touchscreen technology.
- Be a user-friendly system that is easy to learn and requires minimal training.
- Provide management with effective controls for day-to-day management.
- Provide comprehensive, timely, and accurate information.
- Provide comprehensive and flexible reporting and inquiry capabilities.
- As much as possible, maintain a paperless system for record keeping.
- Function using handheld devices for all pool-side outlets.
- Provide operational flexibility to meet the day-to-day challenges and procedural adjustments typical of a new opening.
- Be fully functional with all staff properly trained by opening day.

Although price is an important factor in this process, XYZ places great importance on the quality and dependability of the products reviewed. To determine the quality of systems proposed, emphasis will be placed on the following factors:

- Stability and soundness of the programs (i.e., full-featured, robust, and proven reliability)
- System integrity and security
- The vendor's reputation for quality hardware, software, and service with existing customers

C. Property Overview

Insert as much detail about your property here. Include physical layout, number on staff, target market, and so on. For our purposes, XYZ is a restaurant in a five hundred–room hotel with a pool and golf course. Management also runs a second hotel, which needs a POS in its restaurant.

D. Project Schedule

The following dates reflect estimated timeframe for POS selection, contract negotiation, and installation for the vendor's use in planning responses. This information is subject to change by XYZ.

Dates	Action
5/27/2019	RFP Sent to Vendors
6/17/2019	RFP Received Back
7/15/2019	Decision Made by Owners

9/1/2019	Contract Signed
9/13/2019	Equipment Ordered
11/15/2019	Installation and Training, site 1
12/15/2019	Grand Opening, site 1
6/1/2020	Equipment Ordered, site 2
8/1/2020	Installation and Training, site 2
10/1/2020	Grand Opening, site 2

E. Bidding Guidelines

The bids and proposals in response to this RFP should comply with the following guidelines:

1. All areas of consideration must be answered concisely, following the directions outlined under each subheading. All statements must be supported with concrete examples or explanations. Ambiguous statements such as "…all reasonable support" are not acceptable.

2. Vendors who wish to provide information that is not addressed in the RFP are encouraged to do so as an addendum to the proposal. We realize that the approach of each potential vendor will be unique. We have therefore attempted to present the specifications in general terms. Points that we feel are essential, however, are presented in detail.

3. Vendors are encouraged to provide any additional information, insight, thought, and ideas on how the vendor can help XYZ succeed with this project.

4. XYZ reserves the right to introduce additional factors not contained in this RFP in order to obtain the most suitable solution. After submitting a proposal, each vendor must be prepared to have the operational aspects of their proposed system reviewed in detail by XYZ representatives. A portion of this review may be requested without vendor presence.

5. Questions regarding any information herein should be directed to the project manager from XYZ. Vendors must not contact any XYZ employees directly.

6. Vendors judged to be the most qualified to fulfill XYZ's requirements will be invited to visit for further discussions. This meeting will include a demonstration of the proposed system. At this time, each bidder must be prepared to elaborate upon and clarify its written proposal.

7. XYZ plans to make its initial selection within thirty to forty-five days following the final vendor demonstration meeting.

8. Failure to comply with any of the RFP response requirements may subject a proposal to rejection.

9. Each vendor must be prepared to include any or all statements made in their proposal in a contract for systems and services, or as an addendum to that contract. Acceptance of proposals from any source in no way obligates XYZ to the vendor. Furthermore, such acceptance is not a guarantee of any type for current or future business relations. XYZ reserves the right to accept or reject any and all proposals, in whole or in part, at any time.

10. Each proposal must be signed by a duly authorized officer of the submitting company.

11. Two (2) copies of the response to this RFP must be received at the project manager's office, one (1) hardcopy along with one (1) softcopy, by the date on the cover of this document. Refer to the cover page for complete address information.

12. Any vendor selected to provide systems to XYZ will be required to present an insurance certificate as proof of liability covering the full scope of their work, for at least $1,000,000.

13. Each vendor submitting a proposal must be a direct national representative of the manufacturer, or the actual manufacturer. (If you elect to submit the RFP through your local dealer, please specify the name, address, and number of the dealer chosen to service XYZ.)

14. XYZ requires that vendors provide access, via a software escrow agent, to any applicable software source code, in the event that vendor is no longer able to provide effective support or to continue enhancing the product. Please indicate how this would need to be handled.

15. XYZ reserves the right to adjust the project schedule dates at its sole discretion.

16. The vendor's costs for proposal preparation, demonstration, and testing will be the sole responsibility of the vendor.

II. VENDOR INFORMATION

The following information must be supplied by each vendor:

A. General Information

Respond to all questions detailed in "Vendor Questionnaire."

B. Financial

Provide a copy of your latest annual report or audited financial statements including the balance sheet, income statement, and statement of cash flow. As with all information in your response, this data will be held in confidence. Please note that a "call my banker" type response is not acceptable.

C. Experience

Provide a brief background on your company along with major milestones in the company history.

D. References

Provide a list of customers with a similar configuration, preferably local or regional, using the proposed system along with the list of modules currently in use. Please provide at least two of these references for installations completed in the last year. Also please provide a list of similar installations currently in progress.

Please provide the following for each reference.

- Company name
- Company address
- Contact person (management)
- Company telephone number
- Description of system and use
- Date of implementation

E. Literature

Please attach any additional information that describes your product. Describe what is unique about the proposed solution and what sets it apart from other proposals.

III. GENERAL REQUIREMENTS

The following areas detail some of the general requirements to be considered in the identification of the new POS for XYZ:

A. Network Operating Environment

While the network operating system (OS) will not drive the purchase of the POS system, a graphical user interface (GUI) using Windows 10 at the workstation is the preferred approach. It is critical that vendors should propose the most stable and robust environment for their system with a proven track record. This includes Unix or any form of thin client. All POS terminal locations will be cabled with either Enhanced Cat-5 twisted pair or fiber (still to be determined). The current plan for connecting the networks at the two locations, the country club and the hotel, includes T3 data communications lines.

Server Configuration:

The POS configuration must include the necessary components to ensure that at no time will the system at either location be inoperative in the event of a communications failure between the two locations. For those systems that support continued use of the POS terminal while communication with the server is down, a single server at the hotel is an acceptable configuration. For those that do not, a server will be required at both locations for this configuration). The POS, however, will operate off a single server at the hotel and the POS systems at both locations must interface to the property management system (PMS).

XYZ will be looking to the vendor for assistance with the hardware and networking requirements including:

- Providing specifications for all hardware including terminals, printers, file server, and any other necessary peripherals.
- While XYZ is considering sourcing hardware from a third party, those POS vendors that sell hardware are encouraged to submit hardware prices as well.
- Upon completion of the installation, MIS personnel must be thoroughly trained on all aspects of system maintenance.

B. Device Requirements

Proposed POS terminals should be a PC-based flat-screen active-matrix PC POS terminal with integrated credit card reader. Should be durable, environmentally sealed (protected from spills), and, as much as possible, scratch resistant. Receipt printers should be thermal in the front-of-house, and dot matrix in back (for two colors) at a minimum. Due to frequent electrical problems in the southern Florida area, surge and UPS protection is critical.

C. Modules

The following POS modules and general functionality are required by XYZ:

- Basic F&B POS functionality in the revenue outlets as defined in "IV—FUNCTIONALITY REQUIREMENTS"
- Handheld use for certain outlets
- Comprehensive package tracking (through interface with the PMS)

XYZ will also require the following modules/applications:

- Restaurant management system (RMS) to include:
  - Cash management and reporting
  - Management reporting
  - Inventory and purchasing
  - Report generator
- Retail POS for retail outlets

XYZ is also considering the following applications:

- Frequent diner
- Table management
- Menu management
- Restaurant reservations
- Minibar

Note: As outlined here, XYZ will be selecting numerous F&B-related applications outside of just POS. We realize all vendors will not be able to propose all applications. At a minimum, interfaces with each of these will be required.

D. Interfaces

A very critical component to the POS system will be the interfacing with other hotel systems. Vendors must clearly define the functionality available with each interface:

Depending on the modules being proposed, the new system must provide the following interfaces. Where applicable, vendors currently being considered are listed. Others may be added or removed as necessary.

For all interfaces listed in the following, vendors must provide:

- A detailed description of the features and functionality supported by the interface.
- A listing of those systems to which an interface is already available and installed.

Where applicable, this information should be provided even for those applications being proposed (such as inventory), as XYZ may still decide to purchase the POS system from one vendor and the other system from another.

1. *PMS*

   Due to the resort nature of XYZ along with the extensive offering of activities and F&B, package tracking will be critical. Any systems that offer enhanced interface functionality to include package handling should provide detailed functionality description. On the average, packages are expected to account for approximately 50 percent of the daily occupancy.

2. *Credit Card Processing*

   A single credit card processing system will be used propertywide that has yet to be determined. The selection of this system will be driven by the selected property management system vendor.

3. *In-Room Entertainment*

   Interface will be necessary to allow for room service ordering directly through the in-room entertainment system in the guest room. Vendors currently being considered include:
   - LodgeNet
   - On Command

4. *Minibar*

   If an interface is available with any minibar systems, provide system names and functionality.

5. *Golf Tee Time*

   If an interface is available with any tee time systems, provide system names and functionality.

6. *Purchasing/Inventory*

7. *Menu Management*

8. *Reservations*

9. *Table Management*

10. *Accounting*

    This applies to an interface with Purchasing.

11. *Golf Cart GPS*

    Ability to interface with golf cart GPS system to enable F&B ordering while on the golf course. Designed to allow food prep prior to arrival between the ninth and tenth holes. When planning the interface installations, the vendor must:
    - Give the XYZ project manager adequate advance notice for all tasks for which the hotel is responsible.
    - Vendors must insure that all interfaces will be up and running on each of the opening dates.
    - A permanent backup plan must be in place by GoLive so that no postings are lost in the event of a system problem.
    - Backup procedures must be detailed in writing.

E. Consolidated Reporting

   Due to the unique layout of XYZ, with two separate locations, there are specific reporting requirements that must be supported. Each outlet and each location must be able to report individually and consolidated reporting including both locations must also be available.

IV. FUNCTIONALITY REQUIREMENTS

Please respond to all questions in "Functionality Requirements." While completing the questionnaire, keep in mind all information detailed in sections I through III of this proposal.

To help us better understand your solution, please feel free to add additional descriptions or details as necessary.

If you are able to supply any of the other modules currently being considered (i.e., table management, menu management, reservations, frequent diner, minibar, or retail POS) please provide functionality descriptions for those modules. Provide any screen captures that may help to describe functionality.

V. PROPOSAL FORMAT

All vendors must follow the format described in this section when completing and submitting proposals for consideration. Each section of the proposal must be clearly labeled and separated by an index tab also lettered and labeled as indicated in this section.

The required sections for vendor responses include the following:

A. Vendor Information
B. Scope of Proposal
C. Functionality Requirements
D. Sample Reports and Screen Layouts
E. Operating Environment
F. System Response Time
G. Equipment Configuration
H. Physical and Environmental Requirements
I. Implementation and Training
J. Documentation
K. System Upgrades
L. Contracts
M. System Costs

Section A: Vendor Information

This section should consist of the responses to the questions listed in "II–VENDOR INFORMATION."

Section B: Scope of Proposal

This section of the proposal should be a concise statement of the relevant factors in the vendor's approach to supplying hardware, software, support, and other key elements as each applies to XYZ's requirements and objectives. Briefly describe the proposed system, highlighting major features, functions, and any areas of potential noncompliance with RFP requirements.

State the modules that you are proposing in response to this RFP. Describe the methods that you will use to insure compatibility with the other systems we will be interfacing with.

Section C: Functionality Requirements

This section should consist of the completed requirements form in "Functionality Requirements."

Section D: Sample Reports and Screen Layouts

In Section D, include sample reports and screen layouts.

Section E: Operating Environment

Section E should begin with a description of the proposed operating environment incorporating the requirements as described in "III. A. Network Operating Environment." Vendor proposals should describe the specific version of the OS that would be installed with the proposed system. Indicate how long the vendor applications have been operating on this version of the OS in a live environment. In addition, please provide the following information:

Languages/Development Tools: Indicate the programming languages used to develop your system. State what other tools are used in developing your system.

Database: Describe the file organization/database structure that is supported by your OS.

Section F: System Response Time

Based on vendor experience, please indicate the following response times assuming a hotel and F&B configuration similar to XYZ that has been operating and accumulating data for one year:

Credit Card Approval: Indicate the wait time for a credit card approval from the time of the card swipe assuming that your recommended method of data communications is in place.

Backup: Indicate the backup time for daily, weekly and monthly, backups.

Daily Processing: If applicable, indicate the processing time required for the end-of-day process.

System Startup: In the event of a system failure, indicate the time for the system to be up and fully functional from the time the server powered up.

Section G: Equipment Configuration

In Section E, please detail specific information including itemized cost for all of the hardware that you are proposing referring to "III. B. Device Requirements" for device types and quantities. If you are not proposing hardware, please indicate the same specifications for equipment that would be required to run your application.

Where applicable, please make sure to include the following information:

File Server(s): model number, speed, memory size, hard disk capacity, and configuration. Include size and model of monitor.

Storage: type (disk, tape) model number, cost, and capacity.

Note: The new system must include the bidder's recommendation for either hardware redundancy or fault tolerance. If the hardware proposed is to be redundant, the recommended hardware configuration should specify all redundant components and their quantities required for redundancy.

POS Terminal: model number, speed, memory size, network card, and hard disk capacity. Include size and type of touchscreen monitor along with information about cash drawer.

Printers: model number(s), speed, size, and required accessories. Please indicate which printers will be connected to the network and those that would be slave printers.

Mobile Applications: Please provide further detail on your mobile application/hardware specifications and interfaces.

Other Hardware: Please provide the necessary details for any other recommended hardware including network hubs and uninterrupted power supplies.

Section H: Physical and Environmental Requirements

In this section, present an outline of technical and preinstallation assistance your firm will provide. Also explain what is required but not provided by your company and how it is normally accomplished.

List all site preparation information including server space requirements, any special mounting methods required, special power requirements (including any need for isolated power circuits), and the number and type of required data communication lines. Please include information on cabling requirements along with electrical, architectural, and other special concerns. Indicate the maximum distance that all peripherals may be located from the computer or control unit.

In addition, describe any environmental requirements for the proposed system, including air conditioning, humidity control, power supply, and so on.

Section I: Implementation and Training

The following table details the staff training requirements for each of the two phases:

Phase I			Phase II		
Department	Staff	Management	Department	Staff	Management

Based on these staffing levels (which only includes staffing numbers for employees that will require system training) and the two opening phases as outlined in "Property Overview," please provide detailed information on the proposed training process for XYZ including:

- A sample installation schedule using a calendar without dates
- Total number of training hours for each phase
- Number of vendor trainers required for each phase

Include the recommended number of days for the following:

- Network installation
- Network training for MIS personnel
- Interface installation
- On-site postconversion support

Please also provide the total cost for all implementation and training services outlined here. Using the following format, summarize the assignments, responsibilities, when due and associated costs, and where applicable, for implementing the proposed system. Systems must be fully functional on the dates outlined in "Property Overview." Add any factors not listed in the implementation schedule that are relevant to a successful implementation including detailed customer responsibilities.

Tasks	Assigned to	Time
XYZ	Vendor	

Section J: Documentation

Provide a list of the user and system operating manuals that will be provided. In addition, please include a copy of the table of contents and index for each. Please state if technical writing assistance will be provided to document XYZ-specific policies and procedures relating to your system. This could include any necessary interface procedures and emergency network procedures, and any necessary checklists (such as night audit or front office management procedures). Indicate your policy for documentation of system enhancements or upgrades, how the user base is updated, how often, and so forth.

Section K: System Upgrades

In this section, please provide the following information regarding software upgrades:

- Are new releases with improved and additional functionality provided on a regular basis? If so, how often?
- How would your company handle system upgrades for an installation of this size?
- What kinds of additional training and implementation services are provided for new releases and at what cost?

Section L: Contracts

In this section include samples of all contracts related to your proposal. Include hardware, software, service, support and supplies contracts, and any information needed to assess the scope of each.

Section M: System Costs

In this section, please include all costs associated with the project as defined in this RFP. Provide the complete itemized cost for each hardware and software component of the proposed system. Include unit cost, extended cost, quantity discount scales, and total cost for each item. Also indicate the length of time the quoted prices are valid.

Please make sure to include the following:

- All applications, modules, and interfaces
- Network OS
- Other required utilities
- Programming—Hourly/daily rate for programmers, consultants, and any other individuals that may be necessary if specialty programming is required
- Installation—Itemize all installation costs
- Other Costs—Itemize any other related costs not already listed

REFERENCES

CHAPTER 1

Adcock, Ken, Helms, Marilyn M., and Jih, Wen-Jang Kenny. (1993, Spring). Information technology: Can it provide a sustainable competitive advantage? *Information Strategy: The Executive's Journal*, 10–15.

Applegate, Lynda M., McFarlan, F. Warren, and McKenney, James L. (1996). *Corporate information systems management: The issues facing senior executives* (4th ed.). Chicago: Irwin.

Bakos, J. Yannis and Treacy, Michael E. (1986, June). Information technology and corporate strategy: A research perspective. *MIS Quarterly, 10* (2), 107–119.

Cash, James I., Jr. and Konsynski, Benn R. (1985, March–April). IS redraws competitive boundaries. *Harvard Business Review*, 134–142.

Cho, Wonae. (1996). *A case study: Creating and sustaining competitive advantage through an information technology application in the lodging industry.* Unpublished doctoral dissertation, Virginia Polytechnic Institute and State University.

Clemons, Eric K. and Kimbrough, Steven O. (1986, December). Information systems, telecommunications and their effects on industrial organizations. Proceedings of the Seventh International Conference on Information Systems, San Diego, CA, 99–108.

Clemons, Eric K. and Row, Michael C. (1991, September). Sustaining IT advantage: The role of structural differences. *MIS Quarterly, 15* (3), 275–291.

Copeland, Duncan G. and McKenney, James L. (1988, September). Airline reservations systems: Lessons from history. *MIS Quarterly, 12* (3), 353–370.

D'Aveni, Richard A. (with Gunther, Robert). (1994). *Hyper-competition: Managing the dynamics of strategic maneuvering.* New York: The Free Press.

Feeny, David F. and Ives, Blake. (1990, Summer). In search of sustainability: Reaping long-term advantage from investments in information technology. *Journal of Management Information Systems, 7* (1), 27–46.

Hanks, Richard D., Noland, R. Paul, and Cross, Robert G. (1992, February). Discounting in the hotel industry: A new approach. *Cornell Hotel and Restaurant Administration Quarterly,33* (1), 15–23.

Hitt, Lorin M. and Brynjolfsson, Erik. (1996, June). Productivity, business profitability, and consumer surplus: Three different measures of information technology value. *MIS Quarterly, 20* (2), 121–143.

Hopper, Max D. (1990, May–June). Rattling SABRE—New ways to compete on information. *Harvard Business Review*, 118–125.

Ives, Blake and Learmonth (1984, December). The information system as a competitive weapon. *Communications of the ACM, 27* (12), 1193–1201.

Mata, Francisco J., Fuerst, William L., and Barney, Jay B. (1995, December). Information technology and sustained competitive advantage: A resource-based analysis. *MIS Quarterly, 19* (4), 487–505.

McFarlan, F. Warren. (1984, May–June). Information technology changes the way you compete. Harvard Business Review, 98–103.

Ohmae, Kenichi. (1992). *The mind of the strategist: Business planning for competitive advantage.* New York: Penguin Books.

Parsons, Gregory L. (1983, Fall). Information technology: A new competitive weapon. *Sloan Management Review*, 3–14.

Plimpton, George. (1990). *The X Factor.* Knoxville, TN: Whittle Direct Books.

Porter, Michael E. (1985). *Competitive advantage: Creating and sustaining superior performance.* New York: The Free Press.

Porter, Michael E. and Millar, Victor E. (1985, July–August). How information gives you competitive advantage. *Harvard Business Review,* 149–160.

Segars, Albert H. and Grover, Varun. (1995, May–June). The industry-level impact of information technology: An empirical analysis of three industries. *Decision Sciences, 26* (3), 337–368.

Sethi, Vijay and King, William R. (1994, December). Development of measures to assess the extent to which an information technology application provides competitive advantage. *Management Science, 40* (12), 1601–1626.

Weill, Peter. (1991). The information technology payoff: Implications for investment appraisal. *Australian Accounting Review, 1* (1) 2–11.

CHAPTER 2

Laudon, Kenneth, and Laudon, Jane. 2015. *Management information systems* (14th ed.) Upper Saddle River, NJ: Prentice Hall.

Long, Larry, and Long, Nancy. 2007. *Computers* (6th ed.) Upper Saddle River, NJ: Prentice Hall.

Panko, Raymond R. 2008. *Business data networks and telecommunications* (7th ed.). Upper Saddle River, NJ: Prentice Hall.

CHAPTER 3

VeriSign (2017) "Direct Denial of Service Report," White paper.

What is a Zero-Day Vulnerability? | *Security News—PC Tools* \www.pctools.com/security-news/zero-day-vulnerability/

Verizon's Data Breach Investigations Report 2017

CHAPTER 5

Hotel Technology—Next Generation. (2010, May). Vision and first steps for shared technology services for hospitality: A position paper. Available: http://htng. org/mediacenter/htng_shared_services_position_paper_1.0.pdf.

O'Neill, Siobhan. "Starwood Makes Strong Progress on Sustainability Goals." International Tourism Partnership Presents Green Hotelier. *Green Hotelier*, July 2, 2015. Web. July 15, 2017. http://www .greenhotelier.org/

Soule, Alexander. "Starwood Hotels Hits Environmental Milestone". StamfordAdvocate. Hearst Media Services Connecticut, LLC, February 5, 2015. Web. 15 July 2017. http://www.greenhotelier.org/

CHAPTER 6

APEX. Events Industry Council. Retrieved May 14, 2017, from www.eventscouncil.org/APEX/about-apex.

Bandwidth and Networking Terms for Meeting & Event Professionals, APEX Glossary Supplement. Eventscouncil.org. Retrieved May 14, 2017, from http://www.eventscouncil.org/docs/default-source/apex-bandwidth-and-connectivity/NEW_APEX_Bandwidth_Terminology.pdf?sfvrsn=0

Events Industry Council. Retrieved May 14, 2017, from www.eventscouncil.org.

How the Digital Experience Institute Streamed PCMA Convening Leaders 2017 All Over the Globe. Pcmaconvene.org. Retrieved August 14, 2017, from http://www.pcmaconvene.org/plenary/the-digital-experience-institute-streamed-pcma-convening-leaders-2017/

May weather-Pacquaio fight made Periscope the new Napster. CNN.com. Retrieved May 14, 2017, from http://money.cnn.com/2015/05/04/technology/live-stream-mayweather-pacquiao/index.html

Mobile App Store Revenue To Exceed $139 Billion By 2021: A Look At Mature And Emerging App Markets Worldwide. Dazeinfo.com. Retrieved May 14, 2017, from https://dazeinfo.com/2017/04/17/mobile-app-downloads-revenue-worldwide-2016-2021.

New York Expects Fewer Foreign Tourists, Saying Trump Is to Blame. Nytimes.com. Retrieved May 14, 2017, from https://www.nytimes.com/2017/02/28/nyregion/new-york-foreign-tourists-trump-policies.html?_r=0

Why Hybrid, and Other Highlights From DEI's 2016 Digital Event Benchmark Report. Pcmaconvene.org. Retrieved August 14, 2017, from http://www.pcmaconvene.org/plenary/digital-experience-institute-2016-digital-event-benchmark-report/

CHAPTER 7

Connolly, Daniel J. and Moore, Richard G. (1995). Technology and its impact on global distribution channels in the hotel industry. *Proceedings of the Decision Sciences Institute, USA, 3*, 1563–1565.

Davis, Stan M. and Meyer, Christopher. (1998). *Blur: The speed of change in the connected economy*. New York: Warner Books.

Estis Green, Cindy. (2008). *Demystifying Distribution 2.0: A TIG Global special report*. Washington, DC: HSMAI Foundation.

Evans, Philip and Wurster, Thomas S. (1999). *Blown to bits: How the new economics of information transforms strategy*. Boston: Harvard Business School Press.

Hamel, Gary and Prahalad, C. K. (1994). *Competing for the future*. Boston: Harvard Business School Press.

Kirsner, Scott. (1999, November 1). Very truly yours. *CIO Web Business* (Section 2), 30, 32–33.

Stein, Tom and Sweat, Jeff. (1998, November 9). Killer supply chains. *InformationWeek*, 36–38, 42, 44, 46.

CHAPTER 8

Connolly, Thomas, Carolyn Begg, and Anne Strachan. 1999. *Database systems* (2nd ed.). North Reading, MA: Addison-Wesley.

CHAPTER 9

Davenport, Thomas H. and Harris, Jeanne G. (2007). *Competing on analytics: The new science of winning*. Cambridge: Harvard Business School Publishing.

Gates, Bill (with Hemingway, Collins). (1999). *Business @ the speed of thought: Using a digital nervous system*. New York: Warner Books.

Kaplan, Robert S. and Norton, David P. (1996). *The balanced scorecard: Translating strategy into action*. Boston: Harvard Business School Press.

Norton, David. (2009, June). SAS Predictive Analytics: Harrah's builds customer loyalty. *Information Management Magazine* [Online]. Available: http://www.information-management.com/issues/2007_59/sas_predictive_analytics-10015490-1.html.

CHAPTER 10

Augmented Reality Market by Offering (Hardware (Sensor, Displays & Projectors, Cameras), and Software), Device Type (Head-Mounted, Head-Up, Hand-held), Application (Enterprise, Consumer, Commercial, Automotive) and Geography-Global forecast to 2023. Retrieved August 23, 2017, from http://www.marketwatch.com/story/augmented-reality-market-growing-at-a-cagr-of-5571-during-2017-to-2023—reportsnreports-2017-07-27-6203123.

Azuma, R. T. (1997). A survey of augmented reality. *Presence: Teleoperators and virtual environments, 6* (4), 355–385.

Azuma, R., Baillot, Y., Behringer, R., Feiner, S., Julier, S., and MacIntyre, B. (2001). Recent advances in augmented reality. *IEEE Computer Graphics and Applications, 21* (6), 34–47.

Blascovich, J., & Bailenson, J., (2011). *Infinite reality: The hidden blueprint of our virtual lives.* New York: HarperCollins Publishers.

Burdea Grigore, C., and Coiffet, P. (1994). *Virtual reality technology.* London: Wiley-Interscience.

Daniel A. Guttentag (2010). "Virtual reality: Applications and implications for tourism". *Science Direct. 31* (5).

Goh, C, Mok, H, and Law, R, (2009). Artificial intelligence applications in tourism, in Khosrow-Pour, M. (Ed.), Encyclopedia of information science and technology (2nd ed., Vol. 2), p. 241–247. Hershey, Pa.: Information Science Reference, http://hdl.handle.net/10397/54834

Hale, K.S. and Stanney, K.H., (2014). *Handbook of Virtual Environments: Design, implementation, and applications* (2nd ed.). CRC Press.

Jerald, J., (2016). *The VR Book: Human-centered design for virtual reality.* ACM Books.

Lavalle, S.M., (2015). Virtual reality. Retrieved on August 23, 2017, from http://msl.cs.uiuc.edu/vr/vrch1.pdf.

Lavalle, S. M. (2016). Virtual Reality Lectures. Retrieved on August 23, 2017, from https://www.youtube.com/playlist?list=PL_ezWOhnpakMojiJGm-YiCz5zr4GpuLG_

Milgram, P., and Kishino, F. (1994). A taxonomy of mixed reality visual displays. *IEICE TRANSACTIONS on Information and Systems, 77* (12), 1321–1329.

Schmalstieg, D, and Hollerer, T. (2016). Augmented Reality: Principles and Practice, Addison-Wesley.

Van Krevelen, D. W. F., and Poelman, R. (2010). A survey of augmented reality technologies, applications and limitations. *International Journal of Virtual Reality, 9* (2), 1.

Virtual Reality (VR) Market Analysis by Device, by Technology, by Component, by Application (Aerospace & Defense, Commercial, Consumer Electronics, Industrial, & Medical), by Region, and Segment Forecasts, 2014–2025. Retrieved August 23, 2017, from http://www.grandviewresearch.com/industry-analysis/virtual-reality-vr-market.

CHAPTER 11

Brueggeman, William, and Fisher, Jeffrey. (2001). *Real estate finance and investments* (11th ed.). New York: McGraw-Hill/Irwin.

INDEX